THE
CHRISTIAN
ITS COURSE, ITS
HINDRANCES,
AND ITS HELPS

BY
THOMAS ARNOLD

"As far as the principle on which Archbishop Laud and his followers acted went to re-actuate the idea of the church, as a co-ordinate and living power by right of Christ's institution and express promise, I go along with them; but I soon discover that by the church they meant the clergy, the hierarchy exclusively, and then I fly off from them in a tangent.

"For it is this very interpretation of the church, that, according to my conviction, constituted the first and fundamental apostasy; and I hold it for one of the greatest mistakes of our polemical divines, in their controversies with the Romanists, that they trace all the corruptions of the gospel faith to the Papacy."--COLERIDGE,

Literary Remains, vol. iii. p. 386.

INTRODUCTION.

The contents of this volume will be found, I hope, to be in agreement with its title.

Amongst the helps of Christian life, the highest place is due to the Christian church and its ordinances. I have been greatly misunderstood with respect to my estimate of the Christian church, as distinguished from the Christian religion. I agree so far with those, from whom I in other things most widely differ, that I hold the revival of the church of Christ in its full perfection, to be the one great end to which all our efforts should be directed. This is with me no new belief, but one which I have entertained for many years. It was impressed most strongly upon me, as it appears to have been upon others, by the remarkable state of affairs and of opinions which we witnessed in this country about nine or ten years ago; and everything since that time has confirmed it in my mind more and more.

Others, according to their own statement, received the same impression from the phenomena of the same period. But the movement had begun earlier; nor should I object to call it, as they do, a movement towards "something deeper and truer than satisfied the last century[1]." It began, I suppose, in the last ten years of the last century, and has ever since been working onwards, though for a long time slowly and secretly, and with no distinctly marked direction. But still, in philosophy and general literature, there have been sufficient proofs that the pendulum, which for nearly two hundred years had been swinging one way, was now beginning to swing back again; and as its last oscillation brought it far from the true centre, so it may be, that its present impulse may be no less in excess, and thus may bring on again, in after ages, another corresponding reaction.

[1] See Mr. Newman's Letter to Dr. Jelf, p. 27.

Now if it be asked what, setting aside the metaphor, are the two points between which mankind has been thus moving to and fro; and what are the tendencies in us which, thus alternately predominating, give so different a character to different periods of the human history; the answer is not easy to be given summarily, for the generalisation which it requires is almost beyond the compass of the human mind. Several phenomena appear in each period, and it would be easy to give any one of these as marking its tendency: as, for instance, we might describe one period as having a tendency to despotism, and another to licentiousness: but the true answer lies deeper, and can be only given by discovering that common element in human nature which, in religion, in politics, in philosophy, and in literature, being modified by the subject-matter of each, assumes in each a different form, so that its own proper nature is no longer to be recognized. Again, it would be an error to suppose that either of the two tendencies which so affect the course of human affairs were to be called simply bad or good. Each has its good and evil nicely intermingled; and taking the highest good of each, it would be difficult to say which was the more excellent;--taking the last corruption of each, we could not determine which, was the more hateful. For so far as we can trace back the manifold streams, flowing some from the eastern mountains, and some from the western, to the highest springs from which they rise, we find on the one side the ideas of truth and justice, on the other those of beauty and love;--things so exalted, and so inseparably united in the divine perfections, that to set either two above the other were presumptuous and profane. Yet these most divine things separated from each other, and defiled in their passage through this lower world, do each assume a form in human nature of very great evil: the exclusive and corrupted love of truth and justice becomes in man selfish atheism; the exclusive and corrupted worship of beauty and love becomes in man a bloody and a lying idolatry.

Such would be the general theory of the two great currents in which human affairs may be said to have been successively drifting. But real history, even the history of all mankind, and much more that of any particular age or country, presents a picture far more complicated. First, as to time: as the vessels in a harbour, and in the open sea without it, may be seen swinging with the tide at the same moment in opposite directions; the ebb has begun in the roadstead, while it is not yet high water in the harbour; so one or more nations may be in advance of or behind the general tendency of their age, and from either cause may be moving in the opposite direction. Again, the tendency or movement in itself is liable to frequent interruptions, and short counter-movements: even when the tide is coming in upon the shore, every wave retires after its advance; and he who follows incautiously the retreating waters, may be caught by some stronger billow, overwhelming again for an instant the spot which had just been left dry. A child standing by the sea-shore for a few minutes, and watching this, as it seems, irregular advance and retreat of the water, could not tell whether it was ebb or flood; and we, standing for a few years on the shore of time, can scarcely tell whether the particular movement which we witness is according to or against the general tendency of the whole period. Farther yet, as these great tendencies are often interrupted, so are they continually mixed: that is, not only are their own good and bad elements successively predominant, but they never have the world wholly to themselves: the opposite tendency exists, in an under-current it may be, and not lightly perceptible; but here and there it struggles to the surface, and mingles its own good and evil with the predominant good and evil of its antagonist. Wherefore he who would learn wisdom from the complex experience of history, must question closely all its phenomena, must notice that which is less obvious as well as that which is most palpable; must judge not peremptorily or sweepingly, but with reserves and exceptions; not as lightly overrunning a wide region of the truth, but thankful if after much pains he has advanced his landmarks only a little; if he has gained, as it were, but one or two frontier fortresses, in which he can establish himself for ever.

Now, then, when Mr. Newman describes the movement of the present moment as being directed towards "something better and deeper than satisfied the last century," this description, although in some sense true, is yet in practice delusive; and the delusion which lurks in it is at the root of the errors of Mr. Newman and of his friends. They regard the tendencies of the last century as wholly evil; and they appear to extend this feeling to the whole period of which the last century was the close, and which began nearly with the sixteenth century. Viewing in this light the last three hundred years, they regard naturally with excessive favour the preceding period, with which they are so strongly contrasted; and not the less because this period has been an object of scorn to the times which have followed it. They are drawn towards the enemy of their enemy, and they fancy that it must be in all points their enemy's opposite. And if the faults of its last decline are too palpable to be denied, they ascend to its middle and its earlier course, and finding that its evils are there less flagrant, they abandon themselves wholly to the contemplation of its good points, and end with making it an idol. There are few stranger and sadder sights than to see men judging of whole periods of the history of mankind with the blindness of party-spirit, never naming one century without expressions of contempt or abhorrence, never mentioning another but with extravagant and undistinguishing admiration.

But the worst was yet to come. The period which Mr. Newman and his friends so disliked, had, in its religious character, been distinguished by its professions of extreme veneration for the Scriptures; in its quarrel with the system of the preceding period, it had rested all its cause on the authority of the Scripture,--it had condemned the older system because Scripture could give no warrant for it. On the other hand, the partizans of the older system protested against the exclusive appeal to Scripture; there was, as they maintained, another authority in religious matters; if their system was not supported in all its points by Scripture, it had at least the warrant of Christian antiquity. Thus Mr. Newman and his friends found that the times which they disliked had professed to rely on Scripture alone; the times which they loved had invested the Church with equal authority. It was natural then to connect the evils of the iron age, for so they regarded it, with this notion of the sole supremacy of Scripture; and it was no less natural to associate the blessings of their imagined golden age with its avowed reverence for the Church. If they appealed only to Scripture, they echoed the language of men whom they abhorred; if they exalted the Church and Christian antiquity, they sympathised with a period which they were resolved to love. Their theological writings from the very beginning have too plainly shown in this respect the force both of their sympathies and their antipathies.

Thus previously disposed, and in their sense or apprehension of the evil of their own times already flying as it were for refuge to the system of times past, they were overtaken by the political storm of 1831, and the two following years. That storm rattled loudly, and alarmed many who had viewed the gathering of the clouds with hope and pleasure; no wonder, then, if it produced a stormy effect upon those who viewed it as a mere calamity, an evil monster bred out of an evil time, and fraught with nothing but mischief. Farther, the government of the country was now, for the first time for many years, in the hands of men who admired the spirit of the age, nearly as much as Mr. Newman and his friends abhorred it. Thus all things seemed combined against them: the spirit of the period which they so hated was riding as it were upon the whirlwind; they knew not where its violence might burst; and the government of the country was, as they thought, driving wildly before it, without attempting to moderate its fury. Already they were inclined to recognise the signs of a national apostasy.

But from this point they have themselves written their own history.--Mr. Percival's letter to the editor of the Irish Ecclesiastical Journal, which was reprinted in the Oxford Herald of January 80, 1841, is really a document of the highest value. It acquaints us, from the very best authority, with the immediate occasion of the publication of the Tracts for the Times, and with the objects of their writers. It tells us whither their eyes were turned for deliverance; with what charm they hoped to allay the troubled waters. Ecclesiastical history would be far more valuable than it is, if we could thus learn the real character and views of every church, or sect, or party, from itself, and not from its opponents.

Mr. Percival informs us, that the Irish Church Act of 1833, which abolished several of the Irish Bishoprics, was the immediate occasion of the publication of the Tracts for the Times; and that the objects of that publication were, to enforce the doctrine of the apostolical succession, and to preserve the Prayer Book from "the Socinian leaven, with which we had reason to fear it would be tainted by the parliamentary alteration of it, which at that time was openly talked of." But the second of these objects is not mentioned in the more formal statements which Mr. Percival gives of them; and in what he calls the "matured account" of the principles of the writers, it is only said, "Whereas there seems great danger at present of attempts at unauthorized and inconsiderate innovation as in other matters so especially in the service of our Church, we pledge ourselves to resist any attempt that may be made to alter the Liturgy on insufficient authority: i.e. without the exercise of the free and deliberate judgment of the Church on the alterations proposed." It would seem, therefore, that what was particularly deprecated was "the alteration of the Liturgy on insufficient authority," without reference to any suspected character of the alteration in itself. But at any rate, as all probability of any alteration in the Liturgy vanished very soon after the publication of the tracts began, the other object, the maintaining the doctrine of the apostolical succession, as it had been the principal one from the beginning, became in a very short time the only one.

The great remedy, therefore, for the evils of the times, the "something deeper and truer than satisfied the last century," or, at least, the most effectual means of attaining to it, is declared to be the maintenance of the doctrine of apostolical succession. Now let us hear, for it is most important, the grounds on which this doctrine is to be enforced, and the reason why so much stress is laid on it. I quote again from Mr. Percival's letter.

"Considering, 1. That the only way of salvation is the partaking of the body and blood of our sacrificed Redeemer;

"2. That the mean expressly authorized by him for that purpose is the holy sacrament of his supper;

"3. That the security by him no less expressly authorized, for the continuance and due application of that sacrament, is the apostolical commission of the bishops, and under them the presbyters of the church;

"4. That under the present circumstances of the church in England, there is peculiar danger of these matters being slighted and practically disavowed, and of numbers of Christians being left, or tempted to precarious and unauthorized ways of communion, which must terminate often in vital apostasy:--

"We desire to pledge ourselves one to another, reserving our canonical obedience, as follows:--

"1. To be on the watch for all opportunities of inculcating, on all committed to our charge, a due sense of the inestimable privilege of communion with our Lord, through the successors of the apostles, and of leading them to the resolution to transmit it, by his blessing, unimpaired to their children."

Then follow two other resolutions: one to provide and circulate books and tracts, to familiarize men's minds with this doctrine; and the other, "to do what lies in us towards reviving among churchmen, the practice of daily common prayer, and more frequent participation of the Lord's Supper."

The fourth resolution, "to resist unauthorized alterations of the Liturgy," I have already quoted: the fifth and last engages generally to place within the reach of all men, accounts of such points in our discipline and worship as may appear most likely to be misunderstood or undervalued.

These resolutions were drawn up more than seven years ago, and their practical results have not been contemptible. The Tracts for the Times amount to no fewer than ninety; while the sermons, articles in reviews, stories, essays, poems, and writings of all sorts which have enforced the same doctrines, have been also extremely numerous. Nor have all these labours been without fruit: for it is known that a large proportion of the clergy have adopted, either wholly or in great part, the opinions and spirit of the Tracts for the Times; and many of the laity have embraced them also.

It seems also, that in the various publications of their school, the object originally marked out in the resolutions quoted above, has been followed with great steadiness. The system has been uniform, and its several parts have held well together. It has, perhaps, been carried on of late more boldly, which is the natural consequence of success. It has in all points been the direct opposite of what may be called the spirit of English protestantism of the nineteenth century: upholding whatever that spirit would depreciate; decrying whatever it would admire. A short statement of the principal views held by Mr. Newman and his friends, will show this sufficiently.

"The sacraments, and not preaching, are the sources of divine grace." So it is said in the Advertisement prefixed to the first volume of the Tracts for the Times, in exact conformity with the preamble to the resolutions, which I have already quoted. But the only security for the efficacy of the sacraments, is the apostolical commission of the bishops, and under them, of the presbyters of the Church. So it is said in the preamble to the resolutions. These two doctrines are the foundation of the whole system. God's grace, and our salvation, come to us principally through the virtue of the sacraments; the virtue of the sacraments depends on the apostolical succession of those who administer them. The clergy, therefore, thus holding in their hands the most precious gifts of the Church, acquire naturally the title of the Church itself; the Church, as possessed of so mysterious a virtue as to communicate to the only means of salvation their saving efficacy, becomes at once an object of the deepest reverence. What wonder if to a body endowed with so transcendant a gift, there should be given also the spirit of wisdom to discern all truth; so that the solemn voice of the Church in

4

its creeds, and in the decrees of its general councils, must be received as the voice of God himself. Nor can such a body be supposed to have commended any practices or states of life winch are not really excellent; and the duty either of all Christians, or of those at least who would follow the most excellent way. Fasting, therefore, and the state of celibacy, are the one a christian obligation, the other a christian perfection. Again, being members of a body so exalted, and receiving our very salvation in a way altogether above reason, we must be cautious how we either trust to our individual conscience rather than to the command of the Church, or how we venture to exercise our reason at all in judging of what the Church teaches; childlike faith and childlike obedience are the dispositions which God most loves. What, then, are they who are not of the Church, who do not receive the Sacraments from those who can alone give them their virtue? Surely they are aliens from God, they cannot claim his covenanted mercies; and the goodness which may be apparent in them, may not be real goodness; God may see that it is false, though to us it appears sincere; but it is certain that they do not possess the only appointed means of salvation; and therefore, we must consider their state as dangerous, although, we may not venture to condemn them.

I have not consciously misrepresented the system of Mr. Newman and his friends in a single particular; I have not, to my knowledge, expressed any one of their tenets invidiously. An attentive reader may deduce, I think, all the Subordinate points in their teaching from some one or more of the principles which I have given; but I have not wilfully omitted any doctrine of importance. And, in every point, the opposition to what I may be allowed to call the protestantism of the nineteenth century is so manifest, that we cannot but feel that the peculiar character of the system is to be traced to what I have before noticed--the extreme antipathy of its founders to the spirit which they felt to be predominant in their own age and country.

It is worth our while to observe this, because fear and passion are not the surest guides to truth, and the rule of contraries is not the rule of wisdom. Other men have been indignant against the peculiar evils of their own time, and from their strong impression of these have seemed to lose sight of its good points; but Mr. Newman and his friends appear to hate the nineteenth century for its own sake, and to proscribe all belonging to it, whether good or bad, simply because it does belong to it.--This diseased state of mind is well shown by the immediate occasion of the organization of their party. Mr. Perceval tells us that it was the Act for the dissolution of some of the Irish bishoprics, passed in 1833, winch first made the authors of the Tracts resolve to commence their publication. Mr. Perceval himself cannot even now speak of that Act temperately; he calls it "a wanton act of sacrilege," "a monstrous act," "an outrage upon the Church;" and his friends, it may be presumed, spoke of it at the time in language at least equally vehement. Now, I am not expressing any opinion upon the justice or expediency of that Act; it was opposed by many good men, and its merits or demerits were fairly open to discussion; but would any fair and sensible person speak of it with such extreme abhorrence as it excited in the minds of Mr. Perceval and his friends? The Act deprived the Church of no portion of its property; it simply ordered a different distribution of it, with the avowed object on the part of its framers of saving the Church from the odium and the danger of exacting Church Rates from the Roman Catholics. It did nothing more than what, according to the constitution of the Churches of England and Ireland, was beyond all question within its lawful authority to do. The King's supremacy and the sovereignty of Parliament may be good or bad, but they are undoubted facts in the constitution of the Church of England, and have been so for nearly three hundred years. I repeat that I am stating no opinion as to the merits of the Irish Church Act of 1833; I only contend, that no man of sound judgment would regard it as "a monstrous act," or as "a wanton sacrilege." It bore upon it no marks of flagrant tyranny: nor did it restrain the worship of the Church, nor corrupt its faith, nor command or encourage anything injurious to men's souls in practice. Luther was indignant at the sale of indulgences; and his horror at the selling Church pardons for money was, by God's blessing, the occasion of the Reformation. The occasion of the new counter-reformation was the abolition of a certain number of bishoprics, that their revenues might be applied solely to church purposes; and that the Church might so be saved from a scandal and a danger. The difference of the exciting cause of the two movements gives the measure of the difference between the Reformation of 1517, and the views and objects of Mr. Newman and his friends.

There are states of nervous excitement, when the noise of a light footstep is distracting. In such a condition were the authors of the Tracts in 1833, and all their subsequent proceedings have shown that the disorder was still upon them. Beset by their horror of the nineteenth century, they sought for something most opposite to it, and therefore they turned to what they called Christian antiquity. Had they judged of their own times fairly, had they appreciated the good of the nineteenth century as well as its evil, they would have looked for their remedy not to the second or third or fourth centuries, but the first; they would have tried to restore, not the Church of Cyprian, or Athanasius, or Augustine, but the Church of St. Paul and of St. John. Now, this it is most certain that they have not done. Their appeal has been not to Scripture, but to the opinions and practices of the dominant party in the ancient Church. They have endeavoured to set those opinions and practices, under the name of apostolical tradition, on a level with the authority of the Scriptures. But their unfortunate excitement has made them fail of doing even what they intended to do. It may be true that all their doctrines may be found in the writings of those whom they call the Fathers; but the effect of their teaching is different because its proportions are altered. Along with their doctrines, there are other points and another spirit prominent in the writings of the earlier Christians, which give to the whole a different complexion. The Tracts for the Times do not appear to me to represent faithfully the language of Christian antiquity; they are rather its caricature.

Still more is this the case, when we compare the language of Mr. Newman and his friends with that of the great divines of the Church of England. Granting that many of these believed firmly in apostolical succession; that one or two may have held general councils to be infallible; that some, provoked by the extravagances of the puritans, have spoken over-strongly about the authority of tradition; yet the whole works even of those who agree with. Mr. Newman in these points, give a view of Christianity different from that of the Tracts, because these points, which in the Tracts stand forward without relief, are in our old divines tempered by the admixture of other doctrines, which, without contradicting them, do in fact alter their effect. This applies most strongly, perhaps, to Hooker and Taylor; but it holds good also of Bull and Pearson. Pearson's exposition of the article in the Creed relating to the Holy Catholic Church is very different from the language of Mr. Newman: it is such as, with perhaps one single exception, might be subscribed by a man who did not believe in apostolical succession[2]. Again, Pearson is so far from making the creeds an independent authority, co-ordinate with Scripture, that he declares, contrary, I suppose, to all probability, that the Apostles' Creed itself was but a deduction from our present Scriptures of the New Testament[3]. Undoubtedly the divines of the seventeenth century are more in agreement with the Tracts than the Reformers are; but it is by no means true that this agreement is universal. There is but one set of writers whose minds are exactly represented by Mr. Newman and his friends, and these are the nonjurors.

[2] The sixth and last mark which he gives of the unity of the Church is, "the unity of discipline and government." "All the Churches of God have the same pastoral guides appointed, authorized, sanctified, and set apart by the appointment of God, by the direction of the Spirit, to direct and lead the people of God in the same way of eternal salvation; as, therefore, there is no Church where there is no order, no ministry, so where the same order and ministry is, there is the same Church. And this is the unity of regiment and discipline." Pearson on the Creed, Art. IX. p. 341, seventh edit. fol. 1701. It would be easy to put a construction upon this paragraph which I could agree with; but I suppose that Pearson meant what I hold to be an error. Yet how gently and generally is it expressed; and this doubtful paragraph stands alone amidst seventeen folio pages on the article of the Holy Catholic Church. And in his conclusion, where he delivers what "every one ought to intend when they profess to believe the Holy Catholic Church," there is not a word about its government; nor is Pearson one of those interpreters who pervert the perfectly certain meaning of the word "Catholic" to favour their own notions about episcopacy. I could cordially subscribe to every word of this conclusion.

6

[3] "To believe, therefore, as the word stands in the front of the Creed, ... is to assent to the whole and every part of it as to a certain and infallible truth revealed by God, ... and delivered unto us in the writings of the blessed apostles and prophets immediately inspired, moved, and acted by God, out of whose writings this brief sum of necessary points of faith was first collected." (P. 12.) And in the paragraph immediately preceding, Pearson had said, "The household of God is built upon the foundation of the apostles and prophets, who are continued unto us only in their writings, and by them alone convoy unto us the truths which they received from God, upon whose testimony we believe." It appears, therefore, that Pearson not only subscribed the 6th Article of the Church of England, but also believed it.

Many reasons, therefore, concur to make it doubtful whether the authors of the Tracts have discovered the true remedy for the evils of their age; whether they have really inculcated "something better and deeper than satisfied the last century." The violent prejudice which previously possessed them, and the strong feelings of passion and fear which led immediately to their first systematic publications, must in the first instance awaken a suspicion as to their wisdom; and this suspicion becomes stronger when we find their writings different from the best of those which they profess to admire, and bearing a close resemblance only to those of the nonjurors. A third consideration is also of much weight-- that their doctrines do not enforce any great points of moral or spiritual perfection which other Christians had neglected; nor do they, in any especial manner, "preach Christ." In this they offer a striking contrast to the religious movement, if I may so call it, which began some years since in the University at Cambridge. That movement, whatever human alloy might have mingled with it, bore on it most clear evidence that it was in the main God's work. It called upon men to turn from sin and be reconciled to God; it emphatically preached Christ crucified. But Mr. Newman and his friends have preached as their peculiar doctrine, not Christ but the Church; we must go even farther and say, not the Church, but themselves. What they teach has no moral or spiritual excellence in itself; but it tends greatly to their own exaltation. They exalt the sacraments highly, but all that they say of their virtue, all their admiration of them as so setting forth the excellence of faith, inasmuch as in them the whole work is of God, and man has only to receive and believe, would be quite as true, and quite as well-grounded, if they were to abandon altogether that doctrine which it is their avowed object especially to enforce--the doctrine of apostolical succession. Referring again to the preamble of their original resolutions, already quoted, we see that the two first articles alone relate to our Lord and to his Sacraments; the third, which is the great basis of their system, relates only to the Clergy. Doubtless, if apostolical succession be God's will, it is our duty to receive it and to teach it; but a number of clergymen, claiming themselves to have this succession, and insisting that, without it, neither Christ nor Christ's Sacraments will save us, do, beyond all contradiction, preach themselves, and magnify their own importance. They are quite right in doing so, if God has commanded it; but such preaching has no manifest warrant of God in it; if it be according to God, it stands alone amongst his dispensations; his prophets and his apostles had a different commission. "We preach," said St. Paul, "not ourselves, but Christ Jesus the Lord; and ourselves your servants for Jesus' sake." It is certain that the enforcing apostolical succession as the great object of our teaching is precisely to do that very thing which St. Paul was commissioned not to do.

This, to my mind, affords a very great presumption that the peculiar doctrines of Mr. Newman and his friends, those which they make it their professed business to inculcate, are not of God. I am anxious not to be misunderstood in saying this. Mr. Newman and his friends preach many doctrines which are entirely of God; as Christians, as ministers of Christ's Church, they preach God's word; and thus, a very large portion of their teaching is of God, blessed both to their hearers and to themselves. Nay, even amongst the particular objects to which their own "Resolutions" pledge them, one is indeed most excellent--"the revival of daily common prayer, and more frequent participation of the Lord's Supper." This is their merit, not as Christians generally, but as a party, (I use the word in no offensive sense;) in this respect their efforts have done, and are doing great good. But they have themselves declared that they will especially set themselves to preach apostolical succession; and it is with reference to this, that I charge them with "preaching themselves;" it was of this

I spoke, when I said that there was a very great presumption that their peculiar doctrines were not of God.

Again, the system which they hold up as "better and deeper than satisfied the last century" is a remedy which has been tried once already: and its failure was so palpable, that all the evil of the eighteenth century was but the reaction from that enormous evil which this remedy, if it be one, had at any rate been powerless to cure. Apostolical succession, the dignity of the Clergy, the authority of the Church, were triumphantly maintained for several centuries; and their full development was coincident, to say the least, with the corruption alike of Christ's religion and Christ's Church. So far were they from tending to realize the promises of prophecy, to perfect Christ's body up to the measure of the stature of Christ's own fulness, that Christ's Church declined during their ascendancy more and more;--she fell alike from truth and from holiness; and these doctrines, if they did not cause the evil, were at least quite unable to restrain it. For, in whatever points the fifteenth century differed from the fourth, it cannot be said that it upheld the apostolical succession less peremptorily, or attached a less value to Church tradition, and Church authority. I am greatly understating the case, but I am content for the present to do so: I will not say that Mr. Newman's favourite doctrines were the very Antichrist which corrupted Christianity; I will only say that they did not prevent its corruption,--that when they were most exalted Christian truth and Christian goodness were most depressed.

After all, however, what has failed once may doubtless be successful on a second trial: it is within possibility, perhaps, that a doctrine, although destitute of all internal evidence showing it to come from God, may be divine notwithstanding;--revealed for some purposes which we cannot fathom, or simply as an exercise of our obedience. All this may be so; and if it can be shown to be so, there remains no other course than to believe God's word, and obey his commandments; only the strength of the external evidence must be in proportion to the weakness of the internal. A good man would ask for no sign from heaven to assure him that God commands judgment, mercy, and truth; whatsoever things are pure, and lovely, and of good report, bear in themselves the seal of their origin; a seal which to doubt were blasphemy. But the cloud and the lightnings and thunders, and all the signs and wonders wrought in Egypt and in the Red Sea, were justly required to give divine authority to mere positive ordinances, in which, without such external warrant, none could have recognised the voice of God. We ask of Mr. Newman and his friends to bring some warrant of Scripture for that which they declare to be God's will. They speak very positively and say, that "the security by our Lord no less expressly authorized for the continuance and due application of the Sacrament of the Lord's Supper, is the apostolical commission of the bishops, and under them the presbyters of the Church." They say that our Lord has authorized this "no less expressly" than he has authorized the Holy Supper as the mean of partaking in his body and blood. What our Lord has said concerning the communion is not truly represented: he instituted it as one mean of grace among many; not as *the* mean; neither the sole mean, nor the principal. But allow, for an instant, that it was instituted as *the* mean; and give this sense to those well-known and ever-memorable words in which our Lord commanded his disciples to eat the bread and drink of the cup, in remembrance of him. His words commanding us to do this are express; "not less express," we are told, is his "sanction of the apostolical commission of the bishops, as the security for the continuance and due application of the Sacrament." Surely these writers allow themselves to pervert language so habitually, that they do not consider when, and with regard to whom, they are doing it. They say that our Lord has sanctioned the necessity of apostolical succession, in order to secure the continuance and efficacy of the sacrament, "no less expressly" than he instituted the sacrament itself. If they had merely asserted that he had sanctioned the necessity of apostolical succession, we might have supposed that, by some interpretation of their own, they implied his sanction of it, from words which, to other men, bore no such meaning. But in saying that he has "expressly sanctioned it," they have, most unconsciously, I trust, ascribed their own words to our Lord; they make Mm to say what he has not said, unless they can produce[4] some other credible record of his words besides the books of the four evangelists and the apostolical epistles.

[4] "Scripture alone contains what remains to us of our Lord's teaching. If there be a portion of revelation sacred beyond other portions, distinct and remote in its nature from the rest, it must be the words and works of the eternal Son Incarnate. He is the one Prophet of the Church, as he is our one Priest and King. His history is as far above any other possible revelation, as heaven is above earth: for in it we have literally the sight of Almighty God in his judgments, thoughts, attributes, and deeds, and his mode of dealing with us his creatures. Now, this special revelation is in Scripture, and in Scripture only: tradition has no part in it."--*Newman's Lectures on the Prophetical Office of the Church.* 1837. Pp. 347, 348.

That their statement was untrue, and being untrue, that it is a most grave matter to speak untruly of our Lord's commands, are points absolutely certain. But if they recall the assertion, as to the expressness of our Lord's sanction, and mean to say, that his sanction is implied, and may be reasonably deduced from what he has said, then I answer, that the deduction ought to be clear, because the doctrine in itself bears on it no marks of having had Christ for its author. Yet so far is it from true, that the necessity of apostolical succession, in order to give efficacy to the sacrament, may be clearly deduced from any recorded words of our Lord, that there are no words[5] of his from which it can be deduced, either probably or plausibly; none with which it has any, the faintest, connexion; none from which it could be even conjectured that such a tenet had ever been in existence. I am not speaking, it will be observed, of apostolical succession simply; but of the necessity of apostolical succession, as a security for the efficacy of the sacrament. That this doctrine comes from God, is a position altogether without evidence, probability, or presumption, either internal or external.

[5] Since this was written, I have found out, what certainly it was impossible to anticipate beforehand, that our Lord's words, "Do this in remembrance of me," are supposed to teach the doctrine of the priest's consecrating power. But the passage to which I refer is so remarkable that I must quote it in its author's own words. Mr. Newman, for the tract is apparently one of his, observes, that three out of the four Gospels make no mention of the raising of Lazarus. He then goes on, "As the raising of Lazarus is true, though not contained at all in the first three Gospels; so the gift of consecrating the Eucharist may have been committed by Christ to the priesthood, though only indirectly taught in any of the four. Will you say I am arguing against our own Church, which says the Scripture 'contains all things necessary to be believed to salvation?' Doubtless, Scripture *contains* all things necessary to be *believed*; but there may be things *contained* which are not *on the surface*, and things which belong to the *ritual*, and not to *belief.* Points of faith may lie *under* the surface: points of observance need not be in Scripture *at all.* The consecrating power is a point of ritual, yet it *is* indirectly taught in Scripture, though not brought out, when Christ said, 'Do this,' for he spake to the apostles, who were priests, not to his disciples generally."--*Tracts for the Times.* Tract   85,   p.   46.

This passage is indeed characteristic of the moral and intellectual faults which I have alluded to as marking the writings of the supporters of Mr. Newman's system. But what is become of the assertion, that this security of the apostolical commission was "expressly authorized" by our Lord, when it is admitted that it is only indirectly taught in Scripture? And what becomes of the notion, that what our Lord did or instituted may be learned from another source than Scripture, when Mr. Newman has most truly stated, in the passage quoted in the preceding note, that our Lord's history, the history of his words and works, "is in Scripture, and Scripture only: tradition has no part in it?" I pass over the surprising state of mind which could imagine a distinction between things necessary to be believed, and necessary to be done; and could conceive such a distinction to be according to the meaning of our article. It would appear that this shift has been since abandoned, and others, no way less extraordinary, have been attempted in its place; for an extraordinary process it must be which tries to reconcile Mr. Newman's opinions with the declaration of the sixth article. But now for Mr. Newman's scriptural proof, that our Lord "committed to the priesthood the gift of consecrating the Eucharist." "When Christ said, 'Do this,' he spake to the apostles, who were priests, not to his disciples generally." This would prove too much, for it would prove that none but the clergy were ordered to receive the communion at all: the words, "Do this," referring, not to any consecration, of which there had been no word said, but to the eating

9

the bread, and drinking of the cup. Again, when St. Paul says, "the cup which we bless,'--the bread which we break," it is certain that the word "we," does not refer to himself and Sosthenes, or to himself and Barnabas, but to himself and the whole Corinthian church; for he immediately goes on, "for we, the whole number of us," ([Greek: oi polloi] compare Romans xii. 5,) "are one body, for we all are partakers of the one bread." Thirdly, Tertullian expressly contrasts the original institution of our Lord with the church practice of his own day, in this very point. "Eucharistiæ sacramentum et in tempore victus, et omnibus mandatum a Domino, etiam antelucanis coetibus nec de aliorum manu quam præridentium sumimus." (*De Coronâ Mililis*, 3.) I know that Tertullian believes the alteration to have been founded upon an apostolical tradition; but he no less names it as a change from the original institution of our Lord; nor does he appear to consider it as more than a point of order. Lastly, what shadow of probability is there, and is it not begging the whole question, to assume that our Lord spoke to his apostles as priests, and not as representatives of the whole Christian church? His language makes no distinction between his disciples and those who were without; it repels it as dividing his disciples from each other. His twelve disciples were the apostles of the church, but they were not priests. In such matters our Lord's words apply exactly, "One is your Master, even Christ, and all ye are brethren."

On the whole, then, the movement in the church, excited by Mr. Newman and his friends, appears to be made in a false direction, and to be incapable of satisfying the feeling which prompted it. I have not noticed other presumptions against it, arising from the consequences to which the original doctrines of the party have since led, or from certain moral and intellectual faults which have marked the writings of its supporters. It is enough to say, that the movement originated in minds highly prejudiced beforehand, and under the immediate influence of passion and fear; that its doctrines, as a whole, resemble the teaching of no set of writers entitled to respect, either in the early church, or in our own; that they tend, not to Christ's glory, or to the advancement of holiness, but simply to the exaltation of the clergy; and that they are totally unsupported by the authority of Scripture. They are a plant, therefore, which our heavenly Father has not planted; a speaking in the name of the Lord what the Lord has not commanded; hay and stubble, built upon the foundation of Christ, which are good for nothing but to be burned.

I have spoken quite confidently of the total absence of all support in Scripture for Mr. Newman's favourite doctrine of "the necessity of apostolical succession, in order to ensure the effect of the sacraments." This doctrine is very different from that of the Divine appointment of episcopacy as a form of government, or even from that of the exclusive lawfulness of that episcopacy which has come down by succession from the apostles. Much less is it to be confounded with any notions, however exalted, of the efficacy of the sacraments, even though carried to such a length as we read of in the early church, when living men had themselves baptized as proxies for the dead, and when a portion of the wine of the communion was placed by the side of a corpse in the grave. Such notions may be superstitious and unscriptural, as indeed they are, but they are quite distinct from a belief in the necessity of a human priest to give the sacraments their virtue. And, without going to such lengths as this, men may overestimate the efficacy of the sacraments, to the disparagement of prayer, and preaching, and reading the Scriptures, and yet may be perfectly clear from the opinion which makes this efficacy depend immediately on a human administrator. And so again, men may hold episcopacy to be divine, and the episcopacy of apostolical succession to be the only true episcopacy, but yet they may utterly reject the notion of its being essential to the efficacy of the sacraments. It is of this last doctrine only that I assert, in the strongest terms, that it is wholly without support in Scripture, direct or indirect, and that it does not minister to godliness.

In truth, Mr. Newman and his friends are well aware that the Scripture will not support their doctrine, and therefore it is that they have proceeded to such, lengths in upholding the authority not of the creeds only, but of the opinions and practices of the ancient church generally; and that they try to explain away the clear language of our article, that nothing "which is neither read therein (i.e. in holy Scripture,) nor may be proved thereby, is to be required of any man that it should be believed as an article of faith, or be thought requisite or necessary to salvation." It would be one of the most unaccountable phenomena of the human mind, were any man fairly to come to the conclusion that the Scriptures and the early church were of equal authority, and that the authority of both were truly divine. If any men resolve to maintain doctrines and practices as of divine authority, for which the Scripture offers no countenance, they of course are driven to maintain the authority of the church in their own defence; and where they have an interest in holding any particular opinion, its falsehood, however palpable, is unhappily no bar to its reception. Otherwise it would seem that the natural result of believing the early church to be of equal authority with the Scripture, would be to deny the inspiration of either. For two things so different in several points as the Christianity of the Scriptures and that of the early church, may conceivably be both false, but it is hard to think that they can both be perfectly true.

I am here, however, allowing, what is by no means true, without many qualifications, that Mr. Newman's system is that of the early church. The historical inquiry as to the doctrines of the early church would lead me into far too wide a field; I may only notice, in passing, how many points require to be carefully defined in conducting such an inquiry; as, for instance, what we mean by the term "early church," as to time; for that may be fully true of the church in the fourth century, which is only partially true of it in the third, and only in a very slight degree true of it in the second or first. And again, what do we mean by the term "early church," as to persons; for a few eminent writers are not even the whole clergy; neither is it by any means to be taken on their authority that their views were really those of all the bishops and presbyters of the Christian world; but if they were, the clergy are not the church, nor can their judgments be morally considered as the voice of the church, even if we were to admit that they could at any time constitute its voice legally. But, for my present purpose, we may take for granted that Mr. Newman's system as to the pre-eminence of the sacraments, and the necessity of apostolical succession to give them their efficacy, was the doctrine of the early church; then I say that this system is so different from that of the New Testament, that to invest the two with equal authority is not to make the church system divine, but to make the scriptural system human; or, at the best, perishable and temporary, like the ceremonial law of Moses. Either the church system must be supposed to have superseded the scriptural system[6], and its unknown authors are the real apostles of our present faith, in which case, we do not see why it should not be superseded in its turn, and why the perfect manifestation of Christianity should not be found in the Koran, or in any still later system; or else neither of the two systems can be divine, but the one is merely the human production of the first century, the other that of the second and third. If this be so, it is clearly open to all succeeding centuries to adopt whichever of the two they choose, or neither.

[6] This, it is well known, has been most ably maintained by Rothe, (*Artfänge der Christlichen Kirche und ihrer Verfassung*, Wittenberg, 1837,) with respect to the origin of episcopacy. He contends that it was instituted by the surviving apostles after the destruction of Jerusalem, as an intentional change from the earlier constitution of the church, in order to enable it to meet the peculiar difficulties and dangers of the times. To this belongs the question of the meaning of the expression, [Greek: oi tais deuterais ton Apostolon diataxesi parakolouthaekotes], in the famous Fragments of Irenæus, published by Pfaff, from a manuscript in the library of Turin, and to be found in the Venice edition of Irenæus, 1734, vol. ii. *Fragmentorum*, p. 10. But then Rothe would admit that if the apostles altered what they themselves had appointed, it would follow that neither their earlier nor their later institutions were intended to be for all times and all places, but were simply adapted to a particular state of circumstances, and were alterable when that state was altered: in short, whatever institutions the apostles changed were shown to be essentially changeable; otherwise their early institution was defective, which cannot be conceived. And thus it may well be that the early church may have altered, in some points, the first institutions of the apostles, and may have been guided by God's Spirit in doing so; but the error consists in believing that the now institutions were to be of necessity more permanent than those which they succeeded; in supposing that either the one or the other belong to the eternal truths and laws of Christ's religion, when they belong, in fact, to the essentially changeable regulations of his church.

To such consequences are those driven who maintain the divine authority of the system of Mr. Newman. Assuredly the thirst for "something deeper and truer than satisfied

11

the last century," will not be allayed by a draught so scanty and so vapid; but after the mirage has beguiled and disappointed him for a season, the traveller presses on the more eagerly to the true and living well.

In truth, the evils of the last century were but the inevitable fruits of the long ascendency of Mr. Newman's favourite principles. Christ's religion had been corrupted in the long period before the Reformation, but it had ever retained many of its main truths, and it was easy, when the appeal was once made to Scripture, to sweep away the corruptions, and restore it in its perfect form; but Christ's church had been destroyed so long and so completely, that its very idea was all but lost, and to revive it actually was impossible. What had been known under that name,--I am speaking of Christ's church, be it observed, as distinguished from Christ's religion,--was so great an evil, that, hopeless of drawing any good from it, men looked rather to Christ's religion as all in all; and content with having destroyed the false church, never thought that the scheme of Christianity could not be perfectly developed without the restoration of the true one. But the want was deeply felt, and its consequences were deplorable. At this moment men are truly craving something deeper than satisfied the last century; they crave to have the true church of Christ, which the last century was without. Mr. Newman perceives their want, and again offers them that false church which is worse than none at all.

The truths of the Christian religion are to be sought for in the Scripture alone; they are the same at all times and in all countries. With the Christian church it is otherwise; the church is not a revelation concerning the unchangeable and eternal God, but an institution to enable changeable man to apprehend the unchangeable. Because man is changeable, the church is also changeable; changeable, not in its object, which is for ever one and the same, but in its means for effecting that object; changeable in its details, because the same treatment cannot suit various diseases, various climates, various constitutional peculiarities, various external influences.

The Scripture, then, which is the sole and direct authority for all the truths of the Christian religion, is not in the same way, an authority for the constitution and rules of the Christian church; that is, it does not furnish direct authority, but guides us only by analogy: or it gives us merely certain main principles, which we must apply to our own various circumstances. This is shown by the remarkable fact, that neither our Lord nor his apostles have left any commands with respect to the constitution and administration of the church generally. Commands in abundance they have left us on moral matters; and one commandment of another kind has been added, the commandment, namely, to celebrate the Lord's Supper. "Do this in remembrance of me," are our Lord's words; and St. Paul tells us, if we could otherwise have doubted it, that this remembrance is to be kept up for ever. "As often as ye eat that bread or drink that cup ye do show the Lord's death *till he come.*" This is the one perpetual ordinance of the Christian church, and this is commanded to be kept perpetually. But its other institutions are mentioned historically, as things done once, but not necessarily to be always repeated: nay, they are mentioned without any details, so that we do not always know what their exact form was in their original state, and cannot, therefore, if we would, adopt it as a perpetual model. Nor is it unimportant to observe that institutions are recorded as having been created on the spur of the occasion, if I may so speak, not as having formed a part of an original and universal plan. A great change in the character of the deacon, or subordinate minister's office, is introduced in consequence of the complaints of the Hellenist Christians: the number of the apostles is increased by the addition of Paul and Barnabas, not appointed, as Matthias had been, by the other apostles themselves, but by the prophets and teachers of the church of Antioch. Again, the churches founded by St. Paul were each, at first, placed by him under the government of several presbyters; but after his imprisonment at Rome, finding that they were become greatly corrupted, he sends out single persons, in two instances, with full powers to remodel these churches, and with authority to correct the presbyters themselves: yet it does not appear that these especial[7] visitors were to alter permanently the earlier constitution of the churches; nor that they were sent generally to all the churches which St. Paul had founded. Indeed, it appears evident from the epistle of Clement, that the original constitution of the church of Corinth still subsisted in his time; the government was still vested not in one man, but in many[8]. Yet a few years later the government of a single man, as we see from Ignatius, was become very general; and Ignatius, as is well known, wishes to invest it with absolute power[9]. I believe that he acted quite wisely according to the circumstances of the church at that period; and that nothing less than a vigorous unity of government could have struggled with the difficulties and dangers of that crisis. But no man can doubt that the system which Ignatius so earnestly recommends was very different from that which St. Paul had instituted fifty or sixty years earlier.

[7] The command, "to appoint elders in every city," is given to Titus, according to Paul's practice when he first formed churches of the Gentiles (Acts xiv, 2.) Nor did Timothy, or Titus, remain permanently at Ephesus, or in Crete. Timothy, when St. Paul's second Epistle was written to him, was certainly not at Ephesus, but apparently in Pontus; and Titus, at the same period, was gone to Dalmatia: nor indeed was he to remain in Crete beyond the summer of the year in which St. Paul's Epistle was written; he was to meet Paul, in the winter, at Nicopolis.

[8] Only elders are spoken of as governing the church of Corinth. It is impossible to understand clearly the nature of the contest, and of the party against which Clement's Epistle is directed. Where he wishes the heads of that party to say, [Greek: ei di eme stasis kai eris kai schismata, ekchoro, apeimi, ou ean, boulaesthe, kai poio, ta, prostassomena upo tou plaethous], c. 54, it would seem as if they had been endeavouring to exercise a despotic authority over the church, in defiance of the general feeling, as well as of the existing government, like those earlier persons at Corinth, whom St. Paul describes, in his second Epistle, xi. 20; and like Diotrephes, mentioned by St. John, 3 Epist. 9, 10. But in a society where all power must have depended on the consent of those subject to it, how could any one exercise a tyranny against the will of the majority, as well as against the authority of the Apostles? And [Greek: ta prostassomena upo tou plaethous] must signify, I think, "the bidding of the society at large." Compare for this use of [Greek: plaethos], Ignatius, Smyrna. 8; Trallian. 1, 8. A conjecture might be offered as to the solution of this difficulty, but it would lead mo into too long a discussion.

[9] Insomuch that he wished all marriages to be solemnized with the consent and approbation of the bishop, [Greek: meta gnomaes tou episkopou], that they might be "according to God, and not according to passion;" [Greek: kapa Theon kai mae kat epithomian].--Ad. Polycarp. 5.

On two points, however,--points not of detail, but of principle,--the Scripture does seem to speak decisively. 1st. The whole body of the church was to take an active share in its concerns; the various faculties of its various members were to perform their several parts: it was to be a living society, not an inert mass of mere hearers and subjects, who were to be authoritatively taught and absolutely ruled by one small portion of its members. It is quite consistent with this, that, at particular times, the church should centre all its own power and activity in the persons of its rulers. In the field, the imperium of the Roman consul was unlimited; and even within the city walls, the senate's commission in times of imminent danger, released him from all restraints of law; the whole power of the state was, for the moment, his, and his only. Such temporary despotisms are sometimes not expedient merely, but necessary: without them society would perish. I do not, therefore, regard Ignatius's epistles as really contradictory to the idea of the church conveyed to us in the twelfth chapter of St. Paul's First Epistle to the Corinthians: I believe that the dictatorship, so to speak, which Ignatius claims for the bishop in each church, was required by the circumstances of the case; but to change the temporary into the perpetual dictatorship, was to subvert the Roman constitution; and to make Ignatius's language the rule, instead of the exception, is no less to subvert the Christian church. Wherever the language of Ignatius is repeated with justice, there the church must either be in its infancy, or in its dotage, or in some extraordinary crisis of danger; wherever it is repeated, as of universal application, it destroys, as in fact it has destroyed, the very life of Christ's institution.

But, 2d, the Christian church was absolutely and entirely, at all times, and in all places, to be without a human priesthood. Despotic government and priesthood are things perfectly distinct from one another. Despotic government might be required, from time to time, by this or that portion of the Christian church, as by other societies; for government is essentially changeable, and all forms, in the manifold varieties of the condition of society, are, in their turn, lawful and beneficial. But a priesthood belongs to a matter not so varying-- the relations subsisting between God and man. These relations were fixed for the Christian church from its very foundation, being, in fact, no other than the main truths of the Christian religion; and they bar, for all time, the very notion of an earthly priesthood. They bar it, because they establish the everlasting priesthood of our Lord, which leaves no place for any other; they bar it, because priesthood is essentially mediation; and they establish one Mediator between God and man--the Man Christ Jesus. And, therefore, the notion of Mr. Newman and his friends, that the sacraments derive their efficacy from the apostolical succession of the minister, is so extremely unchristian, that it actually deserves to be called anti-christian; for there is no point of the priestly office, properly so called, in which the claim of the earthly priest is not absolutely precluded. Do we want him for sacrifice? Nay, there is no place for him at all; for our one atoning Sacrifice has been once offered; and by its virtue we are enabled to offer daily our spiritual sacrifices of ourselves, which no other man can by possibility offer for us. Do we want him for intercession? Nay, there is One who ever liveth to make intercession for us, through whom we have access to ([Greek: prosalogaen], admission to the presence of) the Father, and for whose sake, Paul, and Apollos, and Peter, and things present, and things to come, are all ours already. His claim can neither be advanced or received without high dishonour to our true Priest and to his blessed gospel. If circumcision could not be practised, as necessary, by a believer in Christ, without its involving a forfeiture of the benefits of Christ's salvation; how much more does St. Paul's language apply to the invention of an earthly priesthood--a priesthood neither after the order of Aaron, nor yet of Melchisedek; unlawful alike under the law and the gospel.

It is the invention of the human priesthood, which falling in, unhappily, with the absolute power rightfully vested in the Christian church during the troubles of the second century, fixed the exception as the rule, and so in the end destroyed the church. It pretended that the clergy were not simply rulers and teachers,--offices which, necessarily vary according to the state of those who are ruled and taught,--but that they were essentially mediators between God and the church; and as this language would have sounded too profanely,--for the mediator between God and the church can be none but Christ,--so the clergy began to draw to themselves the attributes of the church, and to call the church by a different name, such as the faithful, or the laity; so that to speak of the church mediating for the people did not sound so shocking, and the doctrine so disguised found ready acceptance. Thus the evil work was consummated; the great majority of the members of the church, were virtually disfranchised; the minority retained the name, but the character of the institution was utterly corrupted.

To revive Christ's church, therefore, is to expel the antichrist of priesthood, (which, as it was foretold of him, "as God, sitteth in the temple of God, showing himself that he is God,") and to restore its disfranchised members,--the laity,--to the discharge of their proper duties in it, and to the consciousness of their paramount importance. This is the point which I have dwelt upon in the XXXVIIIth Lecture, and which is closely in connection with the point maintained in the XLth; and all who value the inestimable blessings of Christ's church should labour in arousing the laity to a sense of their great share in them. In particular, that discipline, which is one of the greatest of those blessings, never can, and, indeed, never ought to be restored, till the Church resumes its lawful authority, and puts an end to the usurpation of its powers by the clergy. There is a feeling now awakened amongst the lay members of our Church, which, if it can but be rightly directed, may, by God's blessing, really arrive at something truer and deeper than satisfied the last century, or than satisfied the last seventeen centuries. Otherwise, whatever else may be improved, the laity will take care that church discipline shall continue to slumber, and they will best serve the church by doing so. Much may be done to spread the knowledge of Christ's religion; new churches may be built; new ministers appointed to preach the word and administer the sacraments; those may hear who now cannot hear; many more sick persons may be visited; many more children may receive religious instruction: all this is good, and to be received with sincere thankfulness; but, with a knowledge revealed to us of a still more excellent power in Christ's church, and with the abundant promises of prophecy in our hands, can we rest satisfied with the lesser and imperfect good, which strikes thrice and stays? But, if the zeal of the lay members of our Church be directed by the principles of Mr. Newman, then the result will be, not merely a lesser good, but one fearfully mixed with evil--Christian religion profaned by anti-christian fables, Christian holiness marred by superstition and uncharitableness; Christian wisdom and Christian sincerity scoffed at, reviled, and persecuted out of sight. This is declared to us by the sure voice of experience; this was the fruit of the spirit of priestcraft, with its accompaniments of superstitious rites and lying traditions, in the last decline of the Jewish church; this was the fruit of the same spirit, with the same accompaniments, in the long decay of the Christian church; although, the indestructible virtue of Christ's gospel was manifest in the midst of the evil, and Christ, in every age and in every country, has been known with saving power by some of his people, and his church, in her worst corruptions, has taught many divinest truths, has inculcated many holiest virtues.

When the tide is setting strongly against us, we can scarcely expect to make progress; it is enough if we do not drift along with it. Mr. Newman's system is now at the flood; it is daily making converts; it is daily swelled by many of those who neither love it nor understand it in itself, but who hope to make it serve their purposes, or who like to swim with the stream. A strong profession, therefore, of an opposite system must expect, at the present moment, to meet with little favour; nor, indeed, have I any hope of turning the tide, which will flow for its appointed season, and its ebb does not seem to be at hand. But whilst the hurricane rages, those exposed to it may well encourage one another to hold fast their own foundations against it; and many are exposed to it in whose welfare I naturally have the deepest interest, and in whom old impressions may be supposed to have still so much force that I may claim from them, at least, a patient hearing. I am anxious to show them that Mr. Newman's system is to be opposed not merely on negative grounds, as untrue, but as obstructing that perfect and positive truth, that perfection of Christ's church, which the last century, it may be, neglected, but which I value and desire as earnestly as it can be valued and desired by any man alive. My great objection to Mr. Newman's system is, that it destroys Christ's church, and sets up an evil in its stead. We do not desire merely to hinder the evil from occupying the ground, and to leave it empty; that has been, undoubtedly, the misfortune, and partly the fault of Protestantism; but we desire to build on the holy ground a no less holy temple, not out of our own devices, but according to the teaching of Christ himself, who has given us the outline, and told us what should be its purposes.

The true church of Christ would offer to every faculty of our nature its proper exercise, and would entirely meet all our wants. No wise man doubts that the Reformation was imperfect, or that in the Romish system there were many good institutions, and practices, and feelings, which it would be most desirable to restore amongst ourselves. Daily church services, frequent communions, memorials of our Christian calling continually presented to our notice, in crosses and way-side oratories; commemorations of holy men, of all times and countries; the doctrine of the communion of saints practically taught; religious orders, especially of women, of different kinds, and under different rules, delivered only from the snare and sin of perpetual vows; all these, most of which are of some efficacy for good, even in a corrupt church, belong no less to the true church, and would there be purely beneficial. If Mr. Newman's system attracts good and thinking men, because it seems to promise them all these things, which in our actual Church are not to be found, let them remember, that these things belong to the perfect church no less than to that of the Romanists and of Mr. Newman, and would flourish in the perfect church far more healthily. Or, again, if any man admires Mr. Newman's system for its austerities, if he regards fasting as a positive duty, he should consider that these might be transferred also to the perfect church, and that they have no necessary connexion with the peculiar tenets of Mr. Newman. We know that the Puritans were taunted by their adversaries for their frequent fasts, and the severity of their lives; and they certainly were far enough from agreeing with Mr. Newman. Whatever there is of good, or self-denying, or ennobling, in his system, is altogether independent of his doctrine concerning the priesthood. It is that doctrine which is the peculiarity of his system and of Romanism; it is that doctrine which constitutes the evil of both, which over-weighs all the good accidentally united with it, and makes the systems, as such, false and anti-christian. Nor can any human being find in this doctrine anything of a beneficial tendency either to his intellectual, his moral, or his spiritual nature. If mere reverence be a virtue, without reference to its object, let us, by all means, do honour to the virtue of those who fell down to the stock of a tree; and let us lament the harsh censure which charged them with "having a lie in their right hand[10]."

[10] The language which Mr. Newman and his friends have allowed themselves to hold, in admiration of what they call reverential and submissive faith, might certainly be used in defence of the lowest idolatry; what they have dared to call rationalistic can plead such high and sacred authority in its favour, that if I were to quote some of the language of the "Tracts for the Times," and place by the side of it certain passages from the New Testament, Mr. Newman and his friends would appear to have been writing blasphemy. It seems scarcely possible that they could have remembered what is said in St. Matthew xv. 9-20, and who said it, when they have called it rationalism to deny a spiritual virtue in things that are applied to the body.

What does the true and perfect church want, that she should borrow from the broken cisterns of idolatry? Holding all those truths in which the clear voice of God's word is joined by the accordant confession of God's people in all ages; holding all the means of grace of which she was designed to be the steward--her common prayers, her pure preaching, her uncorrupted sacraments, her free and living society, her wise and searching discipline, her commemorations and memorials of God's mercy and grace, whether shown in her Lord himself, or in his and her members;--looking lovingly upon her elder sisters, the ancient churches, and delighting to be in communion with them, as she hopes that her younger sisters, the churches of later days, will delight to be in communion with her;--what has she not, that Christ's bride should have? what has she not, that Mr. Newman's system can give her? But because she loves her Lord, and stands fast in his faith, and has been enlightened by his truth, she will endure no other mediator than Christ, she will repose her trust only on his word, she will worship in the light, and will abhor the words, no less than the works, of darkness. Her sisters, the elder churches, she loves and respects as she would be herself loved and respected; but she will not, and may not, worship them, nor even, for their sakes, believe error to be truth, or foolishness to be wisdom. She dare not hope that she can be in all things a perfect guide and example to the churches that shall come after her; as neither have the churches before her been in all things a perfect guide and example to herself. She would not impose her yoke upon future generations, nor will she submit her own neck to the yoke of antiquity. She honours all men, but makes none her idol; and she would have her own individual members regard her with honour, but neither would she be an idol to them. She dreads especially that sin of which her Lord has so emphatically warned her--the sin against the Holy Ghost. She will neither lie against him by declaring that he is where his fruits are not manifested; nor blaspheme him, by saying that he is not where his fruits are. Rites and ordinances may be vain, prophets may be false, miracles may be miracles of Satan; but the signs of the Holy Spirit, truth and holiness, can never be ineffectual, can never deceive, can never be evil; where they are, and only where they are, there is God.

There are states of falsehood and wickedness so monstrous, that, to use the language of Eastern mythology, the Destroyer God is greater than the Creator or the Preserver, and no good can be conceived so great as the destruction of the existing evil. But ordinarily in human affairs destruction and creation should go hand in hand; as the evergreen shrubs of our gardens do not cast their old leaves till the young ones are ready to supply their place. Great as is the falsehood of Mr. Newman's system, it would be but an unsatisfactory work to clear it away, if we had no positive truth to offer in its room. But the thousands of good men whom it has beguiled, because it professed to meet the earnest craving of their minds for a restoration of Christ's church with power, need not fear to open their eyes to its hollowness; like the false miracles of fraud or sorcery, it is but the counterfeit of a real truth. The restoration of the church, is, indeed, the best consummation of all our prayers, and all our labours; it is not a dream, not a prospect to be seen only in the remotest distance; it is possible, it lies very near us; with God's blessing it is in the power of this very generation to begin and make some progress in the work. If the many good, and wise, and influential laymen of our Church would but awake to their true position and duties, and would labour heartily to procure for the church a living organization and an effective government, in both,

16

of which the laity should be essential members, then, indeed, the church would become a reality[11]. This is not Erastianism, or rather, it is not what is commonly cried down under that name; it is not the subjection of the church to the state, which, indeed, would be a most miserable and most unchristian condition; but it would be the deliverance of the church, and its exaltation to its own proper sovereignty. The members of one particular profession are most fit to administer a system in part, most unfit to legislate for it or to govern it: we could ill spare the ability and learning of our lawyers, but we surely should not wish to have none but lawyers concerned even, in the administration of justice, much less to have none but lawyers in the government or in parliament. What is true of lawyers with regard to the state, is no less true of the clergy with regard to the church; indispensable as ministers and advisers, they cannot, without great mischief, act as sole judges, sole legislators, sole governors. And this is a truth so palpable, that the clergy, by pressing such a claim, merely deprive the church of its judicial, legislative, and executive functions; whilst the common sense of the church will not allow them to exercise these powers, and, whilst they assert that no one else may exercise them, the result is, that they are not exercised at all, and the essence of the church is destroyed.

[11] The famous saying, "extra ecclesiam nulla salus," is, in its idea, a most divine truth; historically and in fact it may be, and often has been, a practical falsehood. If the truths of Christ's religion were necessarily accessible only to the members of some visible church, then it would be true always, inasmuch as to be out of the church would then be the same thing as to be without Christ; and, as a society, the church ought so to attract to itself all goodness, and by its internal organization, so to encourage all goodness, that nothing would be without its pale but extreme wickedness, or extreme ignorance; and he who were voluntarily to forfeit its spiritual advantages, would be guilty of moral suicide; so St. Paul calls the church the pillar and ground of truth; that is, it was so in its purpose and idea; and he therefore conjures Timothy to walk warily in it, and to take heed that what ought to be the pillar and ground of truth should not be profaned by fables, and so be changed into a pillar of falsehood. But to say universally, as an historical fact, that "extra ecclesiam nulla salus," may be often to utter one of the worst of falsehoods. A ferry is set up to transport men over an unfordable river, and it might be truly said that "extra navem nulla salus;" there is no other safe way, speaking generally, of getting over; but the ferryman has got the plague, and if you go in the boat with him, you will catch it and die. In despair, a man plunges into the water, and swims across; would not the ferryman be guilty of a double falsehood who should call out to this man, "extra navem nulla salus," insisting that he had not swum over, when he had, and saying that his boat would have carried him safely, whereas it would have killed him?

The first step towards the restoration of the church seems to be the revival of the order of deacons; which might be effected without any other change in our present system than a repeal of all laws, canons, or customs which prohibit a deacon from following a secular calling, which confer on him any civil exemptions, or subject him to any civil disqualifications. The Ordination Service, with the subscription to the Articles, would remain perfectly unaltered; and as no deacon can hold any benefice, it is manifest that the proposed measure would in no way interfere with the rights or duties of the order of presbyters, or priests, which would remain precisely what they are at present. But the benefit in large towns would be enormous, if, instead of the present system of district visiting by private individuals, excellent as that is where there is nothing better, we could have a large body of deacons, the ordained ministers of the church, visiting the sick, managing charitable subscriptions, and sharing with their presbyter in those strictly clerical duties, which now, in many cases, are too much for the health and powers of the strongest. Yet a still greater advantage would be found in the link thus formed between the clergy and laity by the revival of an order appertaining in a manner to both. Nor would it be a little thing that many who now become teachers in some dissenting congregation, not because they differ from our Articles, or dislike our Liturgy, but because they cannot afford to go to the universities, and have no prospect of being maintained by the church, if they were to give up their secular callings, would, in all human probability, be glad to join the church, as deacons, and would

17

thus be subject to her authorities, and would be engaged in her service, instead of being aliens to her, if not enemies.

When we look at the condition of our country: at the poverty and wretchedness of so large a portion of the working classes; at the intellectual and moral evils which certainly exist among the poor, but by no means amongst the poor only; and when we witness the many partial attempts to remedy these evils--attempts benevolent indeed and wise, so far as they go, but utterly unable to strike to the heart of the mischief; can any Christian doubt that here is the work for the church of Christ to do; that none else can do it; and that with the blessing of her Almighty Head she can? Looking upon the chaos around us, one power alone can reduce it into order, and fill it with light and life. And does he really apprehend the perfections and high calling of Christ's church; does he indeed fathom the depths of man's wants, or has he learnt to rise to the fulness of the stature of their divine remedy, who comes forward to preach to us the necessity of apostolical succession? Grant even that it was of divine appointment, still as it is demonstrably and palpably unconnected with holiness, as it would be a mere positive and ceremonial ordinance, it cannot be the point of most importance to insist on; even if it be a sin to neglect this, there are so many far weightier matters equally neglected, that it would be assuredly no Christian prophesying which were to strive to direct our chief attention to this. But the wholly unmoral character of this doctrine, which if it were indeed of God, would make it a single mysterious exception to all the other doctrines of the Gospel, is, God be thanked, not more certain than its total want of external evidence; the Scripture disclaims it, Christ himself condemns it.

I have written at considerable length: yet so vast is the subject, that I may seem to some to have written superficially, and to have left my statements without adequate support. I can only say that no one paragraph has been written hastily, nor in fact is there one the substance of which has not been for several years in my mind; indeed, in many instances, not only the substance, but the proofs in detail have been actually written: but to have inserted them here would have been impracticable, as they would have been in themselves a volume. Neither have I knowingly remained in ignorance of any argument which may have been used in defence of Mr. Newman's system; I have always desired to know what he and his friends say, and on what grounds they say it; although, as I have not read the Tracts for the Times regularly, I may have omitted something which it would have been important to notice. Finally, in naming Mr. Newman as the chief author of the system which I have been considering, I have in no degree wished to make the question personal; but Mr. Percival's letter authorizes us to consider him as one of the authors of it; and as I have never had any personal acquaintance with him, I could mention his name with no shock to any private feelings either in him or in myself. But I have spoken of him simply as the maintainer of certain doctrines, not as maintaining them in any particular manner, far less as actuated by any particular motives. I believe him to be in most serious error; I believe his system to be so destructive of Christ's church, that I earnestly pray, and would labour to the utmost of my endeavours for its utter overthrow: but on the other hand, I will not be tempted to confound the authors of the system with the system itself; for I know that the most mischievous errors have been promulgated by men who yet have been neither foolish nor wicked; and I nothing doubt that there are many points in Mr. Newman, in which I might learn truth from his teaching, and should be glad if I could come near him in his practice.

NOTE.

In order to prevent the possibility of misunderstanding, it is proper to repeat what has been often said by others, that the English word "priest" has two significations,--the one according to its etymology, through the French *prêtre*, or *prestre*, and the Latin *presbyterus*, from the Greek [Greek: presbuteros]; in which sense it is used in our Liturgy and Rubrics, and signifies merely "one belonging to the order of Presbyters," as distinguished from the other two orders of bishops and deacons. But the other signification of the word "priest," and which we use, as I think, more commonly, is the same with the meaning of the Latin word *sacerdos,* and the Greek word [Greek: iepeus], and means, "one who stands as a mediator between God and the people, and brings them to God by the virtue of certain ceremonial acts which he performs for them, and which they could not perform for themselves without profanation, because they are at a distance from God, and cannot, in their own persons, venture to approach towards him." In this sense of the word "priest," the term is not applied to the ministers of the Christian church, either by the Scripture, or by the authorized formularies of the Church of England; although, in the other sense, as synonymous with Presbyters, it is used in our Prayer Book repeatedly. Of course, not one word of what I have written is meant to deny the lawfulness and importance of the order of Presbyters in the church; I have only spoken against a priesthood, in the other sense of the word, in which a "priest" means "a mediator between God and man;" in that sense, in short, in which the word is not a translation of [Greek: presbuteros], but [iereus].

LECTURE I.

GENESIS iii. 22.

And the Lord God said, Behold,
the man is become as one of us,
to know good and evil.

This is declared to be man's condition after the Fall. I will not attempt to penetrate into that which is not to be entered into, nor to pretend to discover all that may be concealed beneath the outward, and in many points clearly parabolical, form of the account of man's temptation and sin. But that condition to which his sin brought him is our condition; with that, undoubtedly, we are concerned; that must be the foundation of all sound views of human nature; the double fact employed in the word fall is of the last importance; the fact on the one hand of our present nature being evil, the fact on the other hand that this present nature is not our proper nature; that the whole business of our lives is to cast it off, and to return to that better and holy nature, which, in truth, although not in fact, is the proper nature of man.

All individual experience, then, and all history begins in something which is evil; all our course, whether as individuals or as nations, is a progress, an advance, a leaving behind us something bad, and a going forwards towards something that is good. But individual experience, and history apart from Christianity, would make us regard this progress as fearfully uncertain. Clear it is that we are in an evil case; we have lost our way; we are like men who are bewildered in those endless forests of reeds which line some of the great American rivers; if we stay where we are, the venomous snakes may destroy us; or the deadly marsh air when night comes on will be surely fatal; it is death to remain, but yet if we move, we know not what way will lead us out, and it may be that, while seeming to advance, we shall but be going round and round, and shall at last find ourselves hard by the place from which we set out in the beginning. Nay, we may even feel a doubt,--a doubt, I say, though not a reasonable belief,--but a doubt which at times would press us sorely, whether the tangled thicket in which we are placed has any end at all; whether our fond notions of a clear and open space, a pure air, and a fruitful and habitable country, are not altogether merely imaginary; whether the whole world be not such a region of death as the spot in which we are actually prisoned; whether there remains any thing for us, but to curse our fate, and lie down and die. Under such circumstances, although we should admire the spirit which hoped against hope; which would make an effort for deliverance; which would, at any rate, flee from the actual evil, although, other evil might receive him after all his struggles; yet we could forgive those who yielded at once to their fate, and who sat down quietly to wait for their death, without the unavailing labour of a struggle to avoid it.

But when the declaration has been made to us by God himself, that this dismal swamp in which we are prisoners is but an infinitely small portion of his universe, that there do exist all those goodly forms which we fancied; and more, when God declares too that we were in the first instance designed to enjoy them; that our error brought us into the thicket, having been once out of it; that we may escape from it again; nay, much more still, when He shows us the true path to escape, and tells us, that the obstacles in our way have been cleared, and that he will give us strength to accomplish, the task of escaping, and will guide us that we do not miss the track; then what shall we say to those who insist upon, remaining where they are, but that they are either infatuated, or indolent and cowardly even to insanity; that they are refusing certain salvation, and are, by their own act, giving themselves over to inevitable death.

This, then, is the truth taught us by the doctrine of the Fall; not so much that it is our certain destruction to remain where we are, for that our own sense and reason declare to us, if we will but listen to them; but that our present position is not that for which God designed us, and that to rest satisfied with it is not a yielding to an unavoidable necessity, but the indolently or madly shrinking from the effort which would give us certain deliverance.

Now it is a part of our present evil condition from which we must escape, that we know good and evil. We are in the world where evil exists within us, and about us; we cannot but know it. True it is, that it was our misfortune to become acquainted with it; this noisome wilderness of reeds, this reeking swamp; it would have been far happier for us, no doubt, had we never become aware of their existence. But that wish is now too late. We are in the midst of this dismal place, and the question now is, how to escape from it. We may shut our eyes, and say we will not see objects so unsightly; but what avails it, if the marsh poison finds its way by other senses, if we cannot but draw it in with our breath, and so we must die? And such is the case of those who now in this present world confound ignorance with innocence. This is a fatal mistaking of our present condition for our past; there was a time when to the human race ignorance was innocence; but now it is only folly and sin. For as I supposed that a man lost in one of those noxious swamps might shut his eyes, and so keep himself in some measure in ignorance, yet the poison would be taken in with his breath, and so he would die: even thus, whilst we would fain shut the eyes of our understanding, and would so hope to be in safety, our passions are all the time alive and active, and they catch the poison of the atmosphere around us, and we are not innocent, but foolishly wicked.

We must needs consider this carefully; for, to say nothing of wider questions of national importance, who that sees before him, as we must see it, the gradual change from childhood to boyhood, who that sees added knowledge often accompanied with added sin, can help wishing that the earlier ignorance of evil might still be continued; and fancying that knowledge is at best but a doubtful blessing?

But our path is not backwards, but onwards. Israel in the desert was hungry and thirsty, while in Egypt he had eaten bread to the full; Israel in the desert saw a wide waste of sand, or sandy rock, around him, while in Egypt he had dwelt in those green pastures and watered gardens to which the Nile had given freshness and life. But that wilderness is his appointed way to Canaan; its dreariness must be exchanged for the hills and valleys of Canaan, and must not drive him back again to the low plain of Egypt. There is a moral wilderness which lies in the early part of our Christian course; but we must not hope to escape from it but by penetrating through it to its furthest side.

Undoubtedly this place, and other similar places, which receive us when we have quitted the state of childhood, and before our characters are formed in manhood, do partake somewhat of the character of the wilderness; and it is not unnatural that many should shrink back from them in fear. We see but too often the early beauty of the character sadly marred, its simplicity gone, its confidence chilled, its tenderness hardened; where there was gentleness, we see roughness and coarseness; where there was obedience, we find murmuring, and self-will, and pride; where there was a true and blameless conversation, we find now something of falsehood, something of profaneness, something of impurity. I can well conceive what it must be to a parent to see his child return from school, for the first time, with the marks of this grievous change upon him: I can well conceive how bitterly he must regret having ever sent him to a place of so much, danger; how fondly he must look back to the days of his early innocence. And if a parent feels thus, what must be our feelings, seeing that this evil has been wrought here? Are we not as those who, when pretending to give a wholesome draught, have mixed the cup with poison? How can we go on upholding a system, the effects of which appear to be so merely mischievous?

Believe me, that such questions must and ought to present themselves to the mind of every thinking man who is concerned in the management of a school: and I do think that we could not answer them satisfactorily, that our work would absolutely be unendurable, if we did not bear in mind that our eyes should look forward, and not backward; if we did not remember that the victory of fallen man is to be sought for, not in innocence, but in tried virtue. Comparing only the state of a boy after his first half-year, or year, at school, with his earlier state as a child, and our reflections on the evil of our system would be bitter indeed; but when we compare a boy's state after his first half-year, or year, at school, with what it is afterwards; when we see the clouds again clearing off; when we find coarseness succeeded again by delicacy; hardness and selfishness again broken up, and giving place to affection and benevolence; murmuring and self-will exchanged for humility and self-denial; and the profane, or impure, or false tongue, uttering again only the words of truth and purity; and when we see that all these good things are now, by God's grace, rooted in the character; that they have been tried, and grown up amidst the trial; that the knowledge of evil has made them hate it the more, and be the more aware of it; then we can look upon our calling with patience, and even with thankfulness; we see that the wilderness has been gone through triumphantly, and that its dangers have hardened and strengthened the traveller for all his remaining pilgrimage.

For the truth is, that to the knowledge of good and evil we are born; and it must come upon us sooner or later. In the common course of things, it comes about that age with which we are here most concerned. I do not mean that there are not faults in early childhood--we know that there are;--but we know also that with the strength and rapid growth of boyhood there is a far greater development of these faults, and particularly far less of that submissiveness which belonged naturally to the helplessness of mere childhood. I suppose that, by an extreme care, the period of childhood might be prolonged considerably; but still it must end; and the knowledge of good and evil, in its full force, must come. I believe that this must be; I believe that no care can prevent it, and that an extreme attempt at carefulness, whilst it could not keep off the disorder, would weaken the strength, of the constitution to bear it. But yet you should never forget, and I should never forget, that although the evils of schools in some respects must be, yet, in proportion as they exceed what must be, they do become at once mischievous and guilty. And such, or even worse, is the mischief when, with the evil which must be, there is not the good which ought to be; for, remember, our condition is to know good and evil. If we know only evil, it is the condition of hell; and therefore, if schools present an unmixed experience, if there is temptation in abundance, but no support against temptation, and no examples of overcoming it; if some are losing their child's innocence, but none, or very few, are gaining a man's virtue; are we in a wholesome state then? or can we shelter ourselves under the excuse that our evil is unavoidable, that we do but afford, in a mild form, the experience which must be learned sooner or later? It is here that we must be acquitted or condemned. I can bear to see the overclouding of childish simplicity, if there is a reasonable hope that the character so clouded for a time will brighten again into Christian holiness. But if we do not see this, if innocence is exchanged only for vice, then we have not done our part, then the evil is not unavoidable, but our sin: and we may be assured, that for the souls so lost, there will be an account demanded hereafter both of us and you.

21

LECTURE II.

1 CORINTHIANS xiii. 11.

When I was a child, I spake as a child,
I understood as a child, I thought as a child;
but when I became a man, I put away childish things.

Taking the Apostle's words literally, it might appear that no words in the whole range of Scripture were less applicable to the circumstances of this particular congregation: for they speak of childhood and of manhood; and as all of us have passed the one, so a very large proportion of us have not yet arrived at the other. But when we consider the passage a little more carefully, we shall see that this would be a very narrow and absurd objection. Neither the Apostle, nor any one else, has ever stepped directly from childhood into manhood; it was his purpose here only to notice the two extreme points of the change which had taken place in him, passing over its intermediate stages; but he, like all other men, must have gone through those stages. There must have been a time in his life, as in all ours, when his words, his thoughts, and his understanding were neither all childish, nor all manly: there must have been a period, extending over some years, in which they were gradually becoming the one less and less, and the other more and more. And as it suited the purposes of his comparison to look at the change in himself only when it was completed, so it will suit our object here to regard it while in progress, to consider what it is, to ask the two great questions, how far it can be hastened, and how far it ought to be hastened.

"When I was a child, I spake as a child, I understood as a child, I thought as a child; but when I became a man, I put away childish things." It will be seen at once, that when the Apostle speaks of thought and understanding, ([Greek: erronoun elogizomeaen],) he does not mean the mere intellect but all the notions, feelings, and desires of our minds, which partake of an intellectual and of a moral character together. He is comparing what we should call the whole nature and character of childhood with those of manhood. Let us see, for a moment, in what they most strikingly differ.

Our Lord's well-known words suggest a difference in the first place, which is in favour of childhood. When he says, "Except ye be converted, and become as little children, ye can in no case enter into the kingdom of heaven," he must certainly ascribe some one quality to childhood, in which manhood is generally deficient. And the quality which he means is clearly humility; or to speak perhaps more correctly, teachableness. It is impossible that a child can have that confidence in himself, which disposes him to be his own guide. He must of necessity lean on others, he must follow others, and therefore he must believe others. There is in his mind, properly speaking, nothing which can be called prejudice; he will not as yet refuse to listen, as thinking that he knows better than his adviser. One feeling, therefore, essential to the perfection of every created and reasonable being, childhood has by the very law of its nature; a child cannot help believing that there are some who are greater, wiser, better than himself, and he is disposed to follow their guidance.

This sense of comparative weakness is founded upon truth, for a child is of course unfit to guide himself. Without noticing mere bodily helplessness, a child knows scarcely what is good and what is evil; his desires for the highest good are not yet in existence; his moral sense altogether is exceedingly weak, and would yield readily to the first temptation. And, because those higher feelings, which are the great check to selfishness, have not yet arisen within him, the selfish instinct, connected apparently with all animal life, is exceedingly predominant in him. If a child then on the one hand be teachable, yet he is at the same time morally weak and ignorant, and therefore extremely selfish.

It is also a part of the nature of childhood to be the slave of present impulses. A child is not apt to look backwards or forwards, to reflect or to calculate. In this also he differs entirely from the great quality which befits man as an eternal being, the being able to look before and after.

Not to embarrass ourselves with too many points, we may be content with these four characteristics of childhood, teachableness, ignorance, selfishness, and living only for the present. In the last three of these, the perfect man should put away childish things; in the first point, or teachableness, while he retained it in principle, he should modify it in its application. For while modesty, humility, and a readiness to learn, are becoming to men no less than to children; yet it should be not a simple readiness to follow others, but only to follow the wise and good; not a sense of utter helplessness which catches at the first stay, whether sound or brittle; but such a consciousness of weakness and imperfection, as makes us long to be strengthened by Him who is almighty, to be purified by Him who is all pure.

I said, and it is an obvious truth, that the change from childhood to manhood is gradual; there is a period in our lives, of several years, in which we are, or should be, slowly exchanging the qualities of one state for those of the other. During this intermediate state, then, we should expect to find persons become less teachable, less ignorant, less selfish, less thoughtless. "Less teachable," I would wish to mean, in the sense of being "less indiscriminately teachable;" but as the evil and the good are, in human things, ever mixed up together, we may be obliged to mean "less teachable" simply. And, to say the very truth, if I saw in a young man the changes from childhood in the three other points, if I found him becoming wiser, and less selfish, and more thoughtful, I should not be very much disturbed if I found him for a time less teachable also. For whilst he was really becoming wiser and better, I should not much wonder if the sense of improvement rather than of imperfection possessed him too strongly; if his confidence in himself was a little too over-weening. Let him go on a little farther in life, and if he really does go on improving in wisdom and goodness, this over-confidence will find its proper level. He will perceive not only how much he is doing, or can do, but how much there is which he does not do, and cannot. To a thoughtful mind added years can scarcely fail to teach, humility. And in this the highest wisdom of manhood may be resembling more and more the state of what would be perfect childhood, that is, not simply teachableness, but tractableness with respect to what was good and true, and to that only.

But the danger of the intermediate state between childhood and manhood is too often this, that whilst in the one point of teachableness, the change runs on too fast, in the other three, of wisdom, of unselfishness, and of thoughtfulness, it proceeds much too slowly: that the faults of childhood thus remain in the character, whilst that quality by means of which these faults are meant to be corrected,--namely, teachableness,--is at the same time diminishing. Now, teachableness as an instinct, if I may call it so, diminishes naturally with the consciousness of growing strength. By strength, I mean strength of body, no less than strength of mind, so closely are our body and mind connected with, each other. The helplessness of childhood, which presses upon it every moment, the sense of inability to avoid or resist danger, which makes the child run continually to his nurse or to his mother for protection, cannot but diminish, by the mere growth of the bodily powers. The boy feels himself to be less helpless than the child, and in that very proportion he is apt to become less teachable. As this feeling of decreased helplessness changes into a sense of positive vigour and power, and as this vigour and power confer an importance on their possessor, which is the case especially at schools, so self-confidence must in one point at least, arise in the place of conscious weakness; and as this point is felt to be more important, so will the self-confidence be likely to extend itself more and more over the whole character.

And yet, I am bound to say, that, in general, the teachableness of youth is, after all, much greater than we might at first sight fancy. Along with much self-confidence in many things, it is rare, I think, to find in a young man a deliberate pride that rejects advice and instruction, on the strength of having no need for them. And therefore, the faults of boyhood and youth are more owing, to my mind, to the want of change in the other points of the childish character, than to the too great change in this. The besetting faults of youth appear to me to arise mainly from its retaining too often the ignorance, selfishness, and thoughtlessness of a child, and having arrived at the same time at a degree of bodily vigour and power, equal, or only a very little inferior, to those of manhood.

And in this state of things, the questions become of exceeding interest, whether the change from childhood to manhood can be hastened. That it ought to be hastened, appears to me to be clear; hastened, I mean, from what it is actually, because in this respect, we do not grow in general fast enough; and the danger of over-growth is, therefore, small. Besides, where change of one sort is going on very rapidly; where the limbs are growing and the bones knitting more firmly, where the strength of bodily endurance, as well as of bodily activity, is daily becoming greater; it is self-evident that, if the inward changes which ought to accompany these outward ones are making no progress, there cannot but be derangement and deformity in the system. And, therefore, when I look around, I cannot but wish generally that the change from childhood to manhood in the three great points of wisdom, of unselfishness, and of thoughtfulness, might be hastened from its actual rate of progress in most instances.

But then comes the other great question, "Can it be hastened, and if it can, how is it to be done?" "Can it be hastened" means, of course, can it be hastened healthfully and beneficially, consistently with the due development of our nature in its after stages, from life temporal to life eternal? For as the child should grow up into the man, so also there is a term of years given in which, according to God's will, the natural man should grow up into the spiritual man; and we must not so press the first change as to make it interfere with the wholesome working of the second. The question then is, really, can the change from childhood to manhood be hastened in the case of boys and young men in general from its actual rate of progress in ordinary cases, without injury to the future excellence and full development of the man? that is, without exhausting prematurely the faculties either of body or mind.

And this is a very grave question, one of the deepest interest for us and for you. For us, as, according to the answer to be given to it, should depend our whole conduct and feelings towards you in the matter of your education; for you, inasmuch as it is quite clear, that if the change from childhood to manhood can be hastened safely, it ought to be hastened; and that it is a sin in every one not to try to hasten it: because, to retain the imperfections of childhood when you can get rid of them, is in itself to forfeit the innocence of childhood; to exchange the condition of the innocent infant whom Christ blessed, for that of the unprofitable servant whom Christ condemned. For with the growth of our bodies evil will grow in us unavoidably; and then, if we are not positively good, we are, of necessity, positively sinners.

We will consider, then, what can be done to hasten this change in us healthfully; whether we can grow in wisdom, in love, and in thoughtfulness, faster in youth, than we now commonly do grow: and whether any possible danger can be connected with such increased exertion. This shall be our subject for consideration next Sunday. Meantime, let it be understood, that however extravagant it might be to hope for any general change in any moral point, as the direct result of setting truth before the mind; yet, that it never can be extravagant to hope for a practical result in some one or two particular cases; and that, if one or two even be impressed practically with what they hear, the good achieved, or, rather, the good granted us by God, is really beyond our calculation. It is so strictly; for who can worthily calculate the value of a single human soul? but it is so in this sense also, that the amount of general good which may be done in the end by doing good first in particular cases is really more than we can estimate. It was thus that Christ's original eleven apostles became, in the end, the instruments of the salvation of millions: and it is on this consideration that we never need despair of the most extensive improvements in society, if we are content to wait God's appointed time and order, and look for the salvation of the many as the gradual fruit of the salvation of a few.

LECTURE III.

1 CORINTHIANS xiii. 11.

When I was a child, I spoke as a child,
I understood as a child, I thought as a child;
but when I became a man, I put away childish things.

After having noticed last Sunday what were those particular points in childhood, which in manhood should be put away, and having observed that this change cannot take place all at once, but gradually, during a period of several years, I proposed to consider, as on this day, whether it were possible to hasten this change, that is, whether it could be hastened without injury to the future development of the character; for undoubtedly, there is such, a thing in minds, as well as in bodies, as precocious growth; and although it is not so frequent as precocious growth in the body, nor by any means so generally regarded as an evil, yet it is really a thing to be deprecated; and we ought not to adopt such measures as might be likely to occasion it.

Now I believe the only reason which could make it supposed to be possible that there could be danger in hastening this change, is drawn from the observation of what takes place sometimes with regard to intellectual advancement. It is seen that some young men of great ambition, or remarkable love of knowledge, do really injure their health, and exhaust their minds, by an excess of early study. I always grieve over such cases exceedingly; not only for the individual's sake who is the sufferer, but also for the mischievous effect of his example. It affords a pretence to others to justify their own want of exertion; and those to whom it is in reality the least dangerous, are always the very persons who seem to dread it the most. But we should clearly understand, that this excess of intellectual exertion at an early age, is by no means the same thing with hastening the change from childishness to manliness. We are all enough aware, in common life, that a very clever and forward boy may be, in his conduct, exceeding childish; that those whose talents and book-knowledge are by no means remarkable, may be, in their conduct, exceedingly manly. Examples of both these truths instantly present themselves to my memory, and perhaps may do so to some of yours. I may say farther, that some whose change from childhood to manhood had been, in St. Paul's sense of the terms, the most remarkably advanced, were so far from being distinguished for their cleverness or proficiency in their school-work, that it would almost seem as if their only remaining childishness had been displayed there. What I mean, therefore, by the change from childhood to manhood, is altogether distinct from a premature advance in book-knowledge, and involves in it nothing of that over-study which is dreaded as so injurious.

Yet it is true that I described the change from childhood to manhood, as a change from ignorance to wisdom. I did so, certainly; but yet, rare as knowledge is, wisdom is rarer; and knowledge, unhappily, can exist without wisdom, as wisdom can exist with a very inferior degree of knowledge. We shall see this, if we consider what we mean by knowledge; and, without going into a more general definition of it, let us see what we mean by it here. We mean by it, either a knowledge of points of scholarship, of grammar, and matters connected with grammar; or a knowledge of history and geography; or a knowledge of mathematics: or, it may be, of natural history; or, if we use the term, "knowledge of the world," then we mean, I think, a knowledge of points of manner and fashion; such a knowledge as may save us from exposing ourselves in trifling things, by awkwardness or inexperience. Now the knowledge of none of these things brings us of necessity any nearer to real thoughtfulness, such as alone gives wisdom, than the knowledge of a well-contrived game. Some of you, probably, well know that there are games from which chance is wholly excluded, and skill in which is only the result of much thought and calculation. There is no

25

doubt that the game of chess may properly be called an intellectual study; but why does it not, and cannot, make any man wise? Because, in the first place, the calculations do but respect the movements of little pieces of wood or ivory, and not those of our own minds and hearts; and, again, they are calculations which have nothing to do whatever with our being better men, or worse, with our pleasing God or displeasing him. And what is true of this game, is true no less of the highest calculations of Astronomy, of the profoundest researches into language; nay, what may seem stranger still, it is often true no less of the deepest study even of the actions and principles of man's nature; and, strangest of all, it may be, and is often true, also, of the study of the very Scripture itself; and that, not only of the incidental points of Scripture, its antiquities, chronology, and history, but of its very most divine truths, of man's justification and of God's nature. Here, indeed, we are considering about things where wisdom, so to speak, sits enshrined. We are very near her, we see the place where she abides; but her very self we obtain not. And why?--but because, in the most solemn study, no less than in the lightest, our own moral state may be set apart from our consideration; we may be unconscious all the while of our great want; and forgetting our great business, to be reconciled to God, and to do his will: for wisdom, to speak properly, is to us nothing else than the true answer to the Philippian jailor's question, "What must I do to be saved?"

Now then, as knowledge of all kinds may be gained without being received, or meant at all to be applied, as the answer to this question, so it may be quite distinct from wisdom. And when I use the term thoughtfulness, as opposed to a child's carelessness, I mean it to express an anxiety for the obtaining of this wisdom. And farther, I do not see how this wisdom, or this thoughtfulness, can be premature in any one; or how it can exhaust before their time any faculties, whether of body or mind. This requires no sitting up late at night, no giving up of healthful exercise; it brings no headaches, no feverishness, no strong excitement at first, to be followed by exhaustion afterwards. Hear how it is described by one who spoke of it from experience. "The wisdom that is from above is first pure, then peaceable, gentle, easy to be entreated, full of mercy and good fruits, without partiality and without hypocrisy." There is surely nothing of premature exhaustion connected-with any one of these things.

Or, if we turn to the third point of change from childhood to a Christian manhood, the change from selfishness to unselfishness, neither can we find any possible danger in hastening this. This cannot hurt our health or strain our faculties; it can but make life at every age more peaceful and more happy. Nor indeed do I suppose that any one could fancy that such a change was otherwise than wholesome at the earliest possible period.

There may remain, however, a vague notion, that generally, if what we mean by an early change from childishness to manliness be that we should become religious, then, although it may not exhaust the powers, or injure the health, yet it would destroy the natural liveliness and gaiety of youth, and by bringing on a premature seriousness of manner and language, would be unbecoming and ridiculous. Now, in the first place, there is a great deal of confusion and a great deal of folly in the common notions of the gaiety of youth. If gaiety mean real happiness of mind, I do not believe that there is more of it in youth than in manhood; if for this reason only, that the temper in youth being commonly not yet brought into good order, irritation and passion are felt, probably, oftener than in after life, and these are sad drawbacks, as we all know, to a real cheerfulness of mind. And of the outward gaiety of youth, there is a part also which is like the gaiety of a drunken man; which is riotous, insolent, and annoying to others; which, in short, is a folly and a sin. There remains that which strictly belongs to youth, partly physically--the lighter step and the livelier movement of the growing and vigorous body; partly from circumstances, because a young person's parents or friends stand between him and many of the cares of life, and protect him from feeling them altogether; partly from the abundance of hope which belongs to the beginning of every thing, and which continually hinders the mind from dwelling on past pain. And I know not which of these causes of gaiety would be taken away or lessened by the earlier change from childhood to manhood. True it is, that the question, "What must I do to be saved?" is a grave one, and must be considered seriously; but I do not suppose that any one proposes that a young person should never be serious at all. True it is, again, that if we are living in folly and sin, this question may be a painful one; we might be gayer for a time without it. But, then, the matter is, what is to become of us if we do not think of being saved?--shall we be saved without thinking of it? And what is it to be not saved but lost? I cannot pretend to say that the thought of God would not very much disturb the peace and gaiety of an ungodly and sinful mind; that it would not interfere with the mirth of the bully, or the drunkard, or the reveller, or the glutton, or the idler, or the fool. It would, no doubt; just as the hand that was seen to write on the wall threw a gloom over the guests at Belshazzar's festival. I never meant or mean to say, that the thought of God, or that God himself, can be other than a plague to those who do not love Him. The thought of Him is their plague here; the sight of Him will be their judgment for ever. But I suppose the point is, whether the thought of Him would cloud the gaiety of those who were striving to please Him. It would cloud it as much, and be just as unwelcome and no more, as will be the very actual presence of our Lord to the righteous, when they shall see Him as He is. Can that which we know to be able to make old age, and sickness, and poverty, many times full of comfort,--can that make youth and health gloomy? When to natural cheerfulness and sanguineness, are added a consciousness of God's ever present care, and a knowledge of his rich promises, are we likely to be the more sad or the more unhappy?

What reason, then, is there for any one's not anticipating the common progress of Christian manliness, and hastening; to exchange, as I said before, ignorance for wisdom, selfishness for unselfishness, carelessness for thoughtfulness? I see no reason why we should not; but is there no reason why we should? You are young, and for the most part strong and healthy; I grant that, humanly speaking, the chances of early death to any particular person among you are small. But still, considering what life is, even to the youngest and strongest, it does seem a fearful risk to be living unredeemed; to be living in that state, that if we should happen to die, (it may be very unlikely, but still it is clearly possible,)--that if we should happen to die, we should be most certainly lost for ever. Risks, however, we do not mind; the chances, we think, are in our favour, and we will run the hazard. It may be so; but he who delays to turn to God when the thought has been once put before him, is incurring something more than a risk. He may not die these fifty or sixty years; we cannot tell how that may be; but he is certainly at this very present time hardening his heart, and doing despite unto the Spirit of Grace. By the very wickedness of putting off turning to God till a future time, he lessens his power of turning to Him ever. This is certain; no one can reject God's call without becoming less likely to hear it when it is made to him again. And thus the lingering wilfully in the evil things of childhood, when we might be at work in putting them off, and when God calls us to do so, is an infinite risk, and a certain evil;--an infinite risk, for it is living in such a state that death at any moment would be certain condemnation;--and a certain evil, because, whether we live or not, we are actually raising up barriers between ourselves and our salvation; we not only do not draw nigh to God, but we are going farther from Him, and lessening our power of drawing nigh to Him hereafter.

LECTURE IV.

COLOSSIANS i. 9.

We do not cease to pray for you, and to desire that ye might be filled with the knowledge of his will in all wisdom and spiritual understanding.

This is the first of three verses, all of them forming a part of the Epistle which was read this morning, and containing St. Paul's prayer for the Colossians in all the several points of Christian excellence. And the first thing which he desires for them, as we have heard, is, that they should be filled with the knowledge of God's will in all wisdom and spiritual understanding; or, as he expresses the same thing to the Ephesians, that they should be not unwise, but understanding what the will of the Lord is. He prays for the Colossians that they should not be spiritually foolish, but that they should be spiritually wise.

The state of spiritual folly is, I suppose, one of the most universal evils in the world. For the number of those who are naturally foolish is exceedingly great; of those, I mean, who understand no worldly thing well; of those who are careless about everything, carried about by every breath of opinion, without knowledge, and without principle. But the term spiritual folly includes, unhappily, a great many more than these; it takes in not those only who are in the common sense of the term foolish, but a great many who are in the common sense of the term clever, and many who are even in the common sense of the terms, prudent, sensible, thoughtful, and wise. It is but too evident that some of the ablest men who have ever lived upon earth, have been in no less a degree spiritually fools. And thus, it is not without much truth that Christian writers have dwelt upon the insufficiency of worldly wisdom, and have warned their readers to beware, lest, while professing themselves to be wise, they should be accounted as fools in the sight of God.

But the opposite to this notion, that those who are, as it were, fools in worldly matters are wise before God; although this also is true in a certain sense, and under certain peculiar circumstances, yet taken generally, it is the very reverse of truth; and the careless and incautious language which has been often used on this subject, has been extremely mischievous. On the contrary, he who is foolish in worldly matters is likely also to be, and most commonly is, no less foolish in the things of God. And the opposite belief has arisen mainly from that strange confusion between ignorance and innocence, with which many ignorant persons seem to solace themselves. Whereas, if you take away a man's knowledge, you do not bring him to the state of an infant, but to that of a brute; and of one of the most mischievous and malignant of the brute creation. For you do not lessen or weaken the man's body by lowering his mind; he still retains his strength and his passions, the passions leading to self-indulgence, the strength which enables him to feed them by continued gratification. He will not think it is true to any good purpose; it is very possible to destroy in him the power of reflection, whether as exercised upon outward things, or upon himself and his own nature, or upon God. But you cannot destroy the power of adapting means to ends, nor that of concealing his purposes by fraud or falsehood; you take only his wisdom, and leave that cunning which marks so notoriously both the savage and the madman. He, then, who is a fool as far as regards earthly things, is much more a fool with regard to heavenly things; he who cannot raise himself even to the lower height, how is he to attain to the higher? he who is without reason and conscience, how shall he be endowed with the spirit of God?

It is my deep conviction and long experience of this truth, which makes me so grieve over a want of interest in your own improvement in human learning, whenever I observe it, over the prevalence of a thoughtless and childish spirit amongst you. I grant that as to the first point there are sometimes exceptions to be met with; that is to say, I have known persons certainly whose interest in their work here was not great, and their proficiency consequently was small; but who, I do not doubt, were wise unto God. But then these persons, whilst they were indifferent perhaps about their common school-work, were anything but indifferent as to the knowledge of the Bible: there was no carelessness there; but they read, and read frequently, books of practical improvement, or relating otherwise to religious matters, such as many, I believe, would find even less inviting than the books of their common business. So that although there was a neglect undoubtedly of many parts of the school-work, yet there was no spirit of thoughtlessness or childishness in them, nor of general idleness; and therefore, although I know that their minds did suffer and have suffered from their unwise neglect of a part of their duty, yet there was so much attention bestowed on other parts, and so manifest and earnest a care for the things of God, that it was impossible not to entertain for them the greatest respect and regard. These, however, are such rare cases, that it cannot be necessary to do more than thus notice them. But the idleness and want of interest which I grieve for, is one which extends itself but too impartially to knowledge of every kind: to divine knowledge, as might be expected, even more than to human. Those whom we commonly find careless about their general lessons, are quite as ignorant and as careless about their Bibles; those who have no interest in general literature, in poetry, or in history, or in philosophy, have certainly no greater interest, I do not say in works of theology, but in works of practical devotion, in the lives of holy men, in meditations, or in prayers. Alas, the interest of their minds is bestowed on things far lower than the very lowest of all which I have named; and therefore, to see them desiring something only a little higher than their present pursuits, could not but be encouraging; it would, at least, show that the mind was rising upwards. It may, indeed, stop at a point short of the highest, it may learn to love earthly excellence, and rest there contented, and seek for nothing more perfect; but that, at any rate, is a future and merely contingent evil. It is better to love earthly excellence than earthly folly; it is far better in itself, and it is, by many degrees, nearer to the kingdom of God.

There is another case, however, which I cannot but think is more frequent now than formerly; and if it is so, it may be worth while to direct our attention to it. Common idleness and absolute ignorance are not what I wish to speak of now, but a character advanced above these; a character which does not neglect its school-lessons, but really attains to considerable proficiency in them; a character at once regular and amiable, abstaining from evil, and for evil in its low and grosser forms, having a real abhorrence. What, then, you will say, is wanting here? I will tell you what seems to be wanting--a spirit of manly, and much more of Christian, thoughtfulness. There is quickness and cleverness; much pleasure, perhaps, in distinction, but little in improvement; there is no desire of knowledge for its own sake, whether human or divine. There is, therefore, but little power of combining and digesting what is read; and, consequently, what is read passes away, and takes no root in the mind. This same character shows itself in matters of conduct; it will adopt, without scruple, the most foolish, commonplace notions of boys, about what is right and wrong; it will not, and cannot, from the lightness of its mind, concern itself seriously about what is evil in the conduct of others, because it takes no regular care of its own, with reference to pleasing God; it will not do anything low or wicked, but it will sometimes laugh at those who do; and it will by no means take pains to encourage, nay, it will sometimes thwart and oppose any thing that breathes a higher spirit, and asserts a more manly and Christian standard of duty.

I have thought that this character, with its features more or less strongly marked, has shown itself sometimes amongst us, marring the good and amiable qualities of those in whom we can least bear to see such a defect, because there is in them really so much to interest in their favour. Now the number of persons of extraordinary abilities who may be here at any one time can depend on no calculable causes: nor, again, can we give any reason more than what we call accident, if there were to be amongst us at any one time a number of persons whose whole tendency was decidedly to evil. But if, in these respects, the usual average has continued, if there is no lack of ability, and nothing like a prevalence of vice, then we begin anxiously to inquire into the causes, which, while other things remain the same, have led to a different result. And one cause I do find, which, is certainly capable of producing such a result: a cause undoubtedly in existence now, and as certainly not in existence a few years back; nor can I trace any other besides this which appears likely to have produced the same effect. This cause consists in the number and character and cheapness, and peculiar mode of publication, of the works of amusement of the present day. In all these respects the change is great, and extremely recent. The works of amusement published only a very few years since were comparatively few in number; they were less exciting, and therefore less attractive; they were dearer, and therefore less accessible; and, not being published periodically, they did not occupy the mind for so long a time, nor keep alive so constant an expectation; nor, by thus dwelling upon the mind, and distilling themselves into it as it were drop by drop, did they possess it so largely, colouring even, in many instances, its very language, and affording frequent matter for conversation.

The evil of all these circumstances is actually enormous. The mass of human minds, and much more of the minds of young persons, have no great appetite for intellectual exercise; but they have some, which by careful treatment may be strengthened and increased. But here to this weak and delicate appetite is presented an abundance of the most stimulating and least nourishing food possible. It snatches it greedily, and is not only satisfied, but actually conceives a distaste for anything simpler and more wholesome. That curiosity which is wisely given us to lead us on to knowledge, finds its full gratification in the details of an exciting and protracted story, and then lies down as it were gorged, and goes to sleep. Other faculties claim their turn, and have it. We know that in youth the healthy body and lively spirits require exercise, and in this they may and ought to be indulged: but the time and interest which remain over when the body has had its enjoyment, and the mind desires its share, this has been already wasted and exhausted upon things utterly unprofitable: so that the mind goes to its work hurriedly and languidly, and feels it to be no more than a burden. The mere lessons may be learnt from a sense of duty; but that freshness of power which, in young persons of ability would fasten eagerly upon some one portion or other, of the wide field of knowledge, and there expatiate, drinking in health and strength to the mind, as surely as the natural exercise of the body gives to it bodily vigour,--that is tired prematurely, perverted, and corrupted; and all the knowledge which else it might so covet, it now seems a wearying effort to attain.

Great and grievous as is the evil, it is peculiarly hard to find the remedy for it. If the books to which I have been alluding were books of downright wickedness, we might destroy them wherever we found them; we might forbid their open circulation; we might conjure you to shun them as you would any other clear sin, whether of word or deed. But they are not wicked books for the most part; they are of that class which cannot be actually prohibited; nor can it be pretended that there is a sin in reading them. They are not the more wicked for being published so cheap, and at regular intervals; but yet these two circumstances make them so peculiarly injurious. All that can be done is to point out the evil; that it is real and serious I am very sure, and its effects are most deplorable on the minds of the fairest promise; but the remedy for it rests with yourselves, or rather with each of you individually, so far as he is himself concerned. That an unnatural and constant excitement of the mind is most injurious, there is no doubt; that excitement involves a consequent weakness, is a law of our nature than which none is surer; that the weakness of mind thus produced is and must be adverse to quiet study and thought, to that reflection which alone is wisdom, is also clear in itself, and proved too largely by experience. And that without reflection there can be no spiritual understanding, is at once evident; while without spiritual understanding, that is, without a knowledge and a study of God's will, there can be no spiritual life. And therefore childishness and unthoughtfulness cannot be light evils; and if I have rightly traced the prevalence of these defects to its cause, although that cause may seem to some to be trifling, yet surely it is well to call your attention to it, and to remind you that in reading works of amusement, as in every other lawful pleasure, there is and must be an abiding responsibility in the sight of God; that, like other lawful pleasures, we must beware of excess in it; and not only so, but that if we find it hurtful to us, either because we have used it too freely in times past, or because our nature is too weak to bear it, that then we are bound most solemnly to abstain from it; because, however lawful in itself, or to others who can practise it without injury, whatever is to us an hindrance in the way of our intellectual and moral and spiritual improvement, that is in our case a positive sin.

LECTURE V.

COLOSSIANS i. 9.

We do not cease to pray for you, and to desire
that ye might be filled with the knowledge of his
will in all wisdom and spiritual understanding.

These words, on which I spoke last Sunday, appeared to contain so much, which concerns us all so deeply, and to suit the peculiar case of many of us here so entirely, that I thought they might well furnish us with matter for farther consideration to-day. And though I noticed one particular cause, which seemed to have acted mischievously, in the last few years, upon the growth and freshness of the mind in youth, yet it would be absurd to suppose that before this cause came into existence all was well; or that if it could be removed, our progress even in worldly knowledge would henceforth be unimpeded. There are many other causes no doubt which oppose our growth in worldly wisdom; and still more which oppose our growth in the wisdom of God.

One of these causes meets us at the very beginning; it exists at this very moment; it makes it difficult even to gain your attention for what is to be said. This cause is to be found in the want of sympathy between persons of very different ages, between what must be, therefore, in the common course of nature, different degrees of thoughtfulness. It is the want of sympathy, properly speaking, which creates in these matters a difficulty of understanding; for the attention and memory are alike apt to be careless where the mind is not interested; and how can we understand that to which we scarcely listened, and which we imperfectly remember? Nature herself seems to lead the old and the young two different ways: and when the old call upon the young to be thoughtful, it seems as if they were but calling them to a state contrary to their nature; and the call is not regarded.

Is it then that we have here an invincible obstacle, which renders all attempts to inspire thoughtfulness utterly vain? and if it be so, what use can there be in dwelling upon it? None, certainly, if it were actually and in all cases invincible; but if it be every thing short of invincible, there is much good in noticing it. There is much good surely in trying to impress the great truth, that nature must be overcome by a mightier power, or we perish. There is much good in meeting and allowing to its full extent what we are so apt in our folly to regard as an excuse, and which really is the earnest of our condemnation. It is very true, and to be allowed to the fullest extent, that it is against the nature of youth in all ordinary cases to be thoughtful; that it is very difficult for you even to give your attention to serious things when spoken of, more difficult still to remember them afterwards and always. It is for the very reason because it is so difficult, because it is a work so against nature, to raise the young and careless mind to the thought of God; because it is so certain that, in the common course of things, you will not think of Him, but will follow the bent of your own several fancies or desires, that therefore He, who wills in his love to bring us to himself, knowing that without the knowledge of Him we must perish for ever, was pleased to give his only-begotten Son, that through Him we might overcome nature, and might turn to God and live.

I wish that I could increase, if it were possible, the sense which, you have of the difficulty of becoming thoughtful, so that you could but see that out of this very difficulty, and indissolubly connected with it, comes the grace of Christ's redemption. You have not strength of purpose enough to shake off folly and sin; surely you have not, or else, why should Christ have died? It is so hard to come to God; undoubtedly, so hard that no man can come unto God except God will draw him. Nature herself leads us to be careless, our very strength and spirits of themselves will not allow us to reflect. Most true; for that which is born of the flesh, is flesh; and we inherit a nature derived from him in whom we all die.

I believe that it is not idle to dwell upon tins; for it is scarcely possible but that good and earnest resolutions should often enter the minds of many of you; or, if not resolutions, yet at least wishes, wishes chilled but too soon, I fear, by the thought or feeling, that however much to will may be present with you, yet how to perform it you find not. Now, if this true sense of weakness might but lead any one to seek for strength where it may be found, then indeed it would be a feeling no less blessed than true; for it would urge you to seek God's help and Christ's redemption, instead of desperately yielding to your weakness, and so remaining weak for ever.

You may look at the prospect before you in all its reality: you may see how much must be given up, how much withstood, bow much, endured; how hard it is to alter old ways, not in itself only, but because the change attracts attention, and is received, it may be, with doubts as to its sincerity, with irony, and with sneers. There is all this before you: it cannot be denied; it must not be concealed. The way to life is not broad and easy; it is not that way which is most trodden. To pass from what we are to what we may be hereafter, from an earthly nature to an heavenly, cannot be an easy work, to be done at any time, with no effort, with no pain. It is the greatest work which is done in the whole world, it is the mightiest change; death and birth are, as it were, combined in it; but the Lord of birth and of death is at hand, to enable us to effect it. Think that this is so; and the more you feel how hard a task is set before you, the more you will be able to understand the language of joy and thankfulness with which the Scripture speaks of a human soul's redemption.

This great work may be wrought for every soul here assembled; the want of sympathy in sacred and serious things may be changed to sympathy the most intense; the carelessness of fools may be changed into spiritual wisdom. It may be wrought for all; but it is more happy to think that it will be wrought for some;--for whom, no mortal eye or judgment can discern; but it will be wrought for some. If many should yield in despair to their enemy, yet some will resist him: if Christ be to many no more than foolishness, if his name convey nothing more than a vague sense of something solemn, which passes over the mind for an instant, and then vanishes, yet to some undoubtedly, he will be found to be the wisdom of God, and the power of God. There are some here, we may be quite sure, who will be witnesses for ever to all the world of men and angels, that what truly was impossible to nature, is possible to nature renewed and strengthened by grace.

Without such a change, it is vain, I fear, to look for any thing like wisdom or spiritual understanding; for how can such a seed be expected to grow in a soil so shallow as common thoughtlessness? and how can merely human motives have force to overcome so strong a tendency of nature? nay, how can such motives be brought to act upon the mind? for it is absolutely impossible that the middle-aged and the young should be brought into entire sympathy with each other, unless Christ's love be their common bond. Human wisdom in advanced life may be, and is to persons of strong faculties of mind, naturally pleasant: but how can it be made so to persons of ordinary faculties in early youth? There are faults which society condemns strongly, while the temptation to them in after life is slight. Persons in middle age may resist these easily, and abhor them sincerely; but how can we make young persons do the same when the temptation to commit them is strong, and the condemnation of them by their society is either very slight, or does not exist at all? And, therefore, we find that, do what we will, the same faults' continue to be common in schools, the same faults both of omission and commission; there is the same inherent difficulty of bringing persons of different ages and positions to think and feel alike, unless Christ has become possessed of the thoughts and feelings of both, and so they become one with each other in him.

But it was our Lord's charge to Peter, "Thou, when thou art converted, strengthen thy brethren." As sure as it is that some who hear me are turned, or turning, or will turn, to God, so sure is it that these, be they few or many, will do something towards the strengthening of their brethren. Whatever good is to be done amongst us on a large scale, it must be done only in this way, the many half despairing prayer may be, "Lord, I believe; help thou mine unbelief;" but if any one is moved by Christ's call, and feels within himself that he should like to follow Christ, and to be with him always, let him cherish that work of the Holy Spirit within him, which has given him if it be only so much of the will to be saved. It is a spark which may be quenched in a moment; in itself it can give no assurance; but if any one watches it carefully, and prays that it may live and be kindled into a stronger spark, till at last it break out into a flame, then for him it is full of assurance; God has heard his prayer; and he has received the gift of the Holy Spirit, an earnest of his eternal inheritance. Will he not then watch and pray the more anxiously, lest the fruit which, is now partly formed should never ripen? Will he not see and feel that there is some reality in the things of God, that strength, and peace, and victory, are not vainly promised? Will he not hold fast the things which he has now not heard only, but known, lest by any means he should let them slip? May God strengthen such, whoever they may be, with all the might of his Spirit; and may he be with them even to the end.

But for those,--who they are, again, we know not, nor how many; but here, also, there will too surely be some,--for those who hear now, as they have often heard before, words which, they scarcely heed, which, have at times partially caught their attention, but have not produced in them the slightest real effect, for them the words are coming to an end; they will soon be released from the irksome bondage of hearing them; and another opportunity of grace will have been offered to them in vain. Tomorrow, and the day after, they will walk as they have walked before, the wretched slaves of folly and passion; half despairing prayer may be, "Lord, I believe; help thou mine unbelief;" but if any one is moved by Christ's call, and feels within himself that he should like to follow Christ, and to be with him always, let him cherish that work of the Holy Spirit within him, which has given him if it be only so much of the will to be saved. It is a spark which may be quenched in a moment; in itself it can give no assurance; but if any one watches it carefully, and prays that it may live and be kindled into a stronger spark, till at last it break out into a flame, then for him it is full of assurance; God has heard his prayer; and he has received the gift of the Holy Spirit, an earnest of his eternal inheritance. Will he not then watch and pray the more anxiously, lest the fruit which is now partly formed should never ripen? Will he not see and feel that there is some reality in the things of God, that strength, and peace, and victory, are not vainly promised? Will he not hold fast the things which he has now not heard only, but known, lest by any means he should let them slip? May God strengthen such, whoever they may be, with all the might of his Spirit; and may he be with them even to the end.

But for those,--who they are, again, we know not, nor how many; but here, also, there will too surely be some,--for those who hear now, as they have often heard before, words which they scarcely heed, which have at times partially caught their attention, but have not produced in them the slightest real effect, for them the words are coming to an end; they will soon be released from the irksome bondage of hearing them; and another opportunity of grace will have been offered to them in vain. Tomorrow, and the day after, they will walk as they have walked before, the wretched slaves of folly and passion; leaving undone all Christ's work, and greedily doing his enemy's. Yet even these Christ yet spares, he still calls them, he has died for them. Still the word must be spoken to them, whether they will hear, or whether they will forbear. It may be, that they will some day turn; and if not, Christ has perfected his mercy towards them; and Christ's servants have delivered their own souls in warning them. May there be but few of us on whom this horrible portion will fall; yet, is it not an awful thing to think of, that it will, in all human probability, fall on some? and that whoever hardens his heart, and resists the word spoken to him this day, he is one who has done as much as in him lies to make himself among that number.

LECTURE VI.

COLOSSIANS iii. 3.

Ye are dead, and your life is hid with Christ in God.

When I have spoken, from time to time, of denying ourselves for the sake of relieving others, although self-denial and charity are, in their full growth, amongst the highest of Christian graces, yet I have felt much hope that, up to a certain degree, in their lowest and elementary forms at least, there might be many that would be disposed to practise them. For these are virtues which do undoubtedly commend themselves to our minds as things clearly good: so much so that I am inclined to think that the much-disputed moral sense, the nature of which is said to be so hard to ascertain, exists most clearly in the universal perception that it is good to deny ourselves and to benefit others. I do not say merely that there is a perception that it is good to deny ourselves in order to benefit others; but that there is in self-denial, simply, something which commands respect; an unconscious tribute, I suppose, to the truth, that the self which, is thus denied is one which, if indulged, would run to evil.

But a point of far greater difficulty, of absolutely the greatest difficulty, is to impress upon our minds the excellence of another quality, which is known by the name of spiritual or heavenly-mindedness. In fact, this,--and this almost singly,--is the transcendent part of Christianity; that part of it which is not according to, but above, nature; which, conscience, I think, itself, in the natural man, does not acknowledge. When Christianity speaks of purity, of truth, of justice, of charity, of faith and love to God, it speaks a language which, however belied by our practice, is at once allowed by our consciences: the things so recommended are, beyond all doubt, good and lovely. But when it says, in St. Paul's words, "Set your affections on things above, not on things on the earth: for ye are dead, and your life is hid with Christ in God," the language sounds so strange that it is scarcely intelligible; and if we do get to understand it, yet it seems to give a wrench, as it were, to our whole being, to command a thing extravagant and impossible.

I am persuaded that this would be so, more or less, everywhere; but in how extreme a degree must it hold good amongst us! Even in poverty, in sickness, and old age, where this life would seem to be nothing but a burden, and the command to "set the affections on things above" might appear superfluous, still the known so prevails over the unknown, the familiar over the incomprehensible, that hope and affection find continually their objects in this world, there is still a clinging to life, and an unwillingness to die. But in a state the very opposite to this, in plenty, in health, in youth; with much of enjoyment actually in our hands, and more in prospect; with just so much mystery over our coming life as to keep alive interest, yet with enough known and understood in its prospects to awaken sympathy; what deafest ear of the deaf adder could ever be so closed against the voice of the charmer, as our minds, so engrossed with the enjoyments and the hopes of earth, are closed against the voice which speaks of the things of heaven?

Again, I have said, when speaking of other subjects, that I looked upon the older persons among you as a sort of link between me and the younger, who communicated, in some instances, by their language and example, something of an impression of the meaning of Christian teaching. But when we speak of a thing so high as spiritual-mindedness, it seems as if none of us can be a link between Christ's words and our brethren's minds: as if we all stand alike at an infinite distance from the high and unapproachable truth. The mountain of God becomes veiled, as it were, with the clouds which rested upon Sinai; we cannot approach near it, but stand far off, for a moment, perhaps, in awe; but soon in neglect and indifference.

Let any one capable of thinking, but in the full vigour of health of body and mind, placed far above want, and with the prospect, according to all probability, of many years of happy life before him, let such an one go forth, at this season of the year above all, let him see the vast preparation for life in all nature, amongst all living creatures, in every tree, and in every plant of grass; let him feel the warmth of the sun, becoming every day stronger and stronger; let him be possessed, in every sense, with an impression of the vigour and beauty and glory around him; and let him feel no less a vigour in himself, too, of body and mind, and infinitely varied power of enjoyment in so many faculties of repose and of energy,--and then let him calmly consider what St. Paul could mean, when he says generally to Christians, "Set your affections on things above, not on things on the earth; for ye are dead, and your life is hid with Christ in God."

Let a person capable of thinking, and such as I have supposed in all other respects, consider what St. Paul could mean by calling him "dead." With an almost thrilling consciousness of life, with an almost bounding sense of vigour in body and mind, he is told that he is "dead." And stranger still, he is told so by one whose recorded life, and existing writings declare that he too must have had in himself a consciousness of life no less lively; that there was in him an activity and energy which neither age nor sufferings could quell; that he wielded an influence over the minds of thousands, such as kings or conquerors might envy. If St. Paul could stand by our side, think we that he, any more than ourselves, would be insensible to the power within him, and to the beauty and the glory without? Yet his words are recorded; he bids us not set our affections on things on the earth; he declares of himself, and of us equally, if we are Christ's servants, that we are dead, and that our life is hid with Christ in God.

I have put the difficulty in its strongest form, for it is one well worth considering. What St. Paul here urges is indeed the highest perfection of Christianity, and therefore of human nature; but it is not an impossible perfection, and St. Paul's own life and character are our warrant that it is nothing sickly, or foolish, or fanatical. But let us first hear the whole of St. Paul's language: "If ye, then, be risen with Christ, seek those things which are above, where Christ sitteth at the right hand of God. Set your affections on things above, not on things on the earth. For ye are dead, and your life is hid with Christ in God. When Christ, who is our life, shall appear, then shall we also appear with him in glory. Mortify therefore your members which are upon the earth; fornication, uncleanness, inordinate affection, evil concupiscence, and covetousness, which is idolatry." "Mortify," I need not say, is to make dead, to destroy. "Ye are dead;" therefore let your members on earth be dead; "fornication, uncleanness, inordinate affection," &c. As if he had said, By becoming Christians ye engaged to be dead; and therefore see to it that ye are so. But what he requires us to make dead or to destroy, are our evil affections and desires; it is manifest, then, that it is to these that, by becoming Christians, we engage to become dead.

This is true; and it is most certain that Christ requires us to be dead only to what is evil. But the essence of spiritual-mindedness consists in this, that it is assumed that with earth, and all things earthly, evil or imperfection are closely mixed; so that it is not possible to set our affections keenly upon, or to abandon ourselves to the enjoyment of, any earthly thing without the danger of those affections and that enjoyment becoming evil. In other words, there is that in the state of things within and around us, which renders it needful to be ever watchful; and watchfulness is inconsistent with an intensity of delight and enjoyment.

For, consider the case which I was just supposing; that lively sense of the beauty of all nature, that indescribable feeling of delight which arises out of the consciousness of health, and strength and power. Suppose that we abandon ourselves to such impressions without restraint, and is it not manifest that they are the extreme of godless pride and selfishness? For do we not know that in this world, and close to us wherever we are, there is, along with all the beauty and enjoyment which we witness, a large portion also of evil, and of suffering? And do we not know that He who gave to the earth its richness, and who set the sun to shine in the heavens, and who gave to us that wonderful frame of body and mind, whose healthful workings are So delightful to us, that He gave them that we might use both body and mind in His service; that the soldier has something else to do than to gaze like a child on the splendour of his uniform or the brightness of his sword; that those faculties which we feel as it were burning within us, have their work before them, a work far above their strength, though multiplied a thousand fold; that the call to them to be busy is never silent; that there is an infinite voice in the infinite sins and sufferings of millions which proclaims that the contest is raging around us; that every idle moment is treason; that now it is the time for unceasing efforts; and that not till the victory is gained may Christ's soldiers throw aside their arms, and resign themselves to enjoyment and to rest?

Then when we turn to the words, "our life is hid with Christ in God," the exceeding greatness of Christ's promises rises upon us in something of the fulness of their reality. Some may know the story of that German nobleman[12], whose life had been distinguished alike by genius and worldly distinctions, and by Christian holiness; and who, in the last morning of his life, when the dawn broke into his sick chamber, prayed that he might be supported to the window, and might look once again upon the rising sun. After looking steadily at it for some time, he cried out, "Oh! if the appearance of this earthly and created thing is so beautiful and so quickening, how much more shall I be enraptured at the sight of the unspeakable glory of the Creator Himself!" That was the feeling of a man whose sense of earthly beauty had all the keenness of a poet's enthusiasm; but who, withal, had in his greatest health and vigour preserved the consciousness that his life was hid with Christ in God; that the things seen, how beautiful soever, were as nothing to the things which are not seen. And so, if from the feeling of natural enjoyment we turn, at once thankfully and earnestly, to remember God's service, and to address ourselves to his work; and sadly remember, that, although we can enjoy, yet that many are suffering; and that, whilst they are so, enjoyment in us for more than a brief space of needful rest cannot but be sin; then there must come upon us, most strongly, the impression of that life where sin and suffering are not; where not God's works only, but God Himself is visible; where the vigour and faculties which we feel within us are not the passing strength of a decaying body, nor the brief prime of a mind which in a few years must sink into dotage; but the strength of a body incorruptible and eternal, the ripeness of a spirit which shall go on growing in wisdom and love for ever.

[12] The Baron Von Canitz.

Thus, then, if we consider again St. Paul's meaning, we shall find that, high and pure as it is, it is nothing unreasonable or impossible; that what he requires us to be dead to absolutely is that which is evil; that, because of the mixture of evil with ourselves and all around us, this life must not and cannot be a life of entire enjoyment without becoming godless and selfish; that, therefore, our affections cannot be set upon earthly things so as to enjoy them in and for themselves entirely, without becoming inordinate, and therefore evil. He does require us, old and young alike, to set our affection on things above: to remember that with God, and with Him alone, can be our rest, and the fulness of our joy; and amidst our pleasure in earthly things to retain in our minds, first, a grateful sense of their Giver; secondly, a remembrance of their passing nature; and thirdly, a consciousness of the evil that is in the world, which makes it a sin to resign ourselves to any enjoyment, except as a permitted refreshment to strengthen us for duty to come. Above all, let one feeling be truly cherished, and it will do more, perhaps, than any other to moderate our pleasure in earthly things, and to render it safe, and wholesome, and Christianlike. That feeling is the remembrance of our own faults. Let us bear these in mind as God does; let us consider how displeasing they are in His sight; how often they are repeated; how little they deserve the enjoyments which are given us. If this does not change our selfish pleasure into a zealous gratitude, then, indeed, sin must have a dominion over us; for the natural effect would be, that our hearts should burn within us for very shame, and should enkindle us to be thankful with all our strength for blessings so undeserved; to show something of our love to God who has so richly shown his love to us.

LECTURE VII.

CORINTHIANS iii. 21-23.

All things are yours; whether Paul, or Apollos, or Cephas,
or the world, or life, or death, or things present, or things to come;
all are yours; and ye are Christ's; and Christ is God's.

It is very possible, that all may not distinctly understand the force of the several clauses of this passage, yet, all, I suppose, would derive a general impression from it, that it spoke of the condition of Christians in very exalted language, and made it to extend to things in this world, as well as to things in the world to come. But can it be good for us to dwell on our exaltation? And if we do, may we not dread lest such language might be used towards us as that which St. Paul uses in the very next chapter to the Corinthians, "Now ye are full, now ye are rich, ye have reigned as kings without us; and I would to God ye did reign, that we also might reign with you." It would seem, however, that it would be good for us to dwell on the greatness of our condition and privileges, because St. Paul, who thus upbraids the Corinthians with their pride, had yet himself immediately before laid the picture of their high privileges, in the words of the text, in full detail before them, as if he wished them carefully to consider it. And so indeed it is. It feeds pride to dwell upon our good qualities or advantages, as individuals, or as a class in society, or as a nation, or as a sect or party; but, to speak generally, our advantages and privileges, as Christians, have not a tendency to excite pride; for some reasons in the nature of the case; for this reason amongst ourselves particularly, because the very essence of pride consists in contrast; we are proud that we are, in some one or more points, superior to others who come immediately under our observation. Now, we have so little to do with any who are not Christians, that the contrast is in this case wanting; we have none over whom to be proud; none whom we can glory in surpassing; and, therefore, a consideration of our Christian advantages, in the absence of that one element which might feed pride, is likely with us to work in a better manner, and to lead rather to thankfulness and increased exertion.

I say to increased exertion; for what would stop exertion is pride. It is the turning back, and pausing to look with satisfaction on what is below us, rather than the looking upward to the summit, and thinking how much our actual elevation has brought us on the way towards it. And, further, there is coupled with every consideration of Christian privileges, the thought of what it must be to leave such privileges unimproved. In this respect, how well does the language of the two lessons from Deuteronomy suit the lesson from the Epistle to the Corinthians. We heard the description of the beauty and richness of the land which God gave to his people,--there were their advantages and privileges,--we heard also, the declaration of their unworthiness, and the solemn threatening of vengeance if, after having received good, they did evil. And as the vengeance has fallen upon them to the utmost, so we are taught expressly to apply their example to ourselves. "If God spared not the natural branches," such was St. Paul's language to the church at Rome, "take heed lest he also spare not thee."

Let us not fear, then, to consider more nearly the high privileges which, as Christians, we enjoy: let us endeavour to understand, not merely generally, but in detail, the exalted language of the text, where it is said, that all things are ours; Paul, Apollos, and Cephas, the world, and life, and death, the things of time, and the things of eternity. These are ours because we are Christ's, and Christ is God's; they are ours so long as we are Christ's, and so far as we are his truly. They are not ours so far as we are not his: they are ours in no degree whatever the moment that he shall declare that we are his no longer.

"Paul, and Apollos, and Peter, are ours." This, perhaps, is the expression which we should understand least distinctly of any. It is an expression, however, of deep importance, though perhaps less so here than in congregations of a different sort. I need not, therefore, dwell on it long now. But the Corinthians, as many Christians have done since, were apt to think more of their being Christians of a certain sort, than of being Christians simply: some said, "We have Paul's view of Christianity, the true and sound view of it, free from superstition:" others said, "But we have Peter's view of Christianity, one of Christ's own apostles, who were with him on earth; ours is the true and earliest view of it, free from all innovations:" and others, again, said, "Nay, but we have been taught by Apollos, an eloquent man, and mighty in the Scriptures; one who best understands how to unite the law and the gospel; one who has given us the full perfection of Christianity." No doubt there were some differences of views even between Paul, and Peter, and Apollos; for while, on the one hand, they were all enlightened by the Spirit of God, yet, on the other hand, they retained still their human differences of character and disposition, which must on several occasions have been manifest. But St. Paul does not tell us what these were, nor how far they extended, nor to what degree they had been exaggerated by those who heard them. He does not insist upon the truth of his own view, nor wish the Corinthians to lay aside their divisions, after the manner so zealously enforced by some persons now, namely, that those who said they were of Peter, or of Apollos, should confess that they had been in error, and declare themselves to be now only of Paul. Such a condemnation of schism he would have held to be in itself in the highest degree schismatical. But St. Paul was earnest, that schism should be ended after another way than this, by all parties remembering, that whatever became of the truth or falsehood of their own particular views of Christianity, yet, that Christianity according to any of their views was the one great thing which was their glory and their salvation. "Paul, and

Apollos, and Peter, are all yours: but you are Christ's." You should not glory in men; that you belong to a purer church than other Christians; but that you belong to the church of Christ; that church, which, in its most pure particular branches, has never been free from some mixture of human infirmity and error; nor yet, in its worst branches, has ever lost altogether the seal of Christ's Spirit, nor ceased to believe in Christ crucified.

But the next words are of more particular concern to us here. "The world, and life, and death, and things present, and things to come, are all ours." They are all ours, so far as we are Christ's. The world is ours; its manifold riches and delights, its various wisdom, all are ours. They are ours, not as a thing stolen, and which will be taken from us with a heavy over-payment of penalty, because we stole it when it did not belong to us; but they are ours by God's free gift, to minister to our comfort, and to our good. And this is the great difference; the good things of this world are stolen by many; but they belong, by God's gift, to those only who are Christ's: and there is the sure sign, generally, to be seen of their being stolen,--an unwillingness that He to whom of right they belong should see them. What a man steals, he enjoys, as it were, in fear: if the owner of it finds him with it, then all his enjoyment is gone; he wishes that he had never touched it; it is no source of pleasure to him, but merely one of terror. And so it is often with our stolen pleasures,--stolen, I mean, not in respect of man, but of God,--stolen, because we do not feel them to be God's gift, nor receive them, as from him, with thankfulness. They may be very lawful pleasures, so far as other men are concerned; pleasures bought, it may be, with our own money, or given to us by our own friends, and enjoyed without any injury to any one. They may be the very simplest enjoyments of life, our health, the fresh air, our common food, our common amusements, our common society; things most permitted to us all, as far as man is concerned, but yet things which are constantly stolen by us, because we take them without God's leave, and enjoy them not as his gifts. They are all his, and he gives them freely to his children. If we are his children, he gives them to us; and delights in our enjoyment of them, as any human father loves to see the pleasure of his children in those things which it is good for them to enjoy. But then, is any child afraid of his father so seeing him? or is the thought of his father any interruption to his enjoyment? If it would be, we should be sure that there was something wrong; that the enjoyment, either in itself, or with respect to the particular case of that child, was a stolen one. And even as simple is the state of our dread of God, of our wish to keep his name and his thought away from us. It is the sure sign that our pleasures are stolen, either as being wrong in themselves, or much oftener, because we have taken them without being fit for them, have snatched them for ourselves, instead of receiving them at the hands of God. Two of us may be daily doing the very same thing in most respects,--enjoying actually the very same pleasures, whether of body or of mind; the same exercises, the same studies, the same indulgences, the same society,--and yet these very same things may belong rightfully to the one, and be stolen by the other. To the one they may come with a double blessing, as the assurance of God's greater love hereafter: to the other, they are but an addition to that sad account, when all good things enjoyed here, having been not our own rightly, but stolen, shall be paid for in over measure, by evil things to be suffered hereafter.

And what I have said of the world, will apply also to life and to death. Oh, the infinite difference whether life is ours, or but stolen for an instant; whether death is ours, our subject, ministering only to our good; or our fearful enemy, our ever keen pursuer, from whose grasp we have escaped for a few short years, but who is following fast after us, and when he has once caught us will hold us fast for ever! Have we ever seen his near approach--has he ever forced himself upon our notice whether we would or no? But two days since he was amongst us,--we were, as it were, forced to look upon him. Did we think that he was ours, or that we were his? If we are his, then indeed he is fearful: fearful to the mere consciousness of nature; a consciousness which no arguments can overcome; fearful if it be merely the parting from life, if it be merely the resigning that wonderful thing which we call our being. It is fearful to go from light to darkness, from all that we have ever known and loved, to that of which we know and love nothing. But if death, even thus stingless, is yet full of horror, what is he with his worst sting beside, the sting of our sins? What is he when he is taking us, not to nothingness, but to judgment? He is indeed so fearful then, that no words can paint him half so truly as our foreboding dread of him, and no arguments which the wit of man can furnish can strip him of his terrors.

But what if death too, as well as life, be ours?--which he is, if we are Christ's; for Christ has conquered him. If he be ours, our servant, our minister, sent but to bring us into the presence of our Lord, then, indeed, his terrors, his merely natural terrors, the outside roughness of his aspect, are things which the merest child need not shrink from. Then disease and decay, however painful to living friends to look upon, have but little pain for him who is undergoing them. For it is not only amidst the tortures of actual martyrdom that Christians have been more than conquerors,--in common life, on the quiet or lonely sick bed, under the grasp of fever or of consumption, the conquest has been witnessed as often and as completely. It is not a little thing when the faintest whisper of thought to which expiring nature can give utterance breathes of nothing but of peace and of forgiveness. It is not a little thing when the name of Christ possesses us wholly; not distinctly, it may be, for reason may be too weak for this; but with an indescribable power of support and comfort. Or even if there be a last conflict,--a season of terror and of pain, a valley of the shadow of death, dark and gloomy,--yet even there Christ is with his servants, and as their trial is so is his love. Thus it is, if death be ours; and death is ours, if we be Christ's. And are we not Christ's? We bear his name, we have his outward seal of belonging to his people,--can we refuse to be his in heart and true obedience? Would we rather steal our pleasures than enjoy them as our own; steal life for an instant, rather than have it our sure possession for ever? Would we rather be fugitives from death, fugitives whom he will surely recover and hold fast, than be able to say and to feel that death, as well as life is ours, things to come, as well as things present, because we are truly Christ's?

LECTURE VIII.

GALATIANS V. 16, 17.

Walk in the Spirit, and ye shall not fulfil the lusts of the flesh.
For the flesh lusteth against the Spirit, and the Spirit against the
flesh; and these are contrary the one to the other, so that ye cannot
do the things that ye would.

"We cannot do the things that we would." These are words of familiar and common use; this is the language in which we are all apt to excuse, whether to ourselves or to others, the various faults of our conduct. We should be glad to do better, so we say and think, but the power to do so fails us. And so far it may seem that we are but echoing the apostle's language; for he says the very same thing, "Ye cannot do the things that ye would." Yet the words as we use them, and as the apostle used them, have the most opposite meaning in the world. We use them as a reason why we should be satisfied, the apostle as a reason why we should be alarmed; we intend them to be an excuse, the apostle meant them to be a certain sign of condemnation.

The reasons of this difference may be understood very easily. We, in the common course of justice, should think it hard to punish a man for not doing what he cannot do. We think, therefore, that if we say that we cannot do well, we establish also our own claim to escape from punishment. But God declares that a state of sin is and must be a state of misery; and that if we cannot escape the sin, we cannot escape the misery. According to God's meaning, then, the words, "Ye cannot do the things which ye would," mean no other than this: "Ye cannot escape from hell; ye cannot be redeemed from the power of death and of Satan; the power is wanting in you, however much you may wish it: death has got you, and it will keep you for ever." So that, in this way, sickness or weakness of the soul is very like sickness or weakness of the body. We cannot help being ill or weak in many cases: is that any reason why, according to the laws of God's providence, we should not suffer the pain of illness? Or is it not, rather, clear that we suffer it just because we have not the power to get rid of it; if we had the power to be well, we should be well. A man's evils are not gone because he wishes them away; it is not he who would fain see his chains broken, that escapes from his bondage; but he who has the strength to rend them asunder.

Thus, then, in St. Paul's language, "Ye cannot do the things that ye would," means exactly, "Ye are not redeemed, but in bondage; ye are not saved, but lost." But he goes on to the reason why we cannot do the things which we would, which is, "because the flesh and the Spirit are contrary to one another," and pull us, as it were, different ways. Just as we might say of a man in illness, that the reason why he is not well, as he wishes to be, is because his healthy nature and his disease are contrary to one another, and are striving within him for the mastery. His blood, according to its healthy nature, would flow calmly and steadily; his food, according to his healthy nature, would be received with appetite, and would give him nourishment and strength; but, behold, there is in him now another nature, contrary to his healthy nature: and this other nature makes his blood flow with feverish quickness, and makes food distasteful to him, and makes the food which he has eaten before to become, as it were, poison; it does not nourish him or strengthen, but is a burden, a weakness, and a pain. As long as these two natures thus struggle within him, the man is sick; as soon as the diseased nature prevails, the man sinks and dies. He does not wish to die,--not at all,--most earnestly, it may be, does he wish to live; but his diseased nature has overcome his healthy nature, and so he must die. If he would live, in any sense that deserves to be called life, the diseased nature must not overcome, must not struggle equally; it must be overcome, it must be kept down, it must be rendered powerless; and then, when the healthy nature has prevailed, its victory is health and strength.

So far all is alike; but what follows afterwards? As "ye cannot do the things which ye would, because the flesh and the Spirit are contrary to one another,"--what then? "Therefore," says the apostle, "walk in the Spirit, and ye shall not fulfil the lusts of the flesh." Surely there is some thing marvellous in this. For, let us speak the same language to the sick man: tell him, "Follow thy healthy nature, and thou shalt not be sick," what would the words be but a bitter mockery? "How can you bid me," he would say, "to follow my healthy nature, when ye know that my diseased nature has bound me? Have ye no better comfort than this to offer me? Tell me rather how I may become able to follow my healthy nature; show me the strength which may help my weakness; or else your words are vain, and I never can recover." Most true would be this answer; and therefore disease and death do make havoc of us all, and the healthy nature is in the end borne down by the diseased nature, and sooner or later the great enemy triumphs over us, and, in spite of all our wishes and fond desires for life, we go down, death's conquered subjects, to the common grave of all living.

This happens to the bodies of us all; to the souls of only too many. But why does it not happen also to the souls of all? How is it that some do fulfil the apostle's bidding? that they do walk in the Spirit, and therefore do not fulfil the lusts of the flesh; and therefore having conquered their diseased nature, they do walk according to their healthful nature, and are verily able to do, and do continually, the very things that they would? Surely this so striking difference, between the universal conquest of our diseased nature in the body, and the occasional victory of the healthy nature in the soul, shows us clearly that for the soul there has appeared a Redeemer already, while for the body the redemption is delayed till death shall be swallowed up in victory.

For most true is it that in ourselves we could not deliver ourselves either soul or body. "Walk in the Spirit, and ye shall not fulfil the lusts of the flesh," might have been as cruel a mockery to us, as the similar words addressed to the man bodily sick,--"Walk according to thy healthy nature, and thou shalt not suffer from disease." They might have been a mockery, but blessed be God, they are not. They are not, because God has given us a Redeemer; they are not, because Christ has died, yea rather has risen again; and because the

Spirit of Christ helpeth our infirmities, and gives us that power which by ourselves we had not.

Not by wishing then to be redeemed, but by being redeemed, shall we escape the power of death. Not by saying, "Alas! we cannot do the things that we would!" but by becoming able to do them. Walk in the Spirit, and ye shall not fulfil the lusts of the flesh; but if ye do fulfil them, ye must die.

The power to walk in the Spirit is given by the Spirit; but either all have not this power, or all do not use it. I think rather it is that all have it not, for if they had it, a power so mighty and so beneficent, they surely could not help using it. All have it not; but I do not say that they all might not have it; on the contrary, all might have it, but in point of fact they have it not. They have it not because they seek it not: for an idle wish is one thing; a steady persevering pursuit is another. They seek not the Spirit by the appointed means, the means of prayer and attending to God's holy word, and thinking of life and death and judgment.

Do those seek the spirit of God who never pray to God? Clearly they do not. For they who never pray to God never think of Him; they who never think of Him, by the very force of the terms it follows that they cannot seek his help. And yet they say, "Oh, I wish to be good, but I cannot!" But this, in the language of the Scripture, is a lie. If they did wish to be good they would seek the help that could make them so. There is no boy so young as not to know that, when temptation is on him to evil, prayer to God will strengthen him for good. As sure as we live, if he wished really to overcome the temptation, he would seek the strength.

Consider what prayer is, and see how it cannot but strengthen us. He who stands in a sheltered place, where the wind cannot reach him, and with no branches over his head to cause a damp shade, and then holds up his face or his hands to the sun, in his strength, can he help feeling the sun's warmth? Now, thus it is in prayer: we turn to God, we bring our souls, with all their thoughts and feelings, fully before Him; and by the very act of so doing, we shelter ourselves from every chill of worldly care, we clear away every intercepting screen of worldly thought and pleasure. It is an awful thing so to submit ourselves wholly to the influence of God. But do it; and as surely as the sun will warm us if we stand in the sun, so will the Giver of light and life to the soul pour his Spirit of life into us; even as we pray, we become changed into his image.

This is not spoken extravagantly. I ask of any one who has ever prayed in earnest, whether for that time, and while he was so praying, he did not feel, as it were, another man; a man able to do the things which he would; a man redeemed and free. But most true is it that this feeling passes away but too soon, when the prayer is done. Still for the time, there is the effect; we know what it is to put ourselves, in a manner, beneath the rays of God's grace; but we do not abide there long, and then we feel the damp and the cold of earth again.

Therefore says the Apostle, "Pray without ceasing." If we could literally pray always, it is clear that we should sin never: it may be thus that Christ's redeemed, at his coming, as they will be for ever with him and with the Father, can therefore sin no more. For where God is, there is no place left for sin. But we cannot pray always: we cannot pray the greatest portion of our time; nay, we can pray, in the common sense of the term, only a very small portion of it. Yet, at least, we can take heed that we do pray sometimes, and that our prayer be truly in earnest. We can pray then for God's help to abide with us when we are not praying: we can commit to his care, not only our hours of sleep, but our hours of worldly waking. "I have work to do, I have a busy world around me; eye, ear, and thought will be all needed for that work, done in and amidst that busy world; now, ere I enter upon it, I would commit eye, ear, thought and wish to Thee. Do thou bless them, and keep their work thine; that as, through thy natural laws, my heart beats and my blood flows without my thought for them, so my spiritual life may hold on its course, through, thy help, at those times when my mind cannot consciously turn to Thee to commit each particular thought to thy service."

But I dare not say that by any the most urgent prayers, uttered only at night and morning, God's blessing can thus be gained for the whole intervening day. For, in truth, if we did nothing more, the prayers would soon cease to be urgent; they would become formal, that is, they would be no prayers at all. For prayer lives in the heart, and not in the mouth; it consists not of words, but wishes. And no man can set himself heartily to wish twice a day for things, of which he never thinks at other times in the day. So that prayer requires in a manner to be fed, and its food is to be found in reading and thinking; in reading God's word, and in thinking about him, and about the world as being his work.

Young men and boys are generally, we know, not fond of reading for its own sake; and when they do read for their own pleasure, they naturally read something that interests them. Now, what are called serious books, including certainly the Bible, do not interest them, and therefore they are not commonly read. What shall we say, then? Are they not interested in becoming good, in learning to do the things which, they would? If they are not, if they care not for the bondage of sin and death, there is, of course, nothing to be said; then they are condemned already; they are not the children of God. But one says, "I wish I could find interest in a serious book, but I cannot." Observe again, "Ye cannot do the things that ye would," because the flesh and the Spirit are contrary to one another. However, to return to him who says this, the answer to him is this,--"The interest cannot come without the reading; it may and will come with it." For interest in a subject depends very much on our knowledge of it; and so it is with, the things of Christ. As long as the life and death of Christ are strange to us, how can we be interested about them? but read them, thinking of what they were, and what were their ends, and who can help being interested about them? Read them carefully, and read them often, and they will bring before our minds the very thoughts which we need, and which the world keeps continually from us, the thoughts which naturally feed our prayers; thoughts not of self, nor selfishness, nor pleasure, nor passion, nor folly, but of such things as are truly God's--love, and self-denial, and purity, and wisdom. These thoughts come by reading the Scriptures; and strangely do they mingle at first with the common evil thoughts of our evil nature. But they soon find a home within us, and more good thoughts gather round them, and there comes a time when daily life with its various business, which, once seemed to shut them out altogether, now ministers to their nourishment.

Wherefore, in conclusion, walk in the Spirit, and ye shall not fulfil the lusts of the flesh; but do even the things which ye would. And ye can walk in the Spirit, if ye seek for the Spirit; if ye seek him by prayer, and by reading of Christ, and the things of Christ. If we will do neither, then most assuredly we are not seeking him; if we seek him not, we shall never find him. If we find him not, we shall never be able to do the things that we would; we shall never be redeemed, never made free, but our souls shall be overcome by their evil nature, as surely as our bodies by their diseased nature; till one death shall possess us wholly, a death of body and of soul, the death of eternal misery.

LECTURE IX.

LUKE xiv. 33.

Whosoever he be of you that forsaketh not all that he hath, he cannot be my disciple.

In order to show that these words were not spoken to the apostles alone, but to all Christians, we have only to turn to the 25th and 26th verses, which run thus:--"And there went great multitudes with him, and he turned and said unto them, If any man come to me, and hate not his father and mother, and wife and children, and brethren and sisters, yea and his own life also, he cannot be my disciple." The words were not, then, spoken to the twelve apostles only, as if they contained merely some rule of extraordinary piety, which was not to be required of common Christians; they were spoken to a great multitude; they were spoken to warn all persons in that multitude that not one of them could become a Christian, unless he gave himself up to Christ body and soul. Thus declaring that there is but one rule for all; a rule which the highest Christian can never go beyond; and which the lowest, if he would be a Christian at all, must make the foundation of his whole life.

Now take the words, either of the text or of the 26th verse, and is it possible to avoid seeing that, on the very lowest interpretation, they do insist upon a very high standard; that they do require a very entire and devoted obedience? Is it possible for any one who believes what Christ has said, to rest contented, either for himself or for others, with that very low and very unchristian standard which he sees and knows to prevail generally in the world? Is it possible for him not to wish, for himself and for all in whose welfare he is interested, that they may belong to the small minority in matters of principle and practice, rather than to the large majority?

And because he so wishes, one who endeavours to follow Christ sincerely can never be satisfied with the excuse that he acts and thinks quite as well as the mass of persons about him; it can never give him comfort, with regard to any judgment or practice, to be told, in common language, "Everybody thinks so; everybody does so." If, indeed, this expression "everybody" might be taken literally; if it were quite true, without any exception, that "everybody thought or did so;" then I grant that it would have a very great authority; so great that it would be almost a mark of madness to run counter to it. For what all men, all without a single exception, were to agree in, must be some truth which the human mind could not reject without insanity,--like the axioms of science, or some action which if we did not we could not live, as sleeping and eating; or if there be any moral point so universally agreed upon, then it must be something exceedingly general: as, for instance, that truth is in itself to be preferred to falsehood; which to dispute would be monstrous. But, once admit a single exception, and the infallible virtue of the rule ceases. I can conceive one single good and wise man's judgment and practice, requiring, at any rate, to be carefully attended to, and his reasons examined, although millions upon millions stood against him. But go on with the number of exceptions, and bring the expression "everybody," to its real meaning, which is only "most persons," "the great majority of the world;" then the rule becomes of no virtue at all, but very often the contrary. If in matters of morals many are on one side and some on the other, it is impossible to pronounce at once which are most likely to be right: it depends on the sort of case on which the difference exists; for the victories of truth and of good are but partial. It is not all truth that triumphs in the world, nor all good; but only truth and good up to a certain point. Let them once pass this point, and their progress pauses. Their followers, in the mass, cannot keep up with them thus far: fewer and fewer are those who still press on in their company, till at last even these fail; and there is a perfection at which they are deserted by all men, and are in the presence of God and of Christ alone.

Thus it is that, up to a certain point, in moral matters the majority are right; and thus Christ's gospel, in a great many respects, goes along with public opinion, and the voice of society is the voice of truth. But this, to use the expression of our Lord's parable, this is but half the height of that tower whose top should reach unto heaven. Christianity ascends a great deal higher; and therefore so many who begin to build are never able to finish. Christ's disciples and the world's disciples work for a certain way together; and thus far the world's disciples call themselves Christ's, and so Christ's followers seem to be a great majority. But Christ warns us expressly that we are not his disciples merely by going a certain way on the same road with them. They only are His, who follow Him to the end. They only are His, who follow him in spite of everything, who leave all rather than leave him. For the rest, He does not own them. What the world can give they may enjoy; but Christ's kingdom is shut against them.

Speaking, then, according to Christ's judgment, and we must hold those to be of the world, and not of Him,--and therefore in God's judgment, to be the evil and not the good,-- who do not make up their minds to live in His service, and to refer their actions, words, and thoughts to His will. Who these are it is very true that we many times cannot know: only we may always fear that they are the majority of society; and therefore we are rather anxious in any individual's case to get a proof that he is not one of them, because, as they are very many, there is always a sort of presumption that any given person is of this number, unless there is some evidence, or some presumption at any rate, for thinking the contrary.

When we speak, then, of the good and of the evil side in human life, in any society, whether smaller or larger,--this is what we mean, or should mean. The evil side contains much that is, up to a certain point, good: the good side,--for does it not consist of human beings?--contains, unhappily, much in it that is evil. Not all in the one is to be avoided,--far from it; nor is all in the other by any means to be followed. But still those are called evil in God's judgment who live according to their own impulses, or according to the law of the society around them; and those are to be called good, who, in their principles, whatever may be the imperfections of their practice, endeavour in all things to live according to the will of Christ.

And in this view the characters of Jacob and Esau are, as it seems to me, full of instruction; and above all to us here. For I have often observed that the early age of an individual bears a great resemblance to the early age of the human race, or of any particular nation; so that the characters of the Old Testament are often more suited, in a Christian country, for the instruction of the young than for those of more advanced years. To Christian men, looking at Jacob's life, with the faults recorded of it, it is sometimes strange that he should be spoken of as good. But it seems that in a rude state of society, where knowledge is very low, and passion very strong, the great virtue is to be freed from the dominion of the prevailing low principle, to see and resolve that we ought and will live according to knowledge, and not according to passion or impulse. The knowledge may be very imperfect, and probably is so: the practice may in many respects offend against knowledge, and probably will do so: yet is a great step taken; it is *the* virtue of man, in such a state of society, to follow, though imperfectly, principle, where others follow instinct, or the opinion of their fellows. It is the great distinguishing mark, in such a state of things, between the good and the evil; for this reason, amongst many others, that it is the virtue, under such, circumstances, of the hardest attainment.

Now, the Scripture judgment of Jacob and Esau, should be in an especial manner the basis of our judgment with regard to the young. None can doubt, that amongst the young, when they form a society of their own, the great temptation is to live by impulse, or according to the opinion of those around them. It is like a light breaking in upon darkness, when a young person is led to follow a higher standard, and to live according to God's will. Esau, in his faults and amiable points alike, is the very image of the prevailing character amongst boys; sometimes violently revengeful, as when Esau looked forward with satisfaction to the prospect of his father's death, because then we should be able to slay his brother Jacob; sometimes full of generosity, as when Esau forgot all his grounds of complaint against his brother, and received him on his return from Mesopotamia with open arms;--but habitually careless, and setting the present before the future, the lower gratification before the higher, as when Esau sold his birth-right for a mess of pottage. And the point to be noted is, that, because of this carelessness, this profaneness or ungodliness, as it is truly called in the New Testament, Esau is distinguished from those who were God's people; the promises were not his, nor yet the blessing. This is remarkable, because Esau's faults, undoubtedly were just the faults of his age: he was no worse than the great majority of those around him; he lived as we should say, in our common language, that it was natural for him to live. He had, therefore, precisely all those excuses which are commonly urged for the prevailing faults of boys; yet it is quite certain that the Scripture holds him out as a representative of those who were not on the side of God,

If the Scripture has so judged of Esau and Jacob, it must be the model for our judgments of those whose circumstances, on account of their belonging to a society consisting wholly of persons young in age, greatly resemble the circumstances of the early society of the world. I lay the stress on the belonging to a society wholly formed of young persons; for the case of young persons brought up at home, is extremely different; and their circumstances would be best suited by a different scriptural example. But here, with you, I am quite sure that the great distinguishing mark between good and evil, is the endeavouring, or not endeavouring, to rise above the carelessness of the society of which you are members; the determining, or not determining, to judge of things by another rule than that of school morality or honour; the trying, or not trying, to please God, instead of those around you: for the notions and maxims of a society of young persons are like the notions and maxims of men in a half-civilized age, a strange mixture of right and wrong; or rather wrong in their result, although with some right feeling in them, and therefore as a guide, false and mischievous. That it is natural to follow these maxims, is quite obvious: they are the besetting sin of your particular condition; and it is always according to our corrupt nature to follow our besetting sin. It is quite natural that you should be careless, profane, mistaking evil for good, and good for evil; but salvation is not for those who follow their nature, but for those in whom God's grace has overcome its evil; it is for those, in Christ's language, who take up their cross and follow him; that is, for those who struggle against their evil nature, that they may gain a better nature, and be born, not after the flesh, but after the Spirit of God.

What is to be said to this? or what qualification, or compromise, is to be made in it? The words of the text will authorize us, at any rate, to make none: their language is not that of indulgent allowance; but it is a call, a loud and earnest, even a severe, call, it may be, in the judgment of our evil nature,--to shake off the weight that hangs about us; to deliver our hearts from the dominion of that which cannot profit, and to submit them to Christ alone. This is God's judgment, this is Christ's word; and we cannot and dare not qualify it. They are evil, for God and Christ declare it, who judge and live after the maxims of the society around them, and not after Christ; they are evil who are careless; they are evil who live according to their own blind and capricious feelings, now hot, now cold; they are evil who call evil good, and good evil, because they have not known the Father nor Christ. This, and nothing less, we say, lest we should be found false witnesses of God: but if this language, which is that of Scripture, seem harsh, to any one, oh! let him remember how soon he may change it into the language of the most abundant mercy, of the tenderest love; that if he calls upon God, God is ready to hear; that if he seeks to know and to do God's will, God will be found by him, and will strengthen him; that it is true kindness not to disguise from him his real danger, but earnestly to conjure him to flee from it, and to offer our humblest prayers to God, for him and ourselves, that our judgments and our practice may be formed only after his example.

LECTURE X.

1 TIMOTHY i. 9.

The law is not made for a righteous man, but for the lawless and disobedient, for the ungodly and for sinners, for the unholy and profane.

These words explain the meaning of a great many passages in St. Paul's Epistles, in which also he speaks of the law, and of not being under the law, and other such expressions. And it is clear also, that he is not speaking solely, or chiefly, or, in any considerable degree, of the ceremonial law; but much more of the law of moral good, the law which told men how they ought to live, and how they ought not. This law, he says, is not made for good men, but for evil: a thing so plain, that we may well wonder how any could ever have misunderstood it. It is so manifest, that strict rules are required, just exactly in proportion to our inability or want of will to rule ourselves; it is so very plain, that, with regard to those crimes which we are under no temptation to commit, we feel exactly as if there were no law. Which of us ever thinks, as a matter of personal concern, of the law which sentences to death murderers, or housebreakers, or those who maliciously set fire to their neighbours' property? Do we not feel that, as far as our own conduct is concerned, it would be exactly the same thing if no such law were in existence? We should no more murder, or rob, or set fire to houses and barns, if the law were wholly done away, than we do now that it is in force.

There are, then, some points in which we feel practically that we are not under the law, but dead to it; that the law is not made for us: but do we think, therefore, that we may murder, and rob, and burn? or do we not rather feel that such a notion would be little short of madness? We are not under the law, because we do not need it; not because there is in reality no law to punish us if we do need it. And just of this kind is that general freedom from the law, of which St. Paul speaks, as the high privilege of true Christians.

But yet St. Paul would not at all mean that any Christian is altogether without the law: that is, that there are no points at all in which his inclination is not to evil, and in which, therefore, he needs the fear of God to restrain him from it. When he says of himself, that he kept under his body lest that by any means he should become a castaway; just so far as this fear of being a castaway possessed him, that is, just so far as there were any evil tendencies in him, which required him to keep them under by an effort, just so far was he under the law. And this is so, as we full well know, with us all; for as there is none of us in whom sin is utterly dead, so neither can there be any of us who is altogether dead to the law.

Yet, although this be so, there is no doubt that the gospel wishes to consider us as generally dead to the law, in order that we really may become so continually more and more. It supposes that the Spirit of God, presenting to our minds the sight of God's love in Christ, sets us free from the law of sin and death; that is, that a sense of thankfulness to God, and love of God and of Christ, will be so strong a motive, that we shall, generally speaking, need no other; that it will so work upon us, as to make us feel good, easy, and delightful, and thus to become dead to the law. And there is no doubt also, that that same freedom from the law, which we ourselves experience daily, in respect of some particular great crimes, (for, as I said, we do not feel that it is the fear of the law which keeps us from murder or from robbing,) that very same freedom is felt by good men in many other points, where it may be that we ourselves do not feel it. A common instance may be given with respect to prayer, and the outward worship of God. There are a great many who feel this as a duty; but there are many also to whom it is not so much a duty, as a privilege and a pleasure; and these are dead to the law which commands us to be instant in prayer, just as we, in general, are dead to the law which commands us to do no murder.

This being understood, it will be perfectly plain, why St. Paul, along with all his language as to the law being passed away, and our being become dead to it, yet uses, very frequently, language of another kind, which shows that the law is not dead in itself, but lives, and ever will live. He says, "We must all stand before the judgment seat of Christ, that every one may receive according to what he has done in the body." And he adds, "Knowing therefore the terror of the Lord, we persuade men." But the judgment, and the terror of the Lord, mean precisely what are meant by the law. And this language of St. Paul shows more clearly, that, unless we are first dead to the law, the law is not, and never will be dead to us.

I should not have thought it useless, to have offered merely this explanation of a language, which is very common in the New Testament, which forms one of its characteristic points, (for St. John's expression of "Perfect love casteth out fear," is exactly equivalent to St. Paul's, "That we are dead to the law,") and which has been often misunderstood, or misrepresented. But yet I am well aware, that mere explanations of Scripture cannot be expected to interest those to whom Scripture is not familiar. The answer to a riddle would be very soon forgotten, unless the riddle had first at once amused and puzzled us. Just so, explanations of Scripture, to be at all valued, must suppose a previous knowledge of, and desire to understand, the difficulty; and this we cannot expect to find in very young persons. Thus far, then, what I have said has been necessarily addressed, I do not say, or mean, to the oldest part of my hearers only, but yet to the older, and more considering part of them. But the subject is capable, I think, of being brought much more closely home to us; for what St. Paul says of the law, with reference to all mankind, is precisely that state of mind which one would wish to see here; and the mistakes of his meaning are just such as are often prevalent, and are likely to do great mischief, with regard to the motives to be appealed to in education.

Now, what is the case in the Scripture? Men had been subject to a strict law of rewards and punishments, appealing directly to their hopes, and to their fears. The gospel offered itself to them, as a declaration of God's love to them; so wonderful, that it seemed as though it could not but excite them to love him in return. It also raised their whole nature; their understandings, no less than their affections; and thus led them to do God's will, from another and higher feeling than they had felt heretofore; to do it, not because they must, but because they loved it. And to such as answered to this heavenly call, God laid aside, if I may venture so to speak, all his terrors; he showed himself to them only as a loving father, between whom and his children there was nothing but mutual affection; who would be loved by them, and love them forever. But to those who answered not to it, and far more, who dared to abuse it; who thought that God's love was weakness; that the liberty to which they were called, was the liberty of devils, the liberty of doing evil as they would; to all such, God was still a consuming fire, and their most merciful Saviour himself was a judge to try their very hearts and reins; in short, the gospel was to them, not salvation, but condemnation; it awakened not the better, but the baser parts of their nature; it did not do away, but doubled their guilt, and therefore brought upon them, and will bring through all eternity, a double measure of punishment.

Now all this applies exactly to that earlier and, as it were, preparatory life, which ends not in death, but in manhood. The state of boyhood begins under a law. It is a great mistake to address always the reason of a child, when you ought rather to require his obedience. Do this, do not do that; if you do this, I shall love you; if you do not, I shall punish you;--such is the state, most clearly a state of law, under which we are, and must be, placed at the beginning of education. But we should desire and endeavour to see this state of law succeeded by something better; we should desire so to unfold the love of Christ as to draw the affections towards him; we should desire so to raise the understanding as that it may fasten itself, by its own native tendrils, round the pillar of truth, without requiring to be bound to it by external bands. We should avoid all unnecessary harshness; we should speak and act with all possible kindness; because love, rather than fear, love both of God and man, is the motive which we particularly wish to awaken. Thus, keeping punishment in the background and, as it were, out of sight, and putting forward encouragement and kindness, we should attract, as it were, the good and noble feelings of those with, whom we are dealing, and invite them to open, and to answer to, a system of confidence and kindness, rather than risk the chilling and hardening them by a system of mistrust and severity.

And for those who do answer to this call, how really true is it that they do soon become dead, in great measure, to the law of the place where they are living! How little do they generally feel its restraints, or its tasks, burdensome! How very little have they to do with its punishments! Led on by degrees continually higher and higher, their relations with us become more and more relations of entire confidence and kindness; and when at last their trial is over, and they pass from this first life, as I have ventured to call it, into their second life of manhood, how beautifully are they ripened for that state! how naturally do all the restraints of this first life fall away, like the mortal body of the perfected Christian; and they enter upon the full liberty of manhood, fitted at once to enjoy and to improve it!

But observe, that St. Paul does not suppose even the best Christian to be without the law altogether: there will ever be some points in which he will need to remember it. And so it is unkindness, rather than kindness, and a very mischievous mistake, to forget that here, in this our preparatory life, the law cannot cease altogether with any one; that it is not possible to find a perfect sense and feeling of right existing in every action; nay, that it is even unreasonable to seem to expect it. Little faults, little irregularities, there always will be, with which the law is best fitted to deal; which should be met, I mean, by a system of rules and of punishments, not severe, certainly, nor one at all inconsistent with general respect, kindness, and confidence; but which check the particular faults alluded to better, I think, than could be done by seeming to expect of the individual that he should, in all such cases, be a law to himself. There is a possibility of our over-straining the highest principles, by continually appealing to them on very trifling occasions. It is far better, here, to apply the system of the law; to require obedience to rules, as a matter of discipline; to visit the breach of them by moderate punishment, not given in anger, not at all inconsistent with general confidence and regard, but gently reminding us of that truth which we may never dare wholly to forget,--that punishment will exist eternally so long as there is evil, and that the only way of remaining for ever entirely strangers to it, is by adhering for ever and entirely to good.

This applies to every one amongst us; and is the reason why rules, discipline, and punishments, however much they may be, and are, kept in the background for such, as have become almost wholly dead to them, must yet continue in existence, because none are, or can be, dead to them altogether. But now, suppose that we have a nature to deal with, which, cannot answer to a system of kindness, but abuses it; which, when punishment is kept at a distance, rejoices, as thinking that it may follow evil safely; a nature not to be touched by the love of God or man, not to be guided by any perception of its own as to what is right and true. Is the law dead really to such as these? or should it be so? Is punishment a degradation to a nature which, is so self-degraded as to be incapable of being moved by anything better? For this is the real degradation which we should avoid; not the fear of punishment, which is not at all degrading, but the being insensible to the love of Christ and of goodness; and so being capable of receiving no other motive than the fear of punishment alone. With such natures, to withhold punishment, would be indeed to make Christ the minister of sin; to make mercy, that is, lead to evil, and not to good. For them, the law never is dead, and never will be. Here, of course, in this first life, as I have called it, punishment indeed goes but a little way: it is very easy for a hardened nature to defy all that could be laid upon it here in the way of actual compulsion. Our only course is to cut short the time of trial, when we find a nature in whom that trial cannot end in good. Still there may be those in whom this life here, like their greater life which shall last for ever, will have far more to do with punishment than with kindness; they will be living all their time under the law. Continue this to our second life, and the law then will be no less alive, and they will never be dead to it, nor will it be ever dead to them. And however a hardened nature may well despise the punishments of its first life,--punishments, whose whole object is correction, and not retribution,--yet, where is the nature so hard as to endure, in its relations with God, to feel more of his punishment than of his mercy; to know him for ever as a God of judgment, and not as a Father of love?

LECTURE XI.

ST. LUKE xxi. 36.

Watch ye, therefore, and pray always, that ye may be accounted worthy to escape all these things that shall come to pass, and to stand before the Son of Man.

This might be a text for a history of the Christian Church, from its foundation to this hour, or to the latest hour of the world's existence. We might observe how it had fulfilled its Lord's command; with what steadiness it had gone forward on its course, with the constant hope of meeting Him once again in glory. We might see how it had escaped all these things that were to come to pass: tracing its course amidst the manifold revolutions of the world, inward and outward. In the few words, "all these things that shall come to pass," are contained all the events of the last eighteen hundred years: indistinct and unknown to us, as long as they are thus folded up together; but capable of being unrolled before our eyes in a long order, in which should be displayed all the outward changes of nations, the spread of discovery, the vicissitudes of conquest; and yet more, the inward changes of men's minds, the various schools of philosophy, the successive forms of public opinion, the influences of various races, all the manifold elements by which the moral character of the Christian world has been affected. We might observe how the Church had escaped all these things, or to what degree it had received from any of them good or evil. And then, stopping at the point at which it has actually arrived, we might consider how far it deserves the character of that Church, "without spot, or wrinkle, or any such thing," which should be presented before the Son of Man at his coming again.

This would be a great subject; and one, if worthily executed, full of the deepest instruction to us all. But our Lord's words may also be made the text for a history or inquiry of another sort, far less comprehensive in time and space, far less grand, far less interesting to the understanding; yet, on the other hand, capable of being wrought out far more completely, and far more interesting to the spiritual and eternal welfare of each of us. They may be made the text for an inquiry into the course hitherto held, not by the Church as a body, but by each of us individual members of it; an inquiry how far we, each of us, have watched and prayed always, that we might be accounted worthy to escape all the things which should come to pass, and to stand before the Son of Man. And, in this view of the words, the expression "all these things which shall come to pass" has reference no longer to great political revolutions, nor to schools of philosophy, nor to prominent points of national character; but to those humbler events, to those lesser changes, outward and inward, through which we each, pass between our cradle and our grave. How have we escaped these, or turned them to good account? Have earthly things so ministered to our eternal welfare, that if we were each one of us, by a stroke from heaven, cut off at that very point in our course to which we have severally attained this day, we should be accounted worthy to stand before the Son of Man?

Here is, indeed, a very humble history for us each to study; yet what other history can concern us so nearly? And as, in the history of the world, experience in part supplies the place of prophecy, and the fate of one nation is in a manner a mirror to another, so in our individual history, the experience of the old is a lesson to the middle-aged, and that of the middle-aged a lesson to the young. If you wish to know what are the things which shall come to pass with respect to you, we can draw aside the veil from your coming life, because what you will be is no other than what we are. If we would go onwards, in like manner, and ask what are the things which shall come to pass with respect to us, our coming life may be seen in the past and present life of the old; for what we shall be is no other than what they have been, or than what they are.

Let us take, then, the actual moment with, each of us, and suppose that our Lord speaks to each of us as he did to his first disciples: "Watch and pray always, that ye may be accounted worthy to escape all these things which shall come to pass, and to stand before the Son of Man." We ask, naturally, "What are the things which shall come to pass?" and it is to this question that I am to try to suggest the answer.

Those arrived at middle age may ask the question, "What are the things which shall come to pass to us?" Now, setting aside extraordinary accidents, on which we cannot reckon, and the answer would, I think, be something of this sort: There will not come to pass, it is likely, any great change in our condition or employment in life. In middle age our calling, with all the duties which it involves, must generally be fixed for each of us. Our particular kind of trial will not, it is probable, be much altered. We must not, as in youth, fancy that, although our actual occupation does not suit us, although its temptations are often too strong for us, yet a change may take place to another line of duty, and the temptations in that new line may be less formidable. In middle age it will not do to indulge such fond hopes as these. On the contrary, our hope must lie, not in escape, but in victory. If our temptations press us hard, we cannot expect to have them exchanged for others less powerful: they will remain with us, and we must overcome them, or perish. Have we tastes not fully reconciled to our calling,--faculties which seem not to have found their proper field? We must seek our remedy not from without, humanly speaking, but from within: we must discipline ourselves; we must teach our tastes to cling gracefully around that duty to which else they must be helplessly fastened. If any faculties appear not to have found their proper field, we must think that God has, for certain wise reasons, judged it best for us that they should not be exercised; and we must be content to render him the service of others. In this respect, then, the immediate prospect for middle age is not so much change as steadfastness. Fortune will not suit herself to our wishes: we must learn to suit our wishes to her.

But go on a little farther, and what are the things which must come to pass then? A new and most solemn interest arising to us in the entrance of our children into active life. Hitherto they have lived under our care, and our duty to them was simple; but now there comes the choice of a profession, the watching and guiding them, as well as we can, at this critical moment of their course. What cares await us here; and yet what need of avoiding over care! What a trial for us, how we value our children's worldly interests when compared with their eternal--whether we prefer for them the path which may lead most readily to worldly wealth and honour, or that in, which they may best and safest follow Christ! This is a danger which will come to pass to us ere long: do we watch and pray that we may be delivered from it?

The interest of life, which had, perhaps, something begun to fade for ourselves, will revive with vigour at this period in behalf of our children; but after this it will go on steadily ebbing. What life can offer we have tasted for ourselves; we have seen it tasted, or in the way to be tasted, by them. The harvest is gathered, and the symptoms of the fall appear. Is it that some faculty becomes a little impaired, some taste a little dulled; or is it that the friends and companions of our life are beginning to drop away from us? Long since, those whom we loved of the generation before us have been gathered to the grave; now those of our own generation are falling fast also--brothers, sisters, friends of our early youth, a wife, a husband. We are surrounded by a younger generation, to whom the half of our lives, with all their recollections and sympathies, are a thing unknown. Impatience, weariness, a clinging to the past, a vain wish to prolong it in an earthly future,--these are the things which shall befal us then: and they will befal us too surely, and too irresistibly, unless, by earlier watchfulness and prayer, we may have been enabled to avoid them. For vain will it be, with faculties at once weakened by the decay of nature and perverted by long habits of worldliness, to essay, for the first time, to force our way into the kingdom of heaven. Old age is not the season for contest and victory; nor shall we then be so able to escape unharmed from the temptations of life as to stand before the Son of Man.

These are the things which will come to pass for us and for you. But for you there is much more to come, which to us is not future now, but past or present. With you, for a time, it will be all a course forwards and upwards. From the preparation for life, you will come to the reality; from a state of less importance, you will be passing on to one of greater. Your temptations, whatever they may be now, will not certainly become weaker. As outward restraint is more and more taken off from you, so your need of inward restraint will be greater. Will those who are extravagant now on a small scale, be less extravagant on a large scale? Will those who are selfish now, become less selfish amidst a wider field of enjoyment? Will those who know not or care not for Christ, while yet, as it were, standing quietly on the shore, be led to think of him more amidst the excitement of the first setting sail, amidst the interest of the first newly-seen country?

You know not yet, nor can know, the immense importance of that period of life on which many of you are entering, or have just entered. You are coming, or come, to what may be called the second beginning of life: to which, in the common course of things, there will succeed no third. Ignorance, absence of temptation, the presence of all good impressions, constitute much of the innocence of mere childhood,--so beautiful while it lasts, so sure to be soon blighted! It is blighted in the first experience of life, most commonly when a boy first goes to school. Then his mere innocence, which indeed he may be said to have worn rather instinctively than by choice, becomes grievously polluted. Then come the hardness, the coarseness, the intense selfishness; sometimes, too, the falsehood, the cruelty, the folly of the boy: then comes that period, so trying to the faith of parents, when all their early care seems blasted; when the vineyard, which they had fenced so tenderly, seems all despoiled and trodden under foot. It is indeed a discouraging season, the exact image of the ungenial springs of our natural year. But after this there comes, as it were, a second beginning of life, when principle takes the place of innocence. There is a time,--many of you must have arrived at it,--when thought and inquiry awaken; when, out of the mere chaos of boyhood, the elements of the future character of the man begin to appear. Blessed are they for whom the confusion and disarray of their boyish life is quickened into a true life by the moving of the Spirit of God! Blessed are they for whom the beginnings of thought and inquiry are the beginnings also of faith and love; when the new character receives, as it is forming, the Christian seed, and the man is also the Christian. And, then, this second beginning of life, resting on faith and conscious principle, and not on mere passive innocence, stands sure for the middle and the end: those who so watch and pray as to escape out of this critical period, not merely unharmed, but, as it were, set clearly on their way to heaven, will, with God's grace, escape out of the things which shall befal them afterwards, till they shall stand before the Son of Man.

But the word is, "Watch and pray always, that ye may be accounted worthy to escape." We see the time with many of you come, or immediately coming; out of your present state *a* character will certainly be formed; as surely as the innocence of childhood has perished, so surely will the carelessness of boyhood perish too. *A* character will be formed, whether you watch and pray, or whether you do neither; but the great point is what this character may be. If you do not watch the process, it will surely be the character of death eternal. Thought and inquiry will satisfy themselves very readily with an answer as far as regards spiritual things: their whole vigour will be devoted to the things of this world, to science or to business, or to public matters, all alike hardening rather than softening to the mind, if its thoughts do not go to something higher and deeper still. And as years pass on, we may think on these our favourite or professional subjects more and more earnestly; our views on them may be clearer and sounder, but there comes again nothing like the first free burst of thought in youth; the intellect in later life, if its tone was not rightly taken earlier, becomes narrowed in proportion to its greater vigour; one thing it sees clearly, but it is blind to all beside. It is in youth that the after tone of the mind is happily formed, when that natural burst of thought is sanctified and quickened by God's Spirit, and we set up within us to love and adore, all our days, the one image of the truth of God, our Saviour Jesus. Then, whatever else may befal us afterwards, it rarely happens that our faith will fail; his image, implanted in us, preserves us amid every change; we are counted worthy to escape all the things which may come to pass, and to stand before the Son of Man.

LECTURE XII.

PROVERBS i. 28.

Then shall they call upon me, but I will not answer; they shall seek me early, but they shall not find me.

Christ's gospel gives out the forgiveness of sins; and as this is its very essence, so also in what we read connected with Christ's gospel, the tone of encouragement, of mercy, of loving-kindness to sinners, is ever predominant. What was needed at the beginning of the gospel is no less needed now; we cannot spare one jot or one tittle of this gracious language; now, as ever, the free grace, that most seems to be without the law, does most surely establish the law. But yet there is another language, which is to be found alike in the Old Testament and in the New; a language not indeed so common as the language of mercy, but yet repeated many times; a language which we also need as fully as it was ever needed, and of whose severity we can no more spare one tittle than we can spare anything of the comfort of the other. And yet this language has not, I think, been enforced so often as it should have been. Men have rather shrunk from it, and seemed afraid of it; they have connected it sometimes with certain foolish and presumptuous questions, which we, indeed, do well to turn from; but they have not seen, that with such it has no natural connexion, but belongs to a certain fact in the constitution of our nature, and is most highly moral and practical.

The language to which. I allude is expressed, amongst other passages, by the words of the text. They speak of men's calling upon God, and of his refusing to hear them; of men's seeking God, and not finding him. Remember, at the same time, our Lord's words, "Ask, and ye shall receive; seek, and ye shall find." I purposely put together these opposite passages, because the full character of God's Revelation is thus seen more clearly. Do we doubt that our Lord's words are true, and do we not prize them as some of the most precious which he has left us? We do well to do so; but shall we doubt any more the truth of the words of the text; and shall we not consider them as a warning no less needful than the comfort in the other case? Indeed, as true as it is, that, if we seek God, we shall find him; so true is it that we may seek him, and yet not find him.

Now, then, how to explain this seeming contradiction? We can see at once, that these things are not said of the same persons, or rather of the same characters at the same time. They are said of the same persons: that is, there is no one here assembled who is not concerned with both, and to whom both may not be applicable. Only they are not and cannot be both applicable to the same person at the very same time. If God will be found by us, at any given moment, on our seeking him, it is impossible that, at that same moment, he should also not be found. Thus far is plain to every one.

And now, is it true of us, at this present time, that God will be found by us if we seek him, or that he will not be found? If we say that he will be found, then the words of the text are not applicable to us at present, although at some future time they may be; and then we have that well-known difficulty to encounter, to attempt to draw the mind's attention to a future and only contingent evil. If we say that he will not be found, then of what avail can it be to say any word more? Why sit we in this place, to preach, or to listen to preaching, if God, after all, will not be found? Or, again, should we say that there are some by whom he will not be found, then who are they that are thus horribly marked out from among their brethren? Can we dare to conceive of any one amongst us that he is such an one; that there are some, nay, that there is any one amongst us, to whom it is the same thing whether he will hear, or whether he will forbear; who may close his ears as safely as open them, because God has turned his face from him for ever? It were indeed horrible to suppose that any one of us were in such a state; and happily it is a thought of horror which the truth may allow us to repel.

But what, if I were to say, that now, at this very moment, the words of the text are both applicable to us, and not applicable? Is this a contradiction, and therefore impossible? Or is it but a seeming contradiction only, and not only possible, but true? Let us see how the case appears to be.

We should allow, I suppose, that the words of the text were at no time in any man's earthly life so true as they will be at the day of judgment. The hardest heart, the most obdurate in sin, the most closed against all repentance, is yet more within the reach of grace, we should imagine, whilst he is alive and in health, than he will be at the day of the resurrection. We can admit, then, that the words of the text may be true, in a greater or less degree; that they will be more entirely true at the last day, than at any earlier period, but yet that they may be substantially true, true almost beyond exception, in the life that now is. Now carry this same principle a little farther, and we come to our very own case. The words of the text will be more true at the day of judgment, than they ever are on earth; and yet on earth they are often true substantially and practically. And even so, they may be more true to each of us a few years hence, than they are at this moment; and yet, in a certain degree, they may be true at this moment; true, not absolutely and entirely, but partially; so true as to give a most solemn earnest, if we are not warned in time, of their more entire truth hereafter,-- first, in this earthly life; then most perfectly of all, when we shall arise at the last day.

It may be, then, that the words of the text, although not applicable to us in their full and most fatal sense, may yet be applicable to us in a certain degree: the evil which they speak of may be, not wholly future and contingent, and a thing to be feared, but present in part, actual, and a matter of experience. This is not contradiction: it is not impossible; it *may be* our case. Let us see whether it really is so, that is, whether it is in any degree true of us, that when we call upon God he will not answer; that when we seek him, we shall in any manner be unable to find him.

It is manifest that, in proportion as Christ's words "Seek, and ye shall find," are true to any man, so are the words of the text less true to him; and in proportion as Christ's words are less true to any one, so are the words of the text more true to him. Now, is Christ's promise, "Seek, and ye shall find," equally true to all of us? Conceive of one--the thing is rare, but not impossible,--of one who had been so kept from evil, and so happily led forward in good, that when arrived at boyhood, his soul had scarcely more stain upon it than when it was first fully cleansed, and forgiven, in baptism! Conceive him speaking truth, without any effort, on all occasions; not greedy, not proud, not violent, not selfish, not feeling conscious that he was living a life of sin, and therefore glad to come to God, rather than shrinking away from him! Conceive how completely to such an one would Christ's words be fulfilled, "Seek, and ye shall find!" When would his prayers be unblessed or unfruitful? When would he turn his thoughts to God without feeling pleasure in doing so; without a lively consciousness of God's love to him; without an assured sense of the reality of things not seen, of redemption and grace and glory? Would not the communion with God, enjoyed by one so untainted, come up to the full measure of those high promises, "It shall come to pass, that before they call, I will answer, and while they are yet speaking, I will hear?" Would it not be plain, that God was as truly found, by such a person, as he was sought in sincerity and earnestness?

But now, take the most of us: suppose us not to have been kept carefully from evil, nor led on steadily in good; suppose us to have reached boyhood with bad dispositions, ready for the first temptation, with habits of good uncultivated; suppose us to have no great horror of a lie, when it can serve our turn; with much love of pleasure, and little love of our duty; with much, selfishness, and little or no thought of God: suppose such an one, so sadly altered from a state of baptismal purity, to be saying his prayers as he had been taught to say them, and saying them sometimes with a thought of their meaning and a wish that God would hear them. But does God hear them? I ask of your own consciences, whether you have had any sense that he has heard you? whether death and judgment, Christ and Christ's service, have become more real to you after such prayers? If not, then is it not manifest, that you have sought God, and have not found him; that you have called upon him and he has not heard? You know by experience, that you are not as those true children who are ever with him, who listen to catch the lightest whisper of his Spirit, for whom, he, too, vouchsafes to bless the faintest breathing of their prayer.

Or, again, in trying to turn from evil to good, have you ever found your resolutions give way, the ground which you had gained slide from under your feet, till you fell back again to what you were at the beginning? Has this ever happened to us? If it has, then in that case, also, we sought God, but failed to find him; the victory was not yours, but the enemy's; the Spirit of Christ did not help you so as to conquer.

Take another case yet again. Has it ever happened to any of you, to have done a mischief to yourselves which you could not undo? It need not be one of the very highest kind; but has it ever happened, that, by neglect, you have lost ground in the society in which you are placed, which you cannot recover; that your contemporaries have gained an advance upon you, while you have not time left to overtake them? Does it ever happen that, from neglecting some particular element of learning in its proper season, and other things claiming your attention afterwards, you go on with a disadvantage, which you would fain remove, but cannot? Does it, in short, ever happen to any, that his complete success here is become impossible; that whatever prospects of another kind may be open to him elsewhere, yet that he cannot now be numbered amongst those who have turned the particular advantages here afforded them to that end which they might and ought to have done?

To whomsoever this has happened, the truth of the words of the text is matter of experience, not in their full and most dreadful extent, but yet quite enough to prove that they are true; and that just as he now feels them in part, so, if he continues to be what he is, he will one day feel them wholly. He feels that it is possible to seek God, and not to find him; he has learnt by experience that neglected good, or committed evil, may be beyond the power of after-regret to undo. It is true, that as yet, to him, other prospects may be open:

53

prospects which, probably, he may deem no less fair than those which he has forfeited. This may be so; but the point to observe is, that one prospect was lost so irretrievably by his own fault, that afterwards, when he wished to regain it, he could not. Now God gives him other prospects, which he may realize: but as he forfeited his first prospect beyond recovery, so he may do also with his last: and though ill-success at school may be made up by success in another sphere, yet what is to make up for ill-success in the great business of life, when that, too, has been forfeited as irrecoverably; when his last chance is gone as hopelessly as his first?

Now, surely there is in all this an intelligible lesson. I am not at all exaggerating the importance of the particular prospect forfeited here: but I am pressing upon you, that this prospect may be, and often is, forfeited irrecoverably; that when you wish to regain it, it is too late, and you cannot. And I press this, because it is a true type of the whole of human life; because it is just as possible to forfeit salvation irrecoverably, as to forfeit that earthly good which is the prize of well-doing here, with this infinite difference, that the last forfeit is not only irretrievable, but fatal; it can no more be made up for, than it can be regained. Here, then, your present condition is a type of the complete truth of the text: but there are other points, to which I alluded before, in which it is more than a type; it is the very truth itself, although, happily, only in an imperfect measure. That unanswered prayer, of which I spoke, those broken resolutions,--are they not actually a calling on God, without his hearing us; a seeking him, without finding him? We remember who it was that could say with truth to his Father, "I know that thou hearest me always." We know what it is that hinders God from hearing us always; because we are not thoroughly one in his Son Christ Jesus. But this unanswered prayer is not properly the State of Christ's redeemed: it is an enemy that hath brought us to this; the same enemy who will, in time, make all our prayers to be unanswered, as some are now; who will cause God, not only to be slow to listen, but to refuse to listen for ever. Now we are not heard at once, we must repeat our prayers, with more and more earnestness, that God, at last, may hear, and may bless us. But if, instead of repeating them the more, we do the very contrary, and repeat them the less; if, because we have no comfort, and no seeming good from them, we give them up altogether; then the time will surely come when all prayer will be but the hopeless prayer of Esau, because it will be only the prayer of fear; because it will be only the dread of destruction that will, or can, move us:--the love of good will have gone beyond recall. Such prayer does but ask for pardon without repentance; and this never is, or can be, granted.

So then, in conclusion, that very feeling of coldness, and unwillingness to pray, because we have often prayed in vain, is surely working in us that perfect death, which is the full truth of the words of the text. Of all of us, those who the least like to pray, who have prayed with the least benefit, have the most need to pray again. If they have sought God, without finding him, let them take heed that this be not their case for ever; that the truth, of which the seed is even now in them, may not be ripened to their everlasting destruction, when all their seeking, and all their prayer, will be as rejected by God, as, in part, it has been already.

LECTURE XIII.

MARK xii. 34.

Thou art not far from the kingdom of God.

Whoever has gone up any hill of more than common height, may remember the very different impression which the self-same point, whether bush, or stone, or cliff, has made upon him as he viewed it from below and from above. In going up it seemed so high, that we fancied, if we were once arrived at it, we should be at the summit of our ascent; while, when we had got beyond it, and looked down upon it, it seemed almost sunk to the level of the common plain; and we wondered that it could ever have appeared high to us.

What happens with any natural object according to the different points from which we view it, happens also to any particular stage of advancement in our moral characters. There is a goodness which appears very exalted or very ordinary, according as it is much above or much below our own level. And this is the case with the expression of our Lord in the text, "Thou art not far from the kingdom of God." Does this seem a great thing or a little thing to be said to us? Does it give us a notion of a height which we should think it happiness to have reached; or of a state so little advanced, that it would be misery to be forced to go back to it? For, according as it seems to us the one or the other, so we may judge of the greater or less progress which we have made in ascending the holy mountain of our God.

But while I say this, it is necessary to distinguish between two several senses, in which we may be said to be near to the kingdom of God, or actually in it. These two are in respect of knowledge, and in respect of feeling and practice. And our Lord's words seem to refer particularly to knowledge. The scribe to whom he used them, had expressed so just a sense of the true way of pleasing God, had so risen above the common false notions of his age and country, that his understanding seemed to be ripe for the truths of that kingdom of God, which was to make the worship of God to consist in spirit and in truth. Now as far as the knowledge of the kingdom of God is concerned, although, undoubtedly, there are many amongst us who are deficient in it, yet it is true also, that a great many of us are in possession of it; we are familiar enough with the truths of the kingdom of God, and our understandings fully approve them. But we may be near to or far from the kingdom of God, in respect also of feeling and practice; and this is the great matter that concerns us. It is here, then, that we should ask ourselves what we think of our Lord's words in the text; and whether he to whom they were spoken appears to us an object of envy or of compassion; one whom we envy for having advanced so far, or pity for not being advanced further.

"Not far from the kingdom of God." Again, if we take the words Kingdom of God in their highest sense, then the expression contains all that we could desire to have said of us in this life; hope itself on this side of the grave can go no higher. For as, in this sense, the kingdom of God cannot be actually entered before our death; so the best thing that can be said of us here, is, that we are not far from it; but we are in the land of Beulah, so happily imagined in the Pilgrim's Progress; all of our pilgrimage completed, save the last act of crossing the river; with the city of God full in sight, and with hearts ready to enter into it. In this sense, even St. Paul himself, when he wrote his last epistle from Rome, could say no more, could hope for, could desire no more, than to be not far from the kingdom of God.

Yet again, take the words "Kingdom of God" in their lowest sense, and then it is woe to us all, if the expression in the text is all that can be said of us; if, in this sense, we are only not far from the kingdom of God. For take the kingdom of God as God's visible Church, and then, if we are not Christians at all, but only not far from becoming so; if we have not received Christ, but are not far from receiving him; this is a state so imperfect, that he who is in it, has not yet reached to the beginning of his Christian course; and we need not say how far he must be from its end, if he have not yet come as far as its beginning.

Thus, in one sense, the words express something so high that nothing can be higher; in another, something so low, that, to us, nothing can be lower. We have yet to seek that sense, in which they may afford us a useful criterion of our own several states, by appearing high, perhaps, to some of us, and to others low.

The sense which we seek is given by our Lord, when he declares that the kingdom of God is within us; or by St. Paul, when he tells us, that it is righteousness, peace, and joy in the Holy Ghost. And now it is no more a thing which we cannot yet have reached, or, on the other hand, which we all have reached: there is now a great difference in us, some are far from it, some are near it, and some are in it; and thus it is, that they who are near it, seem in it to those who are afar off, and far from it to those who are in it.

Now, first, do they seem far from it? Then, indeed, ours is a happy state, as many of us as can truly feel that they live so constantly in holy and heavenly tempers, in such lively faith and love, so tasting all the blessings of God's kingdom, its peace, and its hope, and its joy, that they cannot bear to think of that time, when these blessings were not enjoyed except in prospect; when they rather desired to have faith and love, than could be said actually to have them; when their tempers were not holy and heavenly, although they were fully alive to the excellence of their being so, and had seen them already cleansed from the opposites of such a state, from ill-nature, and passion, and pride.

If any such there be, in whom good resolutions have long since ripened into good actions, and the continued good actions have now led to confirmed good habits, how miserable will they think it to be only "not far from the kingdom of God!" How ill could they bear to go over again the struggle which used to accompany every action, when it was done in defiance of habits of evil; or to be called back to that condition when resolutions for good were formed over and over again, because they were so often broken, but had as yet rarely led to any solid fruit! How thankful will they be to have escaped from that season when they were seeking, but had not yet found; when they were asking of God, but had not yet received; when they were knocking, but the door had not yet been opened! They were then, indeed, not far from the kingdom of God, but they were still without its walls; they were still strangers, and not citizens. It had held out to them a refuge, and they had fled to it as suppliants to the sanctuary; but they had not yet had the word of peace spoken, to bid them no more kneel without, as suppliants, but to enter and go in and out freely; for that all things were theirs, because they were Christ's.

I have dwelt purposely somewhat the longer upon this, because the more that we can feel the truth of this picture, the more that we can put ourselves into the position of those who are within the kingdom of God, and who, living in the light of it, look back with pity upon those who are only kneeling without its gates,--the more strongly we shall feel what must be our condition, if those who are without its gates appear to us to be objects of envy rather than pity, because they are so near to that place from which we feel ourselves to be so distant. Or, to speak without a figure, if we could but understand how persons advanced in goodness would shrink from the thought of being now only resolving to be good, then we shall perceive how very evil must be our condition, if this very resolving to be good seems to us to be an advance so desirable; if we are so far from being good actually, that the very setting ourselves in earnest to seek for good strikes us as a point of absolute proficiency in comparison of our present degradation.

Yet is not this the case with many of us? Do we not consider it a great point gained, if we can be brought to think seriously, to pray in earnest, to read the Bible, to begin to look to our own ways and lives? We feel it for ourselves, and others also feel it for us: it is natural, it is unavoidable, that we feel great joy, that we think a great deal is done, if we see any of you, after leading a life of manifest carelessness, and therefore of manifest sin, beginning to take more pains with himself, and so becoming what is called somewhat more steady and more serious. I know that the impression is apt to be too strong upon us: we are but too apt to boast for him who putteth on his armour as for him who putteth it off; because he who putteth on his armour at least shows that he is preparing for the battle, which so many never do at all. We observe some of these signs of seriousness: we see perhaps, that a person begins to attend at the Communion; that he pays more attention to his ordinary duties; that he becomes more regular. We see this, and we are not only thankful for it,--this we ought to be,--but we satisfy ourselves too readily that all is done: we reckon a person, somewhat too hastily, to be already belonging to the kingdom of God, because we have seen him turning towards it. Then, if he afterwards does not appear to be entered into it; if we see that he is not what we expected, that he is no longer serious, no longer attentive to his common duties, we are overmuch disappointed; and, perhaps are tempted too completely to despair for him. Is it not that we confounded together the beginning and the end; the being good, and the trying to become so: the resolution with the act; the act with the habit? Did we not forget that he is not at once out of danger who begins to mend: that the first softening of the dry burning skin, the first abating of the hard quick pulse, is far removed from the coolness, and steadiness, and even vigour of health restored, or never interrupted?

But what made us forget truths so obvious? What made us confound things so different that the most ignorant ought to be able to distinguish them? Cannot we tell why it is? Is it not because there are so many in whom we cannot see even as good signs as these,--of whom we cannot but feel that it would be a great advance for them, a matter of earnest thankfulness, if we could only see that they were not far from the kingdom of God,--nay, even that their steps were tending thither? Let us look ever so earnestly, let us watch ever so carefully, let us hope ever so charitably, we cannot see, we can scarcely fancy that we see, even the desire to turn to God. We do not see gross wickedness; it is well; we see much that is amiable; that is well also: but the desire to turn to God, the tending of the steps towards the kingdom of heaven,--that we cannot see. But this is a thing, it may be said, that man cannot see: it may exist, although we cannot perceive it. Oh, that it might and may be so! Yet, surely, as out of the abundance of the heart the mouth speaketh, so a principle so mighty as the desire of turning to God cannot leave itself without a witness: some symptoms must be shown to those who are eagerly watching for them; some ground for hope must be afforded where hope is so ready to kindle. If no sign of life appears, can the life indeed be stirring? And if the life be not stirring; if the disorder is going on in so many cases, raging, with no symptom of abatement; is it not natural, that when we do see such symptoms, we should rejoice even with over-measure, that we should forget how much is yet to be done, when we see that something has been done.

To such persons, it would be an enviable state, to be not far from the kingdom of God. But what, then, must be their state actually? A hopeful one, according to many standards of judgment; a state that promises well, it may be, for a healthy and prosperous life, with many friends, perhaps with much distinction. We know that all this prospect may be blighted; still it exists at present;--the healthy constitution, the easy fortune, the cheerful and good-humoured temper, the quickness and power of understanding; all these, no doubt, are hopeful signs for a period of forty, or fifty, or perhaps sixty years to come. But what is to come then? what is the prospect for the next period, not of fifty, or sixty, not of a hundred, not of a thousand, years; not of any number that can be numbered, but of time everlasting? Is their actual state one of hopeful promise for this period, for this life which no death shall terminate? Nay, is it a state of any promise at all, of any chance at all? Suppose, for a moment, one with a crippled body, full of the seeds of hereditary disease, poor, friendless, irritable in temper, low in understanding; suppose such an one just entering upon youth, and ask yourselves, for what would you consent that his prospects should be yours? What should you think would be your chance of happiness in life, if you were beginning in such a condition? Yet, I tell you that poor, diseased, irritable, friendless cripple has a far better prospect of passing his fifty, or sixty, years, tolerably, than they who have not begun to turn towards God have of a tolerable eternity. Much more wretched is the promise of their life; much more justly should we be tempted, concerning them, to breathe that fearful thought, that it were good for them if they had never been born. And now if, as by miracle, that cripple's limbs were to be at once made sound, if the seeds of disease were to vanish, if some large fortune were left him, if his temper sweetened, and his mind became vigorous, should not we be excused, considering what he had been and what he now was, if we, for a moment, forgot the uncertainty of the future; if we thought that a promise so changed, was almost equivalent to performance? And may not this same excuse be urged for some over-fondness of confidence for their well-doing whom we see so near to the kingdom of God, when we consider how utter is the misery, how hopeless the condition of those who do not appear to have, as yet, stirred one single step towards it?

LECTURE XIV.

57

For many are called, but few are chosen.

The truth here expressed is one of the most solemn in the world, and would be one of the most overwhelming to us, if habit had not, in a manner, blunted our painful perception of it. There is contained in it matter of thought more than we could exhaust, and deeper than we could ever fathom. But on this I will not attempt to enter. I will rather take that view of the text which concerns us here; I will see in how many senses it is true, and with what feeling we should regard it.

"Many are called, but few are chosen." The direct application of this was to the parable of those invited to the supper; in which it had been related, how a great multitude had been invited, but how one among them--and the application as well as the fact in human life, require that this *one* should be taken only as a specimen of a great number--had been found unworthy to enjoy the feast prepared for them. They had not on the wedding garment; they had not done their part to fit themselves for the offered blessing: therefore they were called, but not chosen. God had willed to do them good, but they would not; and therefore, though he had called them at the beginning, he, in the end, cast them out.

We have to do, then, not with an arbitrary call and an arbitrary choice, as if God called many in mockery, meaning to choose out of them only a few, and making his choice independently of any exertion of theirs. The picture is very different; it is a gracious call to us all, to come and receive the blessing; it is a reluctant casting out the greatest part of us, because we would not try to render ourselves fit for it.

I said, that we would take the words of the text in reference to ourselves, for here, too, it is true, that many are called, but few are chosen. It is a large number of you, which I see before me; and if we add to it all those who, within my memory, have sat in the same places before you, we shall have a number very considerable indeed. All these have been called; they have been sent here to enjoy the same advantages with each other; and those advantages have been put within their reach. They have entered into a great society which, on the one hand, might raise them forward, or, on the other, depress them. There has been a sufficient field for emulation: there have been examples and instructions for good; there have been results of credit and of real improvement made attainable to them, which might have lasted all their lives long. To this, they have been all, in their turns, called; and out of those so called, have all, or nearly all, been chosen? I am not speaking of those, who, I trust, would be a very small number, to whom the trial has failed utterly, who could look back on their stay here with no feelings but those of shame. But would there not be a very large number, to whom their stay here has been a loss, compared with what it might have been; who have reaped but a very small part of those advantages to which they had been at first called? Are there not too many who must look back on a part, at least, of their time here as wasted; on the seeds of bad habits sown, which, if conquered by after-care, yet, for a long time, were injurious to them? Are there not too many who carry away from here, instead of good notions, to be ripened and improved, evil notions, to be weeded out and destroyed? Are there not, in short, a great number who, after having had a great advantage put within their reach, and purchased for them by their friends, at a great expense, have made such insufficient use of their opportunities, to say nothing stronger, as to make it a question afterwards, whether it might not have been better for them had they never come here at all?

Thus far I have been speaking of what are called the advantages of this place in our common language. That argument, which Butler has so nobly handled, in one of the greatest works in our language, the resemblance, namely, between the course of things earthly and that of things spiritual, is one which we should never fail to notice. We can discern the type, as it were, of the highest truth of our Lord's sayings in the experience of our common life in worldly things. When he tells us, speaking of things spiritual, that "many are called, but few are chosen;" that "whoso hath, to him shall be given; but from him that hath not shall be taken away even that which he hath,"--although the highest truth contained in these words be yet, in part, matter of faith, for we have not yet seen the end of God's dealings with us: yet what we do see, the evident truth of the words, that is, in respect to God's dealings with us in the course of his earthly providence, may reasonably assure us of their truth no less in respect to those dealings of God which as yet are future. I began, therefore, with reminding you of the truth of the words of the text with regard to worldly advantages; that even here, on this small scale, the general law holds good; that more things are provided for us than we will consent to use; that, in short, "many are called, but few are chosen."

But it were ill done to limit our view to this: we are called to much more than worldly advantages; and what if here, too, we add one more example to confirm our Lord's words, that "many are called, but few are chosen?" Now here, as I said, it is very true that God's choice is as yet not a matter of sight or of certainty to us; we cannot yet say of ourselves, or of any other set of living men, that "few are chosen." But though the full truth is not yet revealed, still, as there is a type of it in our worldly experience, so there is also a higher type, an earnest, of it in our spiritual experience: there is a sense, and that a very true and a very important one, in which we can say already, say now, actually, in the life that now is; say, even in the early stage of it, that some are, and some are not, "chosen."

We have all been called, in a Christian sense, inasmuch as we have been all introduced into Christ's church by Baptism; and a very large proportion of us have been called again, many of us not very long since, at our Confirmation. We have been thus called to enter into Christ's kingdom: we have been called to lead a life of holiness and happiness from this time forth even for ever. Nothing can be stronger than the language in which the Scripture speaks of the nature of our high calling: "All things," says St. Paul to the Corinthians, "all things are yours; whether Paul, or Apollos, or Peter, or the world, or life, or death, or things present, or things to come, all are yours; and ye are Christ's, and Christ is God's." Now, if this be the prize to which we are called, who are they who are also chosen to it? In the first and most complete sense, no doubt, those who have entered into their rest; who are in no more danger, however slight; with whom the struggle is altogether past, and the victory securely won. These are entered within the veil, whither we can as yet penetrate only in hope. But hope, in its highest degree, differs little from assurance; and even, as we descend lower and lower, still, where hope is clearly predominant, there is, if not assurance, yet a great encouragement; and the Scripture, which delights to carry encouragement to the highest pitch to those who are following God, allows of our saying of even these that they are God's chosen. It gives them, as it were, the title beforehand, to make them feel how doubly miserable it must be not only not to obtain it, but to forfeit it after it had been already ours. So then, there are senses in which we may say that some are chosen now; although, strictly speaking, the term can by us be applied, in its full sense, to those only who are passed beyond the reach of evil.

Those, then, we may call chosen, who, having heard their call, have turned to obey it, and have gone on following it. Those we may call chosen,--I do not say chosen irrevocably, but chosen now; chosen so that we may be very thankful to God on their behalf, and they thankful for themselves,--who, since their Confirmation, or since a period more remote, have kept God before their face, and tried to do His will. Those are, in the same way, chosen, who having found in themselves the sin which did most easily beset them, have struggled with it, and wholly, or in a great measure, have overcome it. Thus, they are chosen, who, having lived either in the frequent practice of selfish, extravagance, or of falsehood, or of idleness, or of excess in eating and drinking, have turned away from these things, and, for Christ's sake, have renounced them. They are chosen, I think, in yet a higher sense, who, having found their besetting sin to be, not so much any one particular fault, as a general ungodly carelessness, a lightness which for ever hindered them from serving God, have struggled with this most fatal enemy; and, even in youth, and health, and happiness, have learnt what it is to be sober-minded, what it is to think. Now, such as these have, in a manner, entered into their inheritance; they are not merely called, but chosen. God and spiritual things are not mere names to them, they are a reality. Such persons have tasted of the promises; they have known the pleasure--and what pleasure is comparable to it?--of feeling the bonds of evil passion or evil habit unwound from about their spirit; they have learnt what is that glorious liberty of being able to abstain from the things which we condemn, to do the things which we approve. They have felt true sense of power succeed to that of weakness. It is a delightful thing, after a long illness, after long helplessness, when our legs have been unable to support our weight, when our arms could lift nothing, our hands grasp nothing, when it was an effort to raise our head from the pillow, and it tired us even to speak in a whisper,--it is a delightful thing to feel every member restored to its proper strength; to find that exercise of limb, of voice, of body, which had been so long a pain, become now a source of perpetual pleasure. This is delightful; it pays for many an hour of previous weakness. But it is infinitely more delightful to feel the change from weakness to strength in our souls; to feel the languor of selfishness changed for the vigour of benevolence; to feel thought, hope, faith, love, which before were lying, as it were, in helplessness, now bounding in vigorous activity; to find the soul, which had been so long stretched as upon the sick bed of this earth, now able to stand upright, and looking and moving steadily towards heaven.

These are chosen; and they to whom this description does in no degree apply, they are not chosen. They are not chosen in any sense, they are called only. And, now, what is the proportion between the one and the other; are there as many chosen as there have been many called? Or do Christ's words apply in our case no less than in others; that though they who are called are many, yet they who are chosen are few?

This I dare not answer; there is a good as well as an evil which is unseen to the world at large, unseen even by all but those who watch us most nearly and most narrowly. All we can say is, that there are too many, who we must fear are not chosen; there are too few, of whom we can feel sure that they are. Yet hope is a wiser feeling than its opposite; it were as wrong as it would be miserable to abandon it. How gladly would we hope the best things of all those whom we saw this morning at Christ's table! How gladly would we believe of all such, that they were more than called merely; that they had listened to the call: that they had obeyed it; that they had already gained some Christian victories; that they were, in some sense, not called only, but chosen. But this we may say; that hope which we so long to entertain, that hope too happy to be at once indulged in, you may authorize us to feel it; you may convert it into confidence. Do you ask how? By going on steadily in good, by advancing from good to better, by not letting impressions fade with time. Now, with many of you, your confirmation is little more than three months distant; when we next meet at Christ's table, it will have passed by nearly half-a-year. It may be, that, in that added interval, it will have lost much of its force; that, from various causes, evil may have abounded in you more than good; that then shame, or a willing surrender of yourselves to carelessness, will keep away from Christ's Communion, many who have this day joined in it. But, if this were not to be so; if those, whom we have seen with joy this day communicating with us in the pledges of Christian fellowship, should continue to do so steadily; if, in the meantime, traits shall appear in you in other things that our hope was well founded; if the hatred of evil and the love of good were to be clearly manifest in you; if by signs not to be mistaken by those who watch earnestly for them, we might be assured that your part was taken, that you were striving with us in that service of our common Master, in which we would fain live and die; if evil was clearly lessened among us--not laughed at, but discouraged and put down; if instead of those turning away, who have now been with us at Christ's table, others, who have now turned away, should then be added to the number; then we should say, not doubtingly, that you were chosen: that you had tasted of the good things of Christ; that the good work of God was clearly begun in you. We might not, indeed, be without care, either for you or for ourselves: God forbid, that, in that sense, any of us should deem that we were chosen, until the grave has put us beyond temptation. But how happy were it to think of you as Christ's chosen, in that sense which should be a constant encouragement to us all: to think of you as going on towards God; to think of you as living to him daily; to think of you as on his side against all his enemies; to think of you as led by his Spirit, as living members of his holy and glorious Church,--militant now, in heaven triumphant!

LECTURE XV.

LUKE xi. 25.

When he cometh, he findeth it swept and garnished.

JOHN v. 42.

I know you, that ye have not the love of God in you.

These passages, of which the first is taken from the gospel of this morning's service, the other from the second lesson, differ in words, but their meaning is very nearly the same. The house which was empty, swept and garnished, was especially one empty of the love of God. Whatever evil there may not have been in it; whatever good there may have been in those of whom Christ spoke in the second passage: yet it and they agreed in this; one thing they had not, which alone was worth, all the rest besides; they had not the love of God.

And so it is still; many are the faults which we have not; many are the good qualities which we have; but the life is wanting. What is so rare as to find one who is not indifferent to God? What so rare, even rarer than the other, as to find one who actually loves him?

Therefore it is that those who go in at the broad gate of destruction are many, and those who go in at the narrow gate of life are few. For destruction and life are but other terms for indifference to God on the one hand, and love to him on the other. All who are indifferent to him, die; a painless death of mere extinction, if, like the brute creation, they have never been made capable of loving him; or a living death of perpetual misery, if, like evil spirits and evil men, they might have loved him and would not. And so all who love him, live a life, from first to last, without sin and sorrow, if, like the holy angels, they have loved him always; a life partaking at first of death, but brightening more and more unto the perfect day, if, like Christians, they were born in sin, but had been redeemed and sanctified to righteousness.

Whoever has watched human character, whether in the young or the old, must be well aware of the truth of this: he will know that the value of any character is in proportion to the existence or to the absence of this feeling, or rather, I should say, this principle. An exception may, perhaps, be made for a small, a very small number of fanatics; an apparent exception likewise exists in the case of many who seem to be religious, but who really are not so. The few exceptions of the former case are so very few, that we need not now stop to consider them, nor to inquire how far even these would be exceptions if we could read the heart as God reads it. The seeming exceptions being cases either of hypocrisy, or of very common self-deceit, we need not regard either; for they are, of course, no real objection to the truth of the general statement. It remains true, then, generally, that the value of any character is in proportion to the existence, or to the absence, in it of the love of God.

But is there not another exception to be made for the case of children, and of very young persons? Are they capable of loving God? and are not their earthly relations, their parents especially, put to them, as it were, in the place of God, as objects of trust, of love, of honour, of obedience, till their minds can open to comprehend the love of their Father who is in heaven? And does not the Scripture itself, in the few places in which it seems directly to address children, content itself with directing them to obey and honour their parents? Some notions of this sort are allowed, I believe, to serve sometimes as an excuse, when young persons are blamed for being utterly wanting in a sense of duty to God.

The passages which direct children to obey their parents, are of the same kind with those, directing slaves to obey their masters, and masters to be kind to their slaves; like those, also, which John the Baptist addressed to the soldiers and publicans: in none of all which there is any command to love God, but merely a command to fulfil that particular duty which most arose out of the particular relation, or calling of the persons addressed. In fact, when parents are addressed, they are directed only to do their duties to their children, just as children are directed to do theirs to their parents; in both cases alike, the common duty of parents and children to God is not dwelt upon, because that is a duty which does not belong to them as parents, or as children, but as human beings; and as such, it belongs to all alike. In fact, the very language of St. Paul's command to children implies this; for he says, "Children, obey your parents in the Lord: for this is right:" right, that is, in the sight of God: so that the very reason for which children are to discharge their earthly duties is, because that earthly duty is commanded by, or involved in, their heavenly duty; if they do not do it, they will not please God. But it is manifest that, in this respect, there is for all of us one only law, so soon as we are able to understand it. The moment that a child becomes capable of understanding anything about God and Christ,--and how early that is, every parent can testify,--that moment the duty to love God and Christ begins. It were absurd to say, that this duty has not begun at the age of boyhood. A boy is able to understand the force of religious motives, as well as he can that of earthly motives: he cannot understand either, perhaps, so well as he will hereafter; but he understands both enough, for the purposes of his salvation; enough, to condemn him before God, if he neglects them; enough to make him derive the greatest benefit from faithfully observing them.

And what can have been the purpose with which the only particular of our Lord's early life has been handed down to us, if it were not to direct our attention to this special truth, that our youth, no less than our riper age, belongs to God? "Wist ye not that I must be about my Father's business?" were words spoken by our Lord when he was no more than twelve years old. At twelve years old, he thought of preparing himself for the duties of his after-life; and of preparing himself for them, because they were God's will. He was to be about his Father's business. This is Christ's example for the young; this, and scarcely anything more than this, is recorded of his early years. Those are not like Christ who, at that same age, or even older, never think at all of the business of their future lives, still less would think of it, not as the means of their own maintenance or advancement, but as the duty which they owe to God.

Such as these are the very persons whose hearts are like the house in the parable, empty, swept, and garnished. The house so described in the parable is one out of which an evil spirit has just departed. In case of the young, the evil spirit in this sense, that is, as representing some one particular favourite sin, may perhaps have never entered it. That empty, swept, and garnished house, how like is it to what I have seen, to what I am seeing so continually, when a boy comes here with much still remaining of the innocence of childhood! Evil spirit, in the sense of any one particular vice, there is none to be found in that heart, nor has there been any ever. It is empty, swept, and garnished: there is the absence of evil; there are the various faculties, the furniture, as they may be called, of the house of our spirits, which the spirit uses either for evil or for good. There is innocence, then; there is, also, the promise of power. God hath richly endowed the earthly house of our tabernacle: various and wonderful is the furniture of body and mind with which it is supplied. How can we help admiring that open and cheerful brow which, as yet, no care or sin has furrowed; those light and active limbs, full of health and vigour; the eye so quick; the ear so undulled; the memory so ready; the young curiosity so eager to take in new knowledge; the young feelings, not yet spoiled by over-excitement, ready to admire, ready to love? There is the house, the house of God's building, the house which must abide for ever; but where is the spirit to inhabit it? Evil spirit there is none: is it, then, possessed by the Spirit of God? Has the fire from heaven as yet descended upon that house,--the living sign of God's presence, which alone can convert the house of perishable clay into the everlasting temple?

Can that blessed Spirit of God be indeed there, and yet no sign of his presence be manifest? It may be so, or to speak more truly, it might have been supposed to be so, if

God's word had not declared the contrary. What God's secret workings are; in how many ways, to us inscrutable, he may pervade all nature; in how many cases he may be near us, and we know it not; may, perhaps, be amongst those real mysteries, those truths revealed to none, nor to be revealed; those yet uncleared forests, so to speak, of the world of nature, into which the light of grace has not been permitted to penetrate. But all such mysteries are to us as if they did not exist at all: we have nothing to do with them. God has told us nothing of his unseen and undiscernible presence; when and where he is so present, he is to us as if he were not present at all. God was in the wilderness of Horeb before the bush was kindled; but he was not there for Moses. God, in some sense discernible, it may be, to other beings, may be in that house which, to us is empty; but God, our own God, the Holy Spirit, into whose service we were baptized, where he is, the house is not empty to us, but full of light. Invisible in himself, the signs of his presence are most visible: where no works, no fruits of the Holy Spirit are to be discerned, there, according to our Lord's express declaration, there the Holy Spirit is not.

But the light which declares his presence may indeed be a little spark; just to be seen, and no more. It may show that he has not abandoned all his right to the house of our tabernacle as yet; that he would desire to possess us fully. Such a little spark, such an evidence of the Holy Spirit's presence, is to be found in the outward profession of Christianity. They who call Jesus Lord, do it by the Holy Ghost; and, therefore, it is quite true in this sense, that in every baptized Christian, who has not utterly apostatized, there is that faint sign of the Holy Spirit's still having a claim upon him; he is not yet utterly cast off. This is true; but it is not to our present purpose; such a feeble sign is a sign of God's yet unwearied mercy, but no sign of our salvation. The presence with which the parable is concerned, is a far more effectual presence than this; the house in which there is no more than such a faint sign of a divine inhabitant, is, in the language of the parable, empty. To no purpose of our salvation is the Spirit of God present in the house, when the light of his presence does not flash forth from every part of it, when it is not manifest, not only that he has not quite cast it off to go to ruin, but that he has been pleased to make it his temple.

In this sense, therefore, in this practical, scriptural, Christian sense, those many young minds, which we have seen so often, may truly be called empty. But will they remain so long? How often have I seen the early innocence of boyhood overcast; the natural simplicity of boyhood, its open truth, its confident affection, its honest shame, perverted, blunted, hardened! How often have I seen the seven evil spirits enter in and dwell there,--I know not, and never may know, whether to be cast out again, or to abide for ever. But I have seen them enter, and, whilst the person was yet within my view, I have not seen them depart. And why have they entered; why have they marred that which was so beautiful? For one only reason,--because the house was empty, because the Spirit of God was not there: there was no love of God, no thought of God. Mere innocence taints and spoils as surely before the influence of the world, as true principle flourishes in spite of it, and strengthens. This, too, I have seen, not once only: I have seen the innocence of early boyhood sanctified by something better than innocence, which gave a promise of abiding. I have seen, in other words, that the house was not empty; that the Spirit of God was there. I have watched the effect of those influences, which you know so well: the second half-year came, a period when mere innocence is sure to be worn away, greatly tainted, if not utterly gone; but still, in the cases which I am now alluding to, the promise of good was not less, but greater, there was a more tried, and, therefore, a stronger goodness. I have watched this, too, till it passed on, out of my sight. I never saw the blessed Spirit of God depart from the house which he had chosen: I well believe that he abides in it still, and will abide in it even to the day of Jesus Christ.

This I have seen, and this I shall continue to see; for still the great work of evil and of good is going on; still the house, at first empty, is possessed by the spirits of evil, or by the Spirit of God. And if we do not see the signs of the Spirit of God, we are but too sure that the evil spirit is there. We know him by the manifold signs of folly, coarseness, carelessness; even when we see not, as yet, his worse fruits of falsehood and profligacy. We know him by the sign of an increased, and increasing selfishness, the everlasting cry of the thousand passions of our nature, all for ever calling out, "Give, give;" all for ever impatient, complaining, when their gratification is withheld, when the call of duty is set before them. We know him by pride and self-importance, as if nothing was so great as self, as if our own opinions, judgment, feelings were to be consulted in all things. We know him by the deep ungodliness which he occasions--no thought of God, much less any love of him; living utterly without him in the world, or, at least, whilst health and prosperity continue. These are the fatal signs which show that the house is no longer empty; that the evil spirits have entered in, and dwell there, to make it theirs, as too often happens, for time and for eternity.

LECTURE XVI.

MATHEW xi. 10.

I send my messenger before thy face, who shall prepare thy way before thee.

If it was part of God's dispensation, that there should be one to prepare the way before Christ's first coming, it may be expected much more, that there should be some to prepare the way before his second. And so it is expressed in the collect for the third Sunday in Advent: "O Lord Jesus Christ, who at thy first coming didst send thy messenger to prepare thy way before thee; grant that the ministers and stewards of thy mysteries may likewise so prepare and make ready thy way, by turning the hearts of the disobedient to the wisdom of the just, that at thy second coming to judge the world we may be found an acceptable people in thy sight, who livest and reignest with the Father and the Holy Spirit, ever one God, world without end. Amen." NOW, in what does this preparing for him consist; and what is its object? The Scripture will inform us as to both. The object is, "Lest he come and smite the earth with a curse;" lest, when he shall come, his coming, which should be our greatest joy and happiness, should be our everlasting destruction; for there can abide before him nothing that is evil. This is the object of preparing for Christ's coming. Next, in what does the preparation consist? It consists in teaching men to live above the common notions of their age and country; to raise their standard higher; to live after what is right in God's judgment, which often casts away, as faulty and bad, what men were accustomed to think good. And as the people of Israel, although they had God's revelation among them, had yet let their standard of good and evil become low, even so it has been in the Christian Israel. We have God's will in our hands, yet our judgments are not formed upon it; and, therefore, they who would prepare us for Christ's coming, must set before us a commandment which is new, although old: in one sense old, in every generation, inasmuch as it is the same which we had from the beginning; in another sense, in every generation more new, inasmuch, as the habits opposed to it have become the more confirmed; and the longer the night has lasted, the more strange to our eyes is the burst of the returning light.

But when we thus speak of the common notions of our age and country being deficient, and thus, in effect, commend notions which would be singular, do we not hold a language inconsistent with our common language and practice? Do we not commonly regard singularity as a fault, and attach a considerable authority to the consent of men in general? Nay, do we not often appeal to this consent as to a proof which a sane mind must admit as decisive? Even in speaking of good and evil, have not the very words gained their present sense because the common consent of mankind has agreed to combine notions of self-satisfaction, of honour, and of love, with what we call good, and the contrary with what we call evil?

A short time may, perhaps, not be misapplied in endeavouring to explain this matter; in showing where, and for what reasons, the common opinion of our society is to be followed, where it is to be suspected, and where it is absolutely to be shunned or trampled under foot, as clearly and certainly evil.

I must begin with little things, in order to show the whole question plainly. Take those tastes in us which most resemble the instincts of a brute; and you will find that in these, as with instinct, common consent becomes a sure rule. When I speak of those tastes which most resemble instincts, I mean those in which nature, doing most for us at first, leaves least for us to learn for ourselves. This seems the character of instinct: it is far more complete than reason in its first stage, but it admits of no after improvement; the brute in the thousandth generation is no way advanced beyond the brute in the first. Of our tastes, even of those belonging to our bodily senses, that which belongs to what are called particularly our organs of taste is the one most resembling an instinct: we have less to do for its improvement than in any other instance. Men being here, then, upon an equality, with a faculty given to all by nature, and improved particularly by none, those who differ from the majority are likely to differ not from excellence but from defect: not because they have a more advanced reason, but because they have a less healthy instinct, than their neighbours. Thus, in those matters which relate to the sense of taste--I am obliged to take this almost trivial instance, because it so well illustrates the principle of the whole question--we hold the consent of men in general to be a good rule. If any one were to choose to feed upon what this common taste had pronounced to be disgusting, we should not hesitate to say that such an appetite was diseased and monstrous.

Now, let us take our senses of sight and hearing, and we shall find that just in the proportion in which these less resemble instincts than the sense of taste, so is common consent a less certain rule. Up to a certain point they are instincts: there are certain sounds which, I suppose, are naturally disagreeable to the ear; while, on the other hand, bright and rich colours are, perhaps, naturally attractive to the eye. But, then, sight and hearing are so connected with our minds that they are susceptible of very great cultivation, and thus differ greatly from instincts. As the mind opens, outward sights and sounds become connected with a great number of associations, and thus we learn to think the one or the other beautiful, for reasons which really depend very much on the range of our own ideas. Consider, for a moment, the beautiful in architecture. If the model of the leaning tower of Pisa were generally adopted in our public buildings, all men's common sense would cry out against it as a deformity, because a leaning wall would convey to every mind the notion of insecurity, and every body would feel that it was unpleasant to see a building look exactly as if it were going to fall down. Now, what I have called common sense is, in a manner, the instinct of our reason: it is that uniform level of reason which all sane persons reach to, and the wisest in matters within its province do not surpass. But go beyond this, and architecture is no longer a matter of mere common sense, but of science, and of cultivated taste. Here the standard of beauty is not fixed by common consent; but, in the first instance, devised or discovered by the few: and, so far as it is received by the many, received by them on the authority of the few, and sanctioned, so to speak, not so much from real sympathy and understanding, as from a reasonable trust and deference to those who are believed the best judges.

Here, then, we suppose that the common judgment is right; but we perceive a difference between this case and the one mentioned before, inasmuch as in the first instance the right judgment of the mass of mankind is their own; in the second instance, they have adopted it out of deference to others. Not only, then, will men's common judgment be right in matters of instinct and of common sense, but also in higher matters, where, although they could not have discovered what was right, yet they were perfectly willing to adopt it, when discovered by others. And this opens a very wide field. For in all matters which come under the dominion of fashion, where the avowed object is the convenience or gratification of society, men listen to those who profess to teach them with almost an excess of docility: they will adopt sometimes fashions which are not convenient. But yet, as men can tell well enough by experience whether they do find a thing convenient and agreeable or not, so it is most likely that fashions which continue long and generally prevalent are founded upon sound principles; because else men, being well capable of knowing what convenience is, and being also well disposed to follow it, would neither have been very long or very generally mistaken in this matter; nor would have acquiesced in their mistake contentedly.

We do perfectly right, then, to regard the common opinion as a rule in all points of dress, in our houses and furniture, in those lighter usages of society which come under the denomination of manners, as distinguished from morals. In all these, if the mass of mankind could not find out what would best suit them, yet they are quite ready to adopt it when it is found out; and so they equally arrive at truth. But take away this readiness, and the whole case is altered. If there be any point in which men are not ready to adopt what is best for them; if they are either indifferent, or still more, if they are averse to it; if they thus have neither the power of discovering it for themselves, nor the will to avail themselves of it, when discovered for them; then it is clear that, in such a point, the common judgment will be of no value, nay, there will even be a presumption that it is wrong.

Now as the common consent of mankind was most sure in matters where their sense most resembled instinct, that is, where nature had done most for them, and left them least to do for themselves; as here, therefore, they who are sound are the great majority, and the exceptions are no better than disease; so if there be any part of us which is the direct opposite to instinct, a part in which nature has done next to nothing for us, and all is to be done by ourselves; then, here the common consent of mankind will be of the least value; here the majority will be helpless and worthless; and they who are happy enough to be exceptions to this majority, will be no other than Christ's redeemed.

Now, again, if this deficient part of our nature could be seen purely distinct from every other; if it alone dictated our language, and inspired our actions, then it would follow, that language which must ever be fixed by the majority, would be, in fact, the language of the world of infinite evil; and our actions those of mere devils. Then, whoever of us would be saved, must needs begin by forswearing, altogether, both the language and the actions of his fellow-men. But this is not so; in almost every instance this deficient part of our nature acts along with others that are not so corrupted; it mars their work, undoubtedly; it often confuses and perverts our language; it always taints our actions; but it does not wholly usurp either the one or the other; and thus, by God's blessing, man's language yet affords a high witness to divine truth, and even men's judgments and actions testify, though with infinite imperfection, to the existence and excellence of goodness.

And this it is which forms one of the great perplexities of life; for as there is enough of what is right in men's judgments and conduct to forbid us from saying, that we must take the very rule of contraries, and think and do just the opposite to the opinions and practice of men in general; so, on the other hand, there is always so much wrong in them, that we may never dare to follow them as a standard, but shall find, that if trusted to as such, they will inevitably betray us. So that in points of greater moment than mere manners and fashion, it will ever be true, that if we would be prepared for Christ's coming, we must rise to a far higher standard than that of society in general; that in the greatest concerns of human life, the practice of the majority, though always containing something of good, is yet in its prevailing character, as regards God, so evil, that they who are content to follow it cannot be saved.

This is the explanation of the apparent difficulty in the general, and thus, while acknowledging that there are points in which men, by common consent, make out what is best; and others in which, although they do not make it out, nor at first appreciate it, yet they are very willing to adopt it upon trust, and so come by experience to value it; while, therefore, there are a great many things in which singularity is either a disease or a foolishness; so again there are other points in which men in general have not the power to make out what is good, nor yet the docility to adopt it; and, therefore, in these points, which relate to the great matters of life, singularity is wisdom and salvation, and he who does as others do, perishes. That is what is called the corruption of human nature. I shall attempt, on another occasion, to go into some further details, and show, by common examples, how strangely our judgment and practice contain, with much that is right, just that one taint or defect which, as a whole, spoils them. And this one defect will be found to be, as the Scripture declares, a defect in our sense of our relation towards God.

1 CORINTHIANS ii. 12.

We have received not the spirit of the world, but the Spirit which is of God.

And, therefore, he goes on to say, our language is different from that of others, and not always understood by them; the natural man receiveth not the things of God, for they are foolishness unto him; neither can he know them, because they are spiritually discerned. That is, they are discerned only by a faculty which he has not, namely, by the Spirit; and, therefore, as beings devoid of reason cannot understand the truths of science, or of man's wisdom, for they are without the faculty which can discern them; so beings devoid of God's Spirit cannot understand the truths of God.

Now, in order to turn this passage to our profit, we need not consider those who are wholly without God's Spirit, or inquire whether, indeed, there be any such; it is not that there are two broadly marked divisions of all men, those who have not the Spirit of God at all, and those who have it abundantly: if it were so, the separation of the great day of judgment would be begun already, nor would it require, in order to effect it rightly, the wisdom of Him who trieth the very hearts and reins. No doubt there will be at last but two divisions of us all, the saved and the lost; but now the divisions are infinite; so much so that the great body of us offer much matter for hope as well as for fear. We cannot say, that they are without the Spirit of God; yet neither can we say that they are led by the Spirit, so as to be God's true servants. We cannot say, that the things of God's are absolutely to them as foolishness; yet certainly, we cannot say either, that they are to them as the divinest wisdom.

And here we return to the subject on which I was speaking last Sunday. It is because we are not led by the Spirit of God, but have within us much of the spirit of the world, that our judgments of right and wrong are so faulty; and that this faultiness is particularly seen in our faint sense of our relations to God. These relations seem continually foolishness to us, because they are spiritually discerned, and we have so little of God's Spirit to enable us to discern them. And our blindness here affects our whole souls; we have, in consequence of it, a much fainter perception even of those truths which reason can discern by herself; or, at any rate, if we do not doubt them, they have over us much less influence.

Now we will first see how much of natural reason, and even of the Spirit of God, does exist in our common judgments; for it is fair to see and to allow what there is of right in our language and sentiments, as well as to note what is wrong. Reason influences thus much, that we not only commend good generally, and blame evil; but even, in particular cases, we commend, I think, each separate virtue, and we blame each separate vice. I never heard of justice, truth, kindness, self-denial, &c., being other than approved of in themselves; or injustice, falsehood, malice, and selfishness being other than condemned. And the Spirit of God influences at least thus much, that we shrink from direct blasphemy and profaneness; we cannot but respect those whom we believe to be living sincerely in the fear of God; and further, if we thought our death near, we should desire to hear of God, and to depart from this life under his favour. No doubt, all such feelings, so far as they go, are the work of God's Spirit: whatever is good and right in our minds towards God, that proceeds not from the spirit of the world, but from the Spirit of God.

Where, then, is the great defect which yet continually makes our practical judgments quite wrong; which makes us, in fact, so often countenance and support evil, and discountenance and discourage good? First, it is owing to the spirit of carelessness. One of the most emphatic terms by which a good man is expressed in the language of the Greek philosophers, is that of [Greek: opdouiaos], "one who is in earnest." To be in earnest is, indeed, with, most of us, the same as to be good; it is not that we love evil, but that we are indifferent both to it and to good. Now, many of us are very seldom in earnest. By this I mean, that the highest part of our minds, and that which judges of the highest things, is generally slumbering or but half awake. We may go through, a very busy day, and yet not be, in this true sense, in earnest at all; our best faculties may, as it were, be all the while sleeping or playing. It is notorious how much this is so in the common intercourse of society in the world. Light anecdotes; playful remarks; discussions, it may be, about the affairs of the neighbourhood, or, in some companies, on questions of science or party politics; all these may be often heard; but we may talk on all these brilliantly and well, and yet our best nature may not once be called to exert itself. So again, in mere routine business, it is the same: the body may toil; the pen move swiftly; the thoughts act in the particular matter before them vigorously; and yet we our proper selves, beings understanding and choosing between good and evil, have never bestirred ourselves at all. It has been but a skirmishing at the outposts; not a sword had been drawn in the main battle. Take younger persons, and the same thing is the case even more palpably. Here there is less of business in the common sense of the term; the mind is almost always unbraced and resting. We pass through the good and evil of our daily life, and our proper self scarcely ever is aroused to notice either the one or the other.

But the worst of it is, that this carelessness is not altogether accidental: it is a carelessness which we do not wish to break. So long as it lasts, we manage to get the activity and interest of life, without a sense of its responsibility. We like exceedingly to lay the reins, as it were, upon the neck of our inclinations, to go where they take us, and to ask no questions whether we are in the right road or no. Inclination is never slumbering: this gives us excitement enough to save us from weariness, without the effort of awakening our conscience too. Therefore society, expressing in its rules the feelings of its individual members, prescribes exactly such a style of conversation as may keep in exercise all other parts of our nature except that one which should be sovereign of all, and whose exercise is employed on things eternal.

Not being, then, properly in earnest,--that is, our conscience and our choice of moral good and evil being in a state of repose,--our language is happily contrived so as that it shall contain nothing to startle our sleeping conscience, if her ears catch any of its sounds. We still commend good and dispraise evil, both in the general and in the particular. But as good and evil are mixed in every man, and in various proportions, he who commends, the little good of a bad man, saying nothing of his evil,--or he who condemns the little evil of a good man, saying nothing of his good,--leads us evidently to a false practical conclusion; he leads us to like the bad man and to dislike the good. Again, the lesser good becomes an evil if it keeps out a greater good; and, in the same way, the lesser evil becomes a good. If we have no thought of comparing good things together, if our sovereign nature be asleep, then we shall most estimate the good to which we are most inclined; and where we find this we shall praise it, not observing that it is taking up the place of a greater good which the case requires, and, therefore, that it is in fact an evil. So that our moral judgments may lead practically to great evil: we may join with bad men and despise good; we may approve of qualities which, are, in fact, ruining a man; and despise others which, in the particular case, are virtues; without ever in plain words condemning virtue or approving vice.

But, farther, this habit of never being in earnest greatly lowers the strength of our feelings even towards the good which we praise and towards the evil which we condemn. It was an admirable definition of that which excites laughter, that it was that which is out of rule, that which is amiss, that which is unsightly, (these three ideas, and other similar ones, are alike contained in the single Greek word [Greek: aischron],) provided that it was unaccompanied by pain. This definition accounts for the otherwise extraordinary fact, that there is something in moral evil which, in some instances, affects the mind ludicrously. That is to say, if moral evil affects us with no pain; if we see in it nothing, so to speak, but its irregularity, its strange contrast with what is beautiful, its jarring with the harmony of the system around us; then it does acquire that character which is well defined as being ridiculous. Thus it is notorious that trifling follies, and even gross vices, are often so represented in works of fiction as to be exceedingly ludicrous. It is enough, as an instance of what I mean, to name the vice of drunkenness. Get rid for the moment of the notions of vice or sin which, accompany it, and which give moral pain; get rid also of those points in it which awaken physical disgust; retain merely the notion of the incoherent language, and the strange capricious gait of intoxication; and we have then an image merely ridiculous, as much, so as the rambling talk and absurd gestures of the old buffoons.

Here, then, we have the secret of vice becoming laughable; and of things which are really wicked, disgusting, hateful, being expressed by names purely ludicrous. Where no great physical pain or distress is occasioned by what is evil, our sense of its ludicrousness will be exactly in proportion to the faintness of our sense of moral evil; or, in other words, to our want of being in earnest. The evil that does not seriously pain or inconvenience man, is very apt to be regarded with feelings approaching to laughter, if we have no sense of pain at the notion of its being an offence against God.

Thus, then, we have seen how, from the want of being in earnest, from the habitual slumber of conscience, or that sovereign part of us which looks upon our whole state with reference to its highest interests, and passes judgment upon all our actions,--how, from the practical absence of these, we may get to follow evil persons, and be indifferent to the good; to admire qualities which, from usurping the place of better ones, are actually ruinous; and, finally, to regard all common evil not so much with deep abhorrence, as with a disposition to laugh at it. And thus the practical judgment and influence of the society around us may be fatally evil; while the society all the time shall contain, even in its very perversion, various elements of truth and of good.

I have kept to general language, to general views, perhaps too much; but all the time my mind has been fixed on the particular application of this, which lies scarcely beneath the surface, but which I cannot well bear more fully to unveil. But whoever has attended to what I have been saying, will be able, I should trust, to make the application, for himself, to those points in our society which most need correction. He will be able to understand how it is that the influence of the place is not better, while it undoubtedly contains so much of good; how the public opinion of a Christian school may yet be, in many respects, very unchristian. If he has attended at all to what I have said about our so rarely being in earnest, he will see something of the mischief of some of those publications, of those books, of that tone of conversation, which, I suppose, are here, as elsewhere, in fashion. Utterly impossible is it to lay down a rule for others in such matters: to say this book is too light, or this is an excess of light reading, or this laugh was too unrestrained, or that tone of trifling too perpetual. But, in these things, we should all judge ourselves; and remember that you are so little under outward restraint, your choice of reading is so free, your intercourse with one another so wholly uncontrolled, that, enjoying thus the full liberty of more advanced years, you incur also their responsibility. There is, doubtless, an excess of light reading, both in kind and in quantity; there is such a thing as a tone of conversation and manner too entirely, and too frequently, trifling. And you must be quite aware that we are placed here for something else than to indulge such a temper as this. Cheerfulness and thoughtlessness have no necessary connexion; the lightest spirits, which are indeed one of the greatest of earthly blessings, often play around the most earnest thought and the tenderest affection, and with far more grace than when they are united with the shallowness and hardness of him who is, in the sight of God, a fool. It were a strange notion, that we could never be merry without intoxication, yet not stranger than to think that mirth is the companion only of folly or of sin. But, setting God in Christ before us, then the conscience is awake; then we are in earnest; then we measure things rightly; then we feel them strongly; then we love those that are good, and shun those that are evil; then we learn that sin is no matter of laughter, that it ill deserves to be clothed under a ludicrous name; for that thing which we laugh at, that which we so miscall, is indeed the cause of infinite evil; for that Christ died; for that there are some who die that death which lasts for ever.

LECTURE XVIII.

GENESIS xxvii. 38.

And Esau said unto his father, Hast thou but one blessing, my father? Bless me, even me also, O my father.

MATTHEW xv. 27.

And she said, Truth, Lord: yet the dogs eat of the crumbs which fall from their master's table.

Of these two passages, the first, as we must all remember, is taken from the first lesson of this morning's service; the second is from the morning's gospel. Both speak the same language, and point out, I think, that particular view of the story of Jacob obtaining the blessing which is most capable of being turned to account; for, as to the conduct of Jacob and his mother, it is manifestly no more capable of affording us benefit, as a matter of example, than the conduct, in some respects similar, of the unjust steward in our Lord's parable. The example, indeed, is of the same kind as that. If the steward was so anxious about his future worldly welfare, and Jacob about the worldly welfare of his descendants, that they did not scruple to obtain their ends, the one by dishonesty, the other by falsehood, much more should we be anxious about the true welfare of ourselves and those belonging to us, which no such unworthy means can be required to gain. But the point of the story to which the text refers, and which is illustrated also by the words of the Syrophoenician woman, is one which very directly concerns us all, being no other than this,--what should be the effect upon our own minds of witnessing others possessed of greater advantages than ourselves, whether obtained by the immediate gift of God, through the course of his ordinary providence, or acquired directly by some unjust or unlawful act of those who are in possession of them?

Now, it is evident that, as equality is not the rule either of nature or of human society, there must be many in every congregation who are so far in the condition of Esau and of the Syrophoenician woman, as to be inferior to others around them in some one or more advantages. The inferiority may consist in what are called worldly advantages, or in natural advantages, or in spiritual advantages, or in some or all of these united. And it is not to be doubted that the sense of this inferiority is a hard trial, both as respects our feelings towards God and towards men. It is a hard trial; but yet, no trial overtakes us but such as is common to man: and here, as in all other cases, God will, with the trial, also make a way for us to escape, that we may be able to bear it.

Let us consider, then, some of the most common cases in which this inferiority exists amongst us. With regard to worldly advantages, the peculiar nature of this congregation makes it less necessary than it generally would be, to dwell upon inequality in these: in fact, speaking generally, we are a very unusual example of equality in these respects; the advantages of station and fortune are enjoyed not, literally, in an equal degree by all of us, but equally as compared with, the lot of the great mass of society; we all enjoy the necessaries, and most of the comforts of life. What differences there are would, probably, appear in instances seemingly trifling, if, indeed, any thing were really trifling by which the temper and feelings, and through them the principles, of any amongst us may be affected for good or for evil. It may possibly happen that, in the indulgences, or means of indulgence, given to you by your friends at home, there may be sometimes, such a difference as to excite discontent or jealousy. It may be, that some are apt to exult over others, by talking of the

70

pleasures, or the liberty, which they enjoy; and which the friends of others, either from necessity or from a sense of duty, are obliged to withhold. If this be ever felt by any of you as a trial; if it gall your pride, as well as restrict your enjoyments; then remember, that here, even in this seemingly little thing, the inferiority of which you complain may be either increased ten-fold, or changed into a blessed superiority. Increased ten-fold, even as from him that hath not, shall be taken away even that which he hath, if by discontent, and evil passions towards God and man, you make yourselves a hundred times more inferior spiritually than you were in outward circumstances; but changed into a blessed superiority, if it be borne with meekness, and patience, and thankfulness, even as it was said of the Gentile centurion, that there had not been found faith equal to his, no, not in Israel.

But turning from worldly advantages to those which are called natural, and the inequality here is at once as great as elsewhere. In all faculties of body and mind; in the vigour of the senses, of the limbs, of the general constitution; in the greater or less liability to disease generally, or to any particular form of it; or, again, in powers of mind, in quickness, in memory, in imagination, in judgment; the differences between different persons in this congregation must be exceedingly wide. But, with regard to bodily powers, the trial is little felt, till the inferiority is shown in actual suffering from pain or from disease. So long as we are in health, our enjoyments are so many, and we so easily accommodate our habits to our powers, that a mere inferiority of strength, whether it be of limb or of constitution, is not apt to make us dissatisfied. But if it comes to actual illness or to pain, if we are deprived of the common enjoyments and occupations of our age, then perhaps the trial begins to be severe; and when we look at others who have taken the same liberties with their health as we have done, and see them notwithstanding perfectly well and strong, while we are disabled or suffering, we may think that God has dealt hardly with us, and may be inclined to ask with Esau, "Hast thou but one blessing, my Father? bless me, even me also, O my Father!" Now this language, according to the sense in which we use it, is either blameable or innocent. If we mean to say, "Hast thou health to give to others only and not to me? give me this blessing also, as thou hast given it to my brethren:" then it has in it somewhat of discontent and murmuring; it implies a claim to which God never listens. But if we mean, "Hast thou only one kind of blessing, my father? If thou hast blest others in one way, I murmur not nor complain: but out of thine infinite store, give me also such a blessing as may be convenient for me;" then God hears the prayer, then he gives the blessing, and gives it so richly, and makes it bear so evidently the mark of his love, that they who were last are become first; if others have health, and we have sickness, yet the spirit of patience and cheerful submission which God gives with it is so great a blessing, and makes us so certainly happy, that the strongest and healthiest of our friends have often far more reason to wish to change places with us, than we with them.

Let us now take inequality in powers of mind. And here, undoubtedly, the difference is apt to be a trial. Not that, probably, it excites discontent or murmuring against God; nor jealousy against those whose faculties are better than our own: the trial is of another kind; we are tempted to make our inferiority an excuse for neglect; because we cannot do so much nor so easily as others, we do far less than we might do. But the parable shows us plainly, that if one talent only has been given us, while others have ten, yet that the one, no less than the ten, must be made to yield its increase. Here is the feeling expressed so earnestly by the woman entreating Christ to heal her daughter. "The dogs eat of the crumbs which fall from their master's table." Small as may be the portion of power given us, when compared with the plenty vouchsafed to others, still it is capable of nourishing us if we make use of it; still it shows that we too have our blessing. And if using it with thankfulness, if doing our very best with it, knowing that "a man is accepted according to what he hath, and not according to what he hath not," we labour humbly and diligently; then, not only does the talent itself become increased, so that our Lord, when he comes to reckon with us, may receive his own with usury: but a blessing of another kind is added to our labours, again, as in the former case, making those who were last to become first. For if there be one thing on earth which is truly admirable, it is to see God's wisdom blessing an inferiority of natural powers, when they have been honestly, humbly, and zealously cultivated. From how many pains are they delivered, to which great natural talents are continually exposed; irritation, jealousy, a morbid and nervous activity, bearing fruits not of peace, but of gall! With what blessings are they crowned, to which, the most powerful natural understanding is a stranger! the love of truth gratified, without the fear that truth will demand the sacrifice of personal vanity; the line of duty clearly discerned, because those mists of passion and selfishness which obscure it so often from the view of the keenest natural perception, have been dispersed by the spirit of humility and love; imperfect knowledge patiently endured, because whatever knowledge is enjoyed is known to be God's gift, and what he gives, or what he withholds, is alike welcome. This is the blessing of those who having had inferior natural powers, have so laboured to improve them according to God's will, that on all there has been grafted, as it were, some better power of grace, to yield a fruit most precious both for earth and heaven.

But I spoke of an equality of spiritual advantages also, and this is perhaps the hardest trial of all. Oh, how great is this inequality in truth, when it seems to be so little! All of you, the children of Christian parents; all members of the Christian Church; all partaking here of the same worship, the same prayers, the same word of God, the same sacrament; are you not all the Israel of God, and not, like Esau, or the Syrophoenician woman, strangers to the covenant of blessing? Yet your real condition is, notwithstanding, very unequal. How unlike are your friends at home; how, unlike, also, are your friends here! Are there not some to whom their homes, both by direct precept and by example, are a far greater help than to others? Are there not some, whose immediate companions here may encourage them in all good far more than may be the case with, others? So, then, there may be some to whom this great blessing has been denied, whilst others enjoy it. What then? Shall we say, that, because we have it not, we will refuse to go in to our Father's house; that we will not walk as our brother walks, unless we have his advantages? Then must we remain cast out; vessels fashioned to dishonour, rejected of God, and cursed. Nay rather let us put a Christian sense on Esau's prayer, and cry, "'Hast thou but one blessing, my Father? bless me, even me also, O my Father.' If thou hast given to others earthly helps, which thou hast denied to me, give me thyself and thy own Spirit the more! If father and mother forsake my most precious interest, do thou take me up. If my nearest friends will not walk with me in the house of God, be thou my friend, and abide with, me always, making my house as thine. Outward and earthly means thou givest or takest away at thy pleasure; but give me help according to my need, that I yet may not lose thee."

How naturally are we interested at the thought of any one so circumstanced, and uttering such a prayer! How earnestly do we wish to help him, to show our respect and true love for a faith so tried and so enduring! And think we that God cares for it less than we do? or have we not already the record of his love towards it, when Christ answered the Syrophoenician woman, "O woman, great is thy faith: be it unto thee even as thou wilt?" He may not, indeed, see fit to give the very same blessing which was in the first instance denied: we may still have fewer spiritual advantages than others, as far as human helps are concerned; fewer good and earnest friends; fewer examples of holiness around us; fewer to join with us in our prayers and in our struggles against evil. But though this particular blessing may be denied,--as Esau could not gain that blessing which had been given to Jacob,--yet there is a blessing for us also, which may prove, in the end, even better than our brother's. He who serves God steadily, amidst many disadvantages, enjoys the blessing of a more confirmed and hardier faith; he has gone through trials, and been found conqueror; and for him that overcometh is reserved a more abundant measure of glory.

But on the other side, we who, like Jacob, or Jacob's posterity, have the blessing,--whether it be natural, worldly, or spiritual,--let us consider what became of it when it was not improved. What was the sin of Esau,--speaking not of the individual, but of the less favoured people of Edom,--compared with the sin of Jacob? Nay, not of Edom only; but it shall be more tolerable for Sodom, in the day of judgment, than for the unbelieving cities of Israel. So it is, not only with the literal, but with the Christian Israel; so it is, not only with the Church as a whole compared with heathens, but with all those individuals amongst us, who enjoy in any larger measure than others any of God's blessings. They are blessings; but they may be made fatal curses. This holds true with blessings of every kind: with station and wealth, with bodily health and vigour, with, great powers of mind, with large means of spiritual improvement. To whom much is given, of him shall be much, required. It is required of us to enjoy our blessings by using them: so will they be blessings indeed. So it is with money and influence, with health, with talents, with spiritual knowledge, and good friends and parents. There are first who shall be last; that is, those who began their course with advantages which set them before their brethren, if they do not exert themselves, will fall grievously behind them: for the blessing denied may be, in effect, a blessing given; and the blessing given, in like manner, becomes too often a blessing taken away.

LECTURE XIX.

MATTHEW xxii. 32.

God is not the God of the dead, but of the living.

We hear these words as a part of our Lord's answer to the Sadducees; and, as their question was put in evident profaneness, and the answer to it is one which to our minds is quite obvious and natural, so we are apt to think that in this particular story there is less than usual that particularly concerns us. But it so happens, that our Lord, in answering the Sadducees, has brought in one of the most universal and most solemn of all truths,--which is indeed implied in many parts of the Old Testament, but which the Gospel has revealed to us in all its fulness,--the truth contained in the words of the text, that "God is not the God of the dead, but of the living."

I would wish to unfold a little what is contained in these words, which we often hear even, perhaps, without quite understanding them; and many times oftener without fully entering into them. And we may take them, first, in their first part, where they say that "God is not the God of the dead."

The word "dead," we know, is constantly used in Scripture in a double sense, as meaning those who are dead spiritually, as well as those who are dead naturally. And, in either sense, the words are alike applicable: "God is not the God of the dead."

God's not being the God of the dead signifies two things: that they who are without him are dead, as well as that they who are dead are also without him. So far as our knowledge goes respecting inferior animals, they appear to be examples of this truth. They appear to us to have no knowledge of God; and we are not told that they have any other life than the short one of which our senses inform us. I am well aware that our ignorance of their condition is so great that, we may not dare to say anything of them positively; there may be a hundred things true respecting them which we neither know nor imagine. I would only say that, according to that most imperfect light in which we see them, the two points of which I have been speaking appear to meet in them: we believe that they have no consciousness of God, and we believe that they will die. And so far, therefore, they afford an example of the agreement, if I may so speak, between these two points; and were intended, perhaps, to be to our view a continual image of it. But we had far better speak of ourselves. And here, too, it is the case that "God is not the God of the dead." If we are without him we are dead; and if we are dead we are without him: in other words, the two ideas of death and absence from God are in fact synonymous.

Thus, in the account given of the fall of man, the sentence of death and of being cast out of Eden go together; and if any one compares the description of the second Eden in the Revelation, and recollects how especially it is there said, that God dwells in the midst of it, and is its light by day and night, he will see that the banishment from the first Eden means a banishment from the presence of God. And thus, in the day that Adam sinned, he died; for he was cast out of Eden immediately, however long he may have moved about afterwards upon the earth where God was not. And how very strong to the same point are the words of Hezekiah's prayer, "The grave cannot praise thee, Death cannot celebrate thee; they that go down into the pit cannot hope for thy truth;" words which express completely the feeling that God is not the God of the dead. This, too, appears to be the sense generally of the expression used in various parts of the Old Testament, "Thou shalt surely die." It is, no doubt, left purposely obscure; nor are we ever told, in so many words, all that is meant by death; but, surely, it always implies a separation from God, and the being--whatever the notion may extend to--the being dead to him. Thus, when David had committed his great sin, and had expressed his repentance for it, Nathan tells him, "The Lord also hath put away thy sin; thou shalt not die:" which means, most expressively, thou shalt not die to God. In one sense, David died, as all men die; nor was he, by any means, freed from the punishment of his sin: he was not, in that sense, forgiven; but he was allowed still to regard God as his God; and, therefore, his punishments were but fatherly chastisements from God's hand, designed for his profit, that he might be partaker of God's holiness. And thus although Saul was sentenced to lose his kingdom, and although he was killed with his sons on Mount Gilboa, yet I do not think that we find the sentence passed upon him, "Thou shalt surely die;" and, therefore, we have no right to say that God had ceased to be his God, although he visited him with severe chastisements, and would not allow him to hand down to his sons the crown of Israel. Observe, also, the language of the eighteenth chapter of Ezekiel, where the expressions occur so often, "He shall surely live," and "He shall surely die." We have no right to refer these to a mere extension, on the one hand, or a cutting short, on the other, of the term of earthly existence. The promise of living long in the land, or, as in Hezekiah's case, of adding to his days fifteen years, is very different from the full and unreserved blessing, "Thou shalt surely live." And we know, undoubtedly, that both the good and the bad to whom Ezekiel spoke, died alike the natural death of the body. But the peculiar force of the promise, and of the threat, was, in the one case, Thou shalt belong to God; in the other, Thou shalt cease to belong to him; although the veil was not yet drawn up which concealed the full import of those terms, "belonging to God," and "ceasing to belong to him:" nay, can we venture to affirm that it is fully drawn aside even now?

I have dwelt on this at some length, because it really seems to place the common state of the minds of too many amongst us in a light which is exceedingly awful; for if it be true, as I think the Scripture implies, that to be dead, and to be without God, are precisely the same thing, then can it be denied, that the symptoms of death are strongly marked upon many of us? Are there not many who never think of God, or care about his service? Are there not many who live, to all appearance, as unconscious of his existence as we fancy the inferior animals to be? And is it not quite clear, that to such persons, God cannot be said to be their God? He may be the God of heaven and earth, the God of the universe, the God of Christ's church; but he is not their God, for they feel to have nothing at all to do with him; and, therefore, as he is not their God, they are, and must be, according to the Scripture, reckoned among the dead.

But God is the God "of the living." That is, as before, all who are alive, live unto him; all who live unto him, are alive. "God said, I am the God of Abraham, and the God of Isaac, and the God of Jacob;" and, therefore, says our Lord, "Abraham, and Isaac, and Jacob, are not and cannot be dead." They cannot be dead, because God owns them: he is not ashamed to be called their God; therefore, they are not cast out from him; therefore, by necessity, they live. Wonderful, indeed, is the truth here implied, in exact agreement, as we have seen, with the general language of Scripture; that, as she who but touched the hem of Christ's garment was, in a moment, relieved from her infirmity, so great was the virtue which went out from him; so they who are not cast out from God, but have any thing whatever to do with him, feel the virtue of his gracious presence penetrating their whole nature; because he lives, they must live also.

Behold, then, life and death set before us; not remote, (if a few years be, indeed, to be called remote,) but even now present before us; even now suffered or enjoyed. Even now, we are alive unto God, or dead unto God; and, as we are either the one or the other, so we are, in the highest possible sense of the terms, alive or dead. In the highest possible sense of the terms; but who can tell what that highest possible sense of the terms is? So much has, indeed, been revealed to us, that we know now that death means a conscious and perpetual death, as life means a conscious and perpetual life. But greatly, indeed, do we deceive ourselves, if we fancy that, by having thus much told us, we have also risen to the infinite heights, or descended to the infinite depths, contained in those little words, life and death. They are far higher, and far deeper, than ever thought or fancy of man has reached to. But, even on the first edge of either, at the visible beginnings of that infinite ascent or descent, there is surely something which may give us a foretaste of what is beyond. Even to us in this moral state, even to you advanced but so short a way on your very earthly journey, life and death have a meaning: to be dead unto God, or to be alive to him, are things perceptibly different.

For, let me ask of those who think least of God, who are most separate from him, and most without him, whether there is not now actually, perceptibly, in their state, something of the coldness, the loneliness, the fearfulness of death? I do not ask them whether they are made unhappy by the fear of God's anger; of course they are not: for they who fear God are not dead to him, nor he to them. The thought of him gives them no disquiet at all; this is the very point we start from. But I would ask them whether they know what it is to feel God's blessing. For instance: we all of us have our troubles of some sort or other, our disappointments, if not our sorrows. In these troubles, in these disappointments,-- I care not how small they may be,--have they known what it is to feel that God's hand is over them; that these little annoyances are but his fatherly correction; that he is all the time loving us, and supporting us? In seasons of joy, such, as they taste very often, have they known what it is to feel that they are tasting the kindness of their heavenly Father, that their good things come from his hand, and are but an infinitely slight foretaste of his love? Sickness, danger,--I know that they come to many of us but rarely; but if we have known them, or at least sickness, even in its lighter form, if not in its graver,--have we felt what it is to know that we are in our Father's hands, that he is with us, and will be with us to the end; that nothing can hurt those whom he loves? Surely, then, if we have never tasted anything of this: if in trouble, or in joy, or in sickness, we are left wholly to ourselves, to bear as we can, and enjoy as we can; if there is no voice that ever speaks out of the heights and the depths around us, to give any answer to our own; if we are thus left to ourselves in this vast world,-- there is in this a coldness and a loneliness; and whenever we come to be, of necessity, driven to be with our own hearts alone, the coldness and the loneliness must be felt. But consider that the things which, we see around us cannot remain with us, nor we with them. The coldness and loneliness of the world, without God, must be felt more and more as life wears on: in every change of our own state, in every separation from or loss of a friend, in every more sensible weakness of our own bodies, in every additional experience of the uncertainty of our own counsels,--the deathlike feeling will come upon us more and more strongly: we shall gain more of that fearful knowledge which tells us that "God is not the God of the dead."

And so, also, the blessed knowledge that he is the God "of the living" grows upon those who are truly alive. Surely he "is not far from every one of us." No occasion of life fails to remind those who live unto him, that he is their God, and that they are his children. On light occasions or on grave ones, in sorrow and in joy, still the warmth of his love is spread, as it were, all through the atmosphere of their lives: they for ever feel his blessing. And if it fills them with joy unspeakable even now, when they so often feel how little they deserve it; if they delight still in being with God, and in living to him, let them be sure that they have in themselves the unerring witness of life eternal: God is the God of the living, and all who are with him must live.

Hard it is, I well know, to bring this home, in any degree, to the minds of those who are dead: for it is of the very nature of the dead that they can hear no words of life. But it has happened that, even whilst writing what I have just been uttering to you, the news reached me that one, who two months ago was one of your number, who this very half-year has shared in all the business and amusements of this place, is passed already into that state where the meanings of the terms life and death are become fully revealed. He knows what it is to live unto God, and what it is to die to him. Those things which are to us unfathomable mysteries, are to him all plain: and yet but two months ago he might have thought himself as far from attaining this knowledge as any of us can do. Wherefore it is clear, that these things, life and death, may hurry their lesson upon us sooner than we deem of, sooner than we are prepared to receive it. And that were indeed awful, if, being dead to God, and yet little feeling it, because of the enjoyments of our worldly life, those enjoyments were on a sudden to be struck away from us, and we should find then that to be dead to God was death, indeed, a death from which there is no waking, and in which there is no sleeping for ever.

LECTURE XX.

EZEKIEL xiii. 22.

With lies ye have made the heart of the righteous sad, whom I have not made sad; and strengthened the hands of the wicked, that he should not return from his wicked way, by promising him life.

The verses which immediately precede this, require explanation, but perhaps our knowledge is hardly sufficient to enable us to give it fully. There are allusions to customs,--to fashions rather,--common amongst the Israelites at the time, which we can now scarcely do more than guess at; but we may observe, that there was a general practice, which even God's own prophets were directed often to comply with, of enforcing what was said in word by some corresponding outward action, in which the speaker made himself, as it were, a living image of the idea which he meant to convey. Thus, when Zedekiah, the son of Chenaanah, was assuring Ahab, that he should drive the Syrians before him, he made himself horns of iron, and said, "With these shalt thou push the Syrians, until thou have consumed them." In the same way, it is imagined that the false prophetesses spoken of in the text were in the habit of wearing pillows, or cushions, fastened to their arms, and directed those who came to consult them to do the same, as a sign of rest and peace; that they who trusted to them had nothing to fear, but might lie down and enjoy themselves at their feasts, or in sleep, with entire security. Or, again, if we connect what is said of the pillows with what immediately follows about the kerchiefs put upon the head, we may suppose that both are but parts of a fantastic dress, such as was often worn by pretended prophets and fortune-tellers, and which they may have made those wear, also, who came before them. We know that the covering on the head was, for instance, a part of the ceremonial law of the Roman augurs, when they began their divinations. But, however this be, the exact understanding of these particular points is not necessary to our deriving the lesson of the passage in general. I know that there is something naturally painful to an active mind in being obliged to content itself with an indistinct notion, or still more, with no notion at all, of the meaning of any words presented to it. But, whilst we should highly value this sensitiveness, as, indeed, few qualities are more essential in the pursuit of truth, yet we must be careful not to let our disappointment carry us too far, so as to pass over a whole passage, or portion, of Scripture, as if in despair, because we cannot understand every part of it. Much of the supposed obscurity of the prophets arises from this cause--that we find in them particular expressions and allusions, which, whether from a, fault in the translation, or from our imperfect knowledge of the times of which the prophets speak, and of the language in which they wrote, are certainly quite unintelligible. But these are only a few expressions, occurring here and there; and it is a great evil to fancy that their writings, in general, are not to be understood, because of the difficulty of particular passages in them. Thus, with the very chapter of which we are now speaking, the expression to which I have alluded can only be uncertainly interpreted, yet the lesson of the chapter, as a whole, is perfectly clear, notwithstanding. The dress, or fashions, or particular rites, of the false prophets of Jerusalem and their votaries, may offer no distinct image to our minds; but the evil of their doings, how they deceived others, and were themselves deceived; the points, that is, which alone concern us practically, these are set before us plainly. "With their lies they made the heart of the righteous sad, whom God had not made sad; and they strengthened the hands of the wicked, that he should not return from his wicked way, by promising him life." Where the way of life was broad, they strove to make it narrow; and where it was narrow, they strove to make it broad: by their solemn and superstitious lies, they frightened and perplexed the good, while, by their lives of ungodliness, they emboldened and encouraged the wicked.

It may not, at first sight, seem necessary that these two things should go together; there might be, it seems, either the fault of making the heart of the righteous sad, without that of strengthening the hands of the wicked: or there might be the strengthening of the hands of the wicked, without making sad the heart of the righteous. And so it sometimes has been: there has been a wickedness which has not tried to keep up superstition: there has been a superstition, the supporters of which have not wilfully encouraged wickedness. Yet, although this has been so, with respect to the intention of the parties concerned, yet in their own nature, the tendency of either evil to produce the other is sure and universal. We cannot exist without some influences of fear and restraint, on the one hand, and without some indulgence of freedom, on the other. God has provided for both these wants, so to speak, of our nature; he has told us whom we should fear, and where we should be restrained, and where, also, we may be safely in freedom: there is the fruit forbidden, and the fruit which we may eat freely. But if the restraint and the liberty be either of them put in the wrong place, the double evil is sure to follow. Restrained in his lawful liberty, debarred from the good and wholesome fruit of the garden, man breaks out into a liberty which is unlawful; he eats of the forbidden fruit, whose taste is death; or, surfeited with an unholy freedom, and let to run wild in a space far too vast for his strength to compass, he turns cravingly for that support to his weariness which a narrowed range would afford him; and he limits himself on that very quarter in which alone he might expatiate freely. Superstition, in fact, is the rest of wickedness, and wickedness is the breaking loose of superstition.

But, however true this may be, are we concerned in it? First of all, when we find an evil dwelt upon often in the Prophets, and find it dwelt upon again by our Lord and his Apostles with no less earnestness, there is, at least, a strong presumption, that an evil of this sort is nothing local or passing, but that it is fixed in man's nature, and is apt to grow up in all times, and in all countries. Now, the double evil spoken of in the text, occurs again in the gospel; there we find men spoken of, who, in like manner, insisted upon what was trifling, and were careless of what was important; and in the epistles, we find, again, the same characters holding up as righteous others than those who worked righteousness: men, who spoke lies in hypocrisy, having their conscience seared with a hot iron. We may presume, therefore, that this evil is of an enduring character; but if we look back to the history of the Christian Church, or look around us, the presumption becomes the sad conviction of experience.

Nor is the evil merely one which exists in the country at large; a thing which might be fully dwelt upon any where but here. On the contrary, I hardly know of an age more exposed to it than youth. There exist in youth, in a very high degree, those opposite feelings of our nature, which I have before spoken of; a tendency to respect, to follow, to be led, on the one hand; and on the other, a lively desire for independence and freedom. These feelings often exist in the greatest strength in the same individual; and when they are not each turned in their proper direction, ruin is the consequence. Nothing is more common than to see great narrowness of mind, great prejudices, and great disorderliness of conduct, united in the same person. Nothing is more common than to see the same mind utterly prostrated before some idol of its own, and supporting that idol with the most furious zeal, and at the same time utterly rebellious to Christ, and rejecting with scorn the enlightening, the purifying, and the loving influences of Christ's Spirit.

The idols of various minds are infinitely various, some seducing the loftiest natures and some the vilest. But of this we may be sure, that every one of us has a tendency to some one idol or other, if not to many; and our business is especially each to watch, ourselves, lest we be enslaved to our peculiar idol. I will now, however, speak of those which, tempt the highest minds; which, by their show of sacredness and excellence, make us fancy, that while following them we are following Christ. And let none be surprised, if I rank among idols many things, which, in themselves and in their proper use and order, are indeed to be loved and reverenced. It was most right to respect the Apostle Peter, and listen to his word; but that great Apostle would have been ruin to Cornelius, and not salvation, if he had suffered him, without reproof, to fall down before him, and render to him the service due to Christ alone. How many good and pious feelings must have been awakened from age to age in many minds, at the sight of the brazen serpent on the pole, the memorial of their fathers' deliverance in the wilderness! But when this awakening, this solemn memorial was corrupted into an idol, when men bowed down before it in superstition, it was the part of true piety to do as Hezekiah did, to dash it, notwithstanding all its solemn associations, into a thousand pieces.

Thus things good, things noble, things sacred, may all become idols. To some minds truth is an idol, to others justice, to others charity or benevolence; and others are beguiled by objects of a different sort of sacredness: some have made Christ's mother their idol; some, Christ's servants; some, again, Christ's sacraments, and Christ's own body, the Church. If these may all be idols, where can we find a name so holy, as that we may surrender up our whole souls to it; before which obedience, reverence, without measure, intense humility, most unreserved adoration, may all be duly rendered. One name there is, and one only; one alone in heaven and in earth; not truth, not justice, not benevolence, not Christ's mother, not his holiest servants, not his blessed sacraments, not his very mystical body, but Himself only, who died for us and rose again, Jesus Christ, both God and Man.

He is truth, and he is righteousness, and he is love; he gives his grace to his sacraments, and his manifold gifts to his Church; whoever hath him hath all things; but if we do not take heed, whenever we turn our mind to any other object, we shall make it an idol and lose him. Take him in all his fulness, not as God merely, not as man merely; not in his life on earth only, not in his death only, not in his exaltation at God's right hand only; but in all his fulness, the Christ of God, God and Man, our Prophet, our Priest, our King and Lord, redeeming us by his blood, sanctifying us by his Spirit; and then worship him and love him with all the heart, and with, all the soul, and with all the strength; and we shall see how all evil will be barred, and all good will abound. No man who worships Christ alone, can be a fanatic, nor yet can be a more philosopher; he cannot be bigoted, nor yet can he be indifferent; he cannot be so the slave of what he calls amiable feelings as to cast truth and justice behind him; nor yet can he so pursue truth and justice as to lose sight of humbler and softer feelings, self-abasement, reverence, devotion. There is no evil tendency in the nature of any one of us, which has not its cure in the true worship of Christ our Saviour. Let us look into our hearts, and consider their besetting faults. Are we indolent, or are we active; are we enthusiastic, or are we cold; zealous or indifferent, devout or reasonable; whatever the inclination, or bias of our nature be, if we follow its kindred idol, it will be magnified and grow on to our ruin; if we worship Christ, it will be pruned and chastened, and made to grow up with opposite tendencies, all alike tempered, none destroyed; none overgrowing the garden, but all filling it with their several fruits; so that it shall be, indeed, the garden of the Lord, and the Spirit of the Lord shall dwell in the midst of it.

And who shall dare to make sad the heart of him who is thus drinking daily of the well-spring of righteousness, by telling him that he is not yet saved, nor can be, unless he will come and bow down before his idol? And if, rather than do so, he break the idol in pieces, who shall dare to call him profane, or cold in love to his Lord, when it was in his very jealousy for his Lord, and in his full purpose to worship him alone, that he threw down all that exalted itself above its due proportion against him? And if a man be not so worshipping Christ only, who shall dare to encourage him in his evil way, by magnifying the sacredness of his idol, and ascribing to it that healing virtue which belongs to Christ alone?

What has been here said might bear to be followed up at far greater length than the present occasion will admit of. But the main point is one, I think, of no small importance, that all fanaticism and superstition on the one hand, and all unbelief and coldness of heart on the other, arise from what is in fact idolatry,--the putting some other object, whether it be called a religious or moral one,--and an object often in itself very excellent,--in the place of Christ himself, as set forth to us fully in the Scriptures. And as no idol can stand in Christ's place, or in any way save us, so whoever worships Christ truly is preserved from all idols and has life eternal. And if any one demand of him further, that he should worship his idol, and tells him that he is not safe if he does not; his answer will be rather that he will perish if he does; that he is safe, fully safe, and only safe, so long as he clings to Christ alone; and that to make anything else necessary to his safety, is not only to minister to superstition, but to ungodliness also; not only to lay on us a yoke which neither our fathers nor we were able to bear; but, by the very act of laying this unchristian yoke upon us, to tear from us the easy yoke and light burden of Christ himself, our Lord and our life.

LECTURE XXI.

ADVENT SUNDAY.

HEBREWS in. 16.

For some, when they had heard, did provoke: howbeit not all that came out of Egypt by Moses.

I take this verse as my text, rather than those which immediately go before or follow it, because it affords one of the most serious instances of mistranslation that are to be met with in the whole New Testament. For the true translation of the words is this: "For who were they who, when they had heard, did provoke? nay, were they not all who came out of Egypt through Moses?" And then it goes on--"And with whom was he grieved forty years? was it not with them that had sinned, whose carcases fell in the wilderness? And to whom sware he that they should not enter into his rest, but to them that believed not?" I call this a serious mistranslation, because it lessens the force of the writer's comparison. So far from meaning to say that "some, but not all did provoke," he lays a stress on the universality of the evil: it was not only a few, but the whole people who came out of Egypt, with only the two individual exceptions of Caleb and Joshua. All the rest who were grown up when they came out of Egypt did provoke God; and the carcases of that whole generation, fell in the wilderness.

Had the lesson from the Hebrews been actually chosen for the service of this day, it could hardly have suited it better. For this day is the New-year's day of the Christian year; and it is probably for this reason that the service of the first day of the common year is confined entirely to the commemoration of our Lord's circumcision, and takes no notice of the beginning of a new year. It is manifest that it could not do so without confusion: for the first of January is not the beginning of the Christian year, but Advent Sunday; the last Sunday of the Christian year is not Christmas-day, as it would be this year if we reckoned by the common divisions of time; but it is the last Sunday after Trinity. Now, then, we are at the beginning of our year; and well it is that, as our trial is now become shorter by another year, as another division of our lives has passed away, we should fix our eyes on that which makes every year so valuable,--the Judgment, for which it ought to be a preparation. In fact, if we observe, we shall see that these Sundays in Advent are much more regarded by the Church as the beginning of a new year, than as a mere prelude to the celebration of the festival of Christmas. That is, Christmas-day is regarded, so to speak, in a two-fold light, as representing both the comings of our Lord, his first coming in the flesh, and his second coming to judgment. When the day actually arrives, it commemorates our Lord's first coming: and this is the beginning of the Christian year, historically regarded, that is, so far as it is a

79

commemoration of the several events of our Lord's life on earth. But before it comes, it is regarded as commemorating our Lord's second coming: and wisely, for his first coming requires now no previous preparation for it; we cannot well put ourselves into the position of those who lived before Christ appeared. But our whole life is, or ought to be, a preparation for his second coming; and it is this state, of which the season of Advent in the Church services is intended to be the representation.

There is something striking in the season of the natural year at which we thus celebrate the beginning of another Christian year. It is a true type of our condition, of the insensible manner in which all the changes of our lives steal upon us, that nature, at this moment, gives no outward signs of beginning: it is a period which does not manifest any striking change in the state of things around us. The Christian Spring begins ere we have reached the half of the natural winter. Nature is not bursting into life, but rather preparing itself for a long period of death. And this is a type of an universal truth, that the signs and warnings which we must look to, must come from within us, not from without: that neither sky nor earth, will arouse us from our deadly slumber, unless we are ourselves aroused already, and more disposed to make warnings for ourselves than to find them.

If this be true of nature, it is true also of all the efforts of man. As nature will give no sign, so man cannot. Let the Church do all that she may; let her keep her solemn anniversaries, and choose out for her services all such passages of Scripture as may be most fitted to impress the lesson which she would teach; still we know that these are alike powerless and unheeded; that unless there be in our own minds something beforehand disposed to profit by them, they are but the words of unavailing affection, vainly spoken to the ears of the dead.

Oh that we would remember this, all of us; that there is no voice in nature, no voice in man, that can really awaken the sleeping soul. That is the work of a far mightier power, to be sought for with most earnest prayers for ourselves and for each other: that the Holy Spirit of God would speak, and would dispose our hearts to hear; that so being awakened from death and our ears being truly opened, all things outward may now join in language which we can hear; and nature, and man, life and death, things present and things to come, may be but the manifold voices of the Spirit of God, all working for us together for good. Till this be so, we speak in vain; our words neither reach our own hearts, nor the hearts of our hearers; they are but recorded in God's book of judgment, to be brought forward hereafter for the condemnation of us both.

Yet we must still speak; for the Spirit of God, who alone works in us effectually, works also secretly; we know not when, nor how, nor where. But we know, that as the Father worketh hitherto, and the Son worketh hitherto, so the Holy Spirit worketh hitherto, and is still working daily. We know that, every year, he creates in thousands of God's people that work which alone shall abide for ever. We know that in the year that is just past he has done this; that in the year which is just beginning he will do it. Have we not here, also, many in whom he has wrought this work? may we not hope, and surely believe, that there are many in whom he is even now preparing to work it?

We know not who these are; still less do we know, what were the occasions which the Holy Spirit so blessed as to work in them his work of life. But this we know, that we are bound to minister all the occasions which we can; we must not spare our labour, although it is God alone who gives the increase. We must speak of life and of death, of Christ and of judgment, not forgetting that we speak often, and shall speak, utterly in vain; yet knowing that it is by these very thoughts, though long unheeded, that God's Spirit does in his own good time awaken the heart; he takes of the things of Christ and shows them to us; and then, what was before like a book in a strange language--we saw the figures, but they conveyed no meaning to our minds--becomes, on a sudden, instinct with the language of God, which we hear and understand as readily as if it were our own tongue wherein we were born.

Therefore, we speak and say, that another year has now dawned upon us; and we would remind you, and remember, ourselves, in what words the various Scriptures of this day's service point out its inestimable value. "Now is our salvation nearer than when we believed." So says St. Paul in the epistle of this day; and how blessed are all those amongst us who can feel that this is truly said of them! Then, indeed, a new year's day is a day of rejoicing; we are so much nearer that period when all care, all anxiety, all painful labour will be for ever ended. But there is other language of a different sort, which, it may be, will suit us better. "I have nourished and brought up children, and they have rebelled against me." "Their land is full of idols; they worship the work of their own hands, that which their own fingers have made;" which means to us, the work of our own hearts, that which our own fancies and desires have made. "Enter into the rock, and hide thee in the dust, for fear of the Lord, and for the glory of his majesty." For in the very temple of God, his Church, all manner of profane thoughts and words and works are crowded together; the din of covetousness and worldliness is loud and constant, and will ill abide the day of his coming, who will, a second time, cast out of his temple all that is unclean. And is there not also in us that evil heart of unbelief and disobedience which departs from the living God? are there not here those who are becoming daily hardened through the deceitfulness of sin? How are they passing their time in the wilderness, and with what prospects when they come to the end of it? God said, "I sware in my wrath, that they shall not enter into my rest." By the way that they came, by the same shall they return; they shall go back to that bondage from which they were once redeemed, and from which they will be redeemed again no more for ever.

These are some of the passages of this day's service which speaks to us at the beginning of this new Christian year. Let me add to all this language of warning, the language in which God, by his apostle Paul, answers every one of us, if we ask of him in sincerity of heart, "Lord, what wilt thou have me to do?" He answers, "The night is far spent, the day is at hand: let us walk honestly, as in the day; not in rioting and drunkenness, not in chambering and wantonness, not in strife and envying: but put ye on the Lord Jesus Christ, and make not provision for the flesh, to fulfil the works thereof." Now, I grant, that this day, of which the apostle speaks, has never yet shone so brightly, as he had hoped and imagined; clouds have, up to this hour, continually overshadowed it. I mean, that the lives of Christians have hindered them from being the light of the world. It has been a light pale and dim, and therefore the works of darkness have continued to abound. But admit this, and what follows? Is it, or can it be, anything else but a more earnest desire not to be ourselves children of darkness, lest what we see to have happened in part should happen altogether; namely, that the day should never shine on us at all? We see that God's promises have been in part forfeited; we see that Christ's kingdom has not been what it was prophesied it should be. Is not this a solemn warning, that for us, too, individually, God's promises may be forfeited? that all we read in Scripture of light, and life, and glory, and happiness, should really prove to us words only, and no reality? that whereas the promise of salvation has been made to us, we should be in the end, not saved, but lost? If, indeed, God's kingdom were shining around us, in its full beauty; if every evil thing were driven out of his temple; if we saw nothing but holy lives and happy, the fruits of his Spirit, truth, and love, and joy; then we might be less anxious for ourselves; our course would be far smoother; the very stream would carry us along to the end of our voyage without our labour: what evil thoughts would not be withered, and die long ere they could ripen into action, if the very air which we breathed were of such, keen and heavenly purity! It is because all this is not so, that we have need of so much watchfulness; it is because the faults of every one of us make our brethren's task harder; because there is not one bad or careless person amongst us who is not a hindrance in his brother's path, and does not oblige him to exert himself the more. Therefore, because the day is not bright, but overclouded; because it is but too like the night, and too many use it as the night for all works of darkness; let us take the more heed that we do not ourselves so mistake it; let us watch each of us the light within us, lest, indeed, we should wholly stumble; let us put on the Lord Jesus Christ. You know how often I have dwelt on this; how often I have tried to show that Christ is all in all to us; that to put on Christ, is a truer and fuller expression, by far, than if we had been told to put on truth, or holiness, or goodness. It includes all these, with something more, that nothing but itself can give--the sense of safety, and joy unspeakable, in feeling ourselves sheltered in our Saviour's arms, and taken even into himself. Assuredly, if we put on the Lord Jesus Christ, we shall not make provision for the flesh to fulfil the lusts thereof; such a warning would then be wholly unnecessary. Or, if we do not like language thus figurative, let us put it, if we will, into the plainest words that shall express the same meaning; let us call it praying to Christ, thinking of him, hoping in him, earnestly loving him; these, at least, are words without a figure, which all can surely understand. Let us be Christ's this year that is now beginning; be his servants, be his disciples, be his redeemed in deed; let us live to him, and for him; setting him before us every day to do his will, and to live in his blessing. Then, indeed, if it be his pleasure that we should serve him throughout this year, even to its end, we may repeat, with a deeper feeling of their truth, the words of St. Paul; we may say, when next Advent Sunday shall appear, that now is our salvation nearer than when we became believers.

LECTURE XXII.

CHRISTMAS DAY.

JOHN i. 10.

He was in the world, and the world was made by Him, and the world knew Him not.

When we use ourselves, or hear others use, the term "mystery," as applied to things belonging to the gospel, we should do well to consider what is meant by it. For our common notion of the word mystery is of something dark; whereas Christ and his gospel are continually spoken of as being, above all other things, light. Then come others, and say, "Light and darkness cannot go together: what you call the mysteries of Christianity are no part of it, but the fond inventions of man: Christianity is all simple and clear:" and thus they strike away some of the very greatest truths which God has revealed to us. Thus they deal in particular with the great truth declared in the text, that He who made the world visited it in the likeness of man. Now, if this truth were a mystery, in the common notion of that term; if it were a thing full of darkness, defying our minds to understand it, or to draw any good from it; then, indeed, it would be of little consequence whether we received it or no. It is because it is a mystery in a very different sense, in the sense in which the word is used commonly in the Scriptures; that is, a thing which was a secret, but which God has been pleased to reveal, and to reveal for our benefit, that therefore the loss of it would be the loss of a real blessing, a loss at once of light and comfort.

But we must go a little further, and explain from what this sad confusion in the use of the term "mystery" has arisen. There are many things relating to ourselves and to things around us, which by nature we cannot understand; and of God we can scarcely understand anything. Now, while the gospel has revealed much that we did not know before, it yet has not revealed everything: of God, in particular, it has given us much most precious knowledge, yet it has not removed all the veil. It has furnished us with a glass, indeed, to use the apostle's comparison; but the glass, although, a great help, although reflecting a likeness of what, without it, we could not see at all, is yet a dark and imperfect manner of seeing, compared with, the seeing face to face. So, when the gospel tells us that He who made the world visited it in our nature, it does not indeed enable us yet fully to conceive what He is who made us, and then became as one of us; there is still left around the name of God that light inaccessible which is to our imperfections darkness; and so far as we cannot understand or conceive rightly of God, so far it is true that we cannot understand all that is conveyed in the expression that God was in the world dwelling among us. Yet it is still most true that by the revelation thus made to us we have gained immensely. God, as he is in himself, we cannot understand; but Jesus Christ we can. When we are told to love God, if we look to the life and death of Christ, we can understand and feel how truly he deserves our love; when we are told to be perfect as God is perfect, we have the image of this perfection so truly set before us in his Son Jesus, that it may be well said, "Whoso hath seen Him hath seen the Father;" and why, then, should we ask with Philip, that "He should show us the Father?"

What, then, the festival of Christmas presents to us, as distinct from that of Easter, is generally the revelation of God in the flesh. True it is, that we may make it, if we will, the same as Easter: that is, we may celebrate it as the birth of our Saviour, of him who died and rose again for us; but then we only celebrate our Lord's birth with reference to his death and resurrection: that is, we make Christmas to be Easter under another name. And so everything relating to our Lord may be made to refer to his death and resurrection; for in them consists our redemption, and for that reason Easter has ever been considered as the great festival of the Christian year. But yet apart from this, Christmas has something peculiarly its own: namely, as I said before, the revelation of God in the flesh, not only to make atonement for our sins,--which is the peculiar subject of the celebration of the season of Easter,--but to give us notions of God at once distinct and lively; to enable us to have One in the invisible world, whom we could conceive of as distinctly as of a mere man, yet whom we might love with all our hearts, and trust with all our hearts, and yet be guilty of no idolatry.

It is not, then, only as the beginning of an earthly life of little more than thirty years, that we may celebrate the day of our Lord's birth in the flesh. His own words express what this day has brought to us: "Henceforth shall ye see heaven opened, and the angels of God ascending and descending upon the Son of man." The words here, like so many of our Lord's, are expressed in a parable; but their meaning is not the less clear. They allude evidently to Jacob's vision, to the ladder reaching from earth to heaven, on which the angels were ascending and descending continually. But this vision is itself a parable; showing, under the figure of the ladder reaching from earth to heaven, and the angels going up and down on it, a free communication, as it were, between God and man, heaven brought nearer to earth, and heavenly things made more familiar. Now, this is done, in a manner, by every revelation from God; most of all, by the revelation of his Son. Nor is it only by his Spirit that Christ communicates with us even now; though, he is ascended again into heaven, yet the benefits of his having become man, over and above those of his dying and rising again for us, have not yet passed away. It is still the man Christ Jesus who brings heaven near to earth, and earth near to heaven.

It has been well said by Augustine, that babes in Christ should so think of the Son of man as not to lose sight of the Son of God; that more advanced Christians should so think of the Son of God as not to lose sight of the Son of man. Augustine well understood how the thought of the Son of man is fitted to our weakness; and that the best and most advanced of us in this mortal life are never so strong as to be able to do without it. Have we ever tried this with our children? We tell them that God made them, and takes care of them, and loves them, and hears their prayers, and knows what is in their hearts, and cannot bear what is evil. These are such notions of God as a child requires, and can understand. But, if we join with them some of those other notions which belong to God as he is in himself; that he is a Spirit, not to be seen, not to be conceived of as in any one place, or in any one form; what do we but embarrass our child's mind, and lessen that sense of near and dear relation to God which, our earlier accounts of God had given him? Yet we must teach him something of this sort, if we would prevent him from forming unworthy notions of God, such as have been the beginning of all idolatry. Here, then, is the blessing of the revelation of God in Christ. All that he can understand of God, or love in him, or fear in him--that is to be found in Christ. Christ made him, takes care of him, can hear his prayers, can read his little heart, loves him tenderly; yet cannot bear what is evil, and will strictly judge him at the last day. But what we must teach when we speak of God, yet which has a tendency to lessen the liveliness of our impressions of him, this has no place when we speak of Christ. Christ has a body, incorruptible and glorified indeed, such as they who are Christ's shall also wear at his coming, yet still a body. Christ is not to be seen, indeed, for the clouds have received him out of our sight: yet he may be conceived of as in one place--at the right hand of God; as in one certain and well-known form--the form of the Son of man. Yet let us observe again, and be thankful for the perfect wisdom of God. Even while presenting to us God in Christ; that is to say, God with all those attributes which we can understand, and fear, and love; and without those which, throw us, as it were, to an infinite distance, overwhelming our minds, and baffling all our conceptions; even then the utmost care is taken to make us remember that God in himself is really that infinite and incomprehensible Being to whom we cannot, in our present state, approach; that even his manifestation of himself in Christ Jesus, is one less perfect than we shall be permitted to see hereafter; that Christ stands at the right hand of the Majesty on high; that he has received from the Father all his kingdom and his glory; finally, that the Father is greater than he, inasmuch as any other nature added to the pure and perfect essence of God, must, in a certain measure, if I may venture so to speak, be a coming down to a lower point, from the very and unmixed Divinity.

I have purposely mentioned this last circumstance, although it is not the view that I wish particularly to take to-day, because such passages as that which I quoted, where Christ tells his disciples that his Father was greater than he, and many others of the same sort, throughout the New Testament, are sometimes apt to embarrass and perplex us, if we do not consider their peculiar object. It was very necessary, especially at a time when men were so accustomed to worship their highest gods under the form of men, that whilst the gospel was itself holding out the man Christ Jesus as the object of religious faith, and fear, and love, and teaching that all power was given to him, in heaven and in earth,--it should, also, guard us against supposing that it meant to represent God as, in himself, wearing a human form, or having a nature partaking of our infirmities; and, therefore, it always speaks of there being something in God higher, and more perfect, than could possibly be revealed to man; and for this eternal and infinite, and inconceivable Being, it claims the reserve of our highest thoughts, or, rather, it commands us to believe, that they who shall hereafter see God face to face, shall be allowed to see something still greater than is now revealed to us, even in him who is the express image of God, and the brightness of his glory.

But, now, to return to what I was dwelling on before. It is not only for children, that the revelation of God in Christ is so valuable; it is fitted to the wants of us all, at all times, and under all circumstances. Say, that we are in joy; say, that we are enjoying some of the festivities of this season. It is quite plain, that, at whatever moment the thought of God is unwelcome to us, that moment is one of sin or unbelief: yet, how can we dare to mix up the notion of the most high God with any earthly merriment, or festivity? Then, if we think of him who was present at the marriage in Cana of Galilee, and who worked a miracle for no other object than to increase the enjoyment of that marriage supper, do we not feel how the highest thoughts may be joined with the most common occasions? how we may bring Christ home with, us to our social meetings, to bless us, and to sanctify them? Imagine him in our feasts as he was in Cana:--we may do it without profaneness; being sure, from that example, that he condemns not innocent mirth; that it is not merely because there is a feast, or because friends and neighbours are gathered together, that Christ cannot, therefore, be in the midst of us. This alone does not drive him away; but, oh consider, with what ears would he have listened to any words of unkindness, of profaneness, or of impurity! with what eyes would he have viewed any intemperance, or revelling; any such, immoderate yielding up of the night to pleasure, that a less portion of the next day can be given to duty and to God! Even as he would have heard or seen such things in Cana of Galilee, so does he hear and see them amongst us; the same gracious eye of love is on our moderate and permitted enjoyments; the same turning away from, the same firm and just displeasure at every word or deed which turns pleasure into sin.

But if I seek for instances to show how God in Christ is brought very near to us, what can I choose more striking than that most solemn act of Christian communion to which we are called this day? For, what is there in our mortal life, what joy, what sorrow, what feeling elated or subdued, which is not in that communion brought near to Christ to receive his blessing? What is the first and outward thing of which it reminds us? Is it not that last supper in Jerusalem, in which men,--the twelve disciples, the first members of our Christian brotherhood,--were brought into such solemn nearness to God, as seems to have begun the privileges of heaven upon earth? They were brought near at once to Christ and to one another: united to one another in him, in that double bond which, is the perfection at once of our duty and of our happiness. And so in our communion we, too, draw near to Christ and to each other; we feel--who is there at that moment, at least, that does not feel?--

what a tie there is to bind each of us to his brother, when we come to the table of our common Lord. So far, the Lord's Supper is but a type of what every Christian meeting should be: never should any of us be gathered together on any occasion of common life, in our families or with our neighbours; we should sit down to no meal; we should meet in no company, without having Christ also in the midst of us; without remembering what we all are to him, and what we each therefore are to our brethren. But when we further recollect what there is in the Lord's Supper beyond the mere meeting of Christ and his disciples; what it is which the bread and the wine commemorate; of what we partake when, as true Christians, we eat of that bread, and drink of that cup; then we shall understand that God indeed is brought very near to us; inasmuch, as he who is a Christian, and partakes sincerely of Christian communion, is a partaker also of Christ: and as belonging to his body, his living spiritual body, the universal Church, receives his share of all those blessings, of all that infinite love which the Father shows continually to the head of that body, his own well-beloved Son.

Say not then in your hearts, Who can ascend up into heaven, that is, to bring Christ down? As on this day, when he took our nature upon him, he came down to abide with us for ever; to abide with, us, even when we should see him with our eyes no more: for whilst he was on earth he so took part in all the concerns of life, in all its duties, its sorrows, and its joys, that memory, when looking back on the past, can fancy him present still; and then let the liveliest fancy do its work to the utmost, it cannot go beyond the reality; he is present still, for that belongs to his almightiness; he is present with us, because he is God; and we can fancy him with us, because he is man. This is the way to lessen our distance from God and heaven, by bringing Christ continually to us on earth: the sky is closed, and shows no sign; all things continue as they were from the beginning of the world; evil abounds, and therefore the faith of many waxes cold; but Christ was and is amongst us; and we need no surer sign than that sign of the prophet Jonah--Christ crucified and Christ risen--to make us feel that we may live with God daily upon earth, and doing so, shall live with him for an eternal life, in a country that cannot pass away.

LECTURE XXIII.

SUNDAY NEXT BEFORE EASTER.

MATTHEW xxvi. 40, 41.

What, could ye not watch with me one hour? Watch and pray, that ye enter not into temptation: the spirit indeed is willing, but the flesh is weak.

These words, we cannot doubt, have an application to ourselves, and to all Christians, far beyond the particular occasion on which they were actually spoken. They are, in fact, the words which Christ addresses daily to all of us. Every day, when he sees how often we have gone astray from him, he repeats to us, Could ye not watch with me one hour? Every day he commands us to watch and pray, that we enter not into temptation; every day he reminds us, that however willing may be our spirits, yet our flesh is weak; and that through that weakness, sin prevails over it, and having triumphed over our flesh, proceeds to enslave our spirit also.

And as the words are applicable to us every day, so also are they in a particular manner suitable now, when the season of Lent is so nearly over, and Easter is so fast approaching. Have we been unable to watch, with Christ one hour? Already are the good resolutions with which, we, perhaps, began Lent, broken in many instances; and the impressions, if any such were made in us, are already weakened. They have been a burden, which we have shaken off, because the weakness of our nature found it too heavy to bear. Sad it is to think how often this same process has been repeated in all time, how often it will be repeated to the end.

Let us just review what the course of this process has probably been. Now, as the parable of the Sower describes three several sorts of persons, who never bring forth, fruit; so in the very same persons, there is at different times something of each of the three characters there described. We, the very same persons, are at one time hard, at another careless, and at another over-busy; although, if compared with, other persons, and in the general form of their characters, some are hard, and others are careless, and others over-busy; different persons having different faults predominantly. But even the hardness of the road side, although God forbid that it should be our prevailing temper, yet surely it does sometimes exist in too many of us. In common speech, we talk of a person showing a hard temper, meaning, generally, a hard temper towards other men. We have done wrong, but being angry when we are reproved for it, we will not acknowledge it at all, and cheat our consciences, by dwelling upon the supposed wrong that has been done to us in some over-severity of reproof or punishment, instead of confessing and repenting of the original wrong which we ourselves did. But is it not true, that a hard temper towards man is very often, even consciously, a hard temper towards God? Does it never happen, that if conscience presents to us the thought of God, whether as a God of judgment to terrify us, or as a God of love to melt us, we repel it with impatience, or with sullenness? Does not the heart sometimes almost speak aloud the language of blasphemy: Who is God, that I should mind him? I do not care what may happen, I will not be softened. Do not all sorts of unbelieving thoughts pass rapidly through the mind at such moments; first in their less daring form, whispering, as the serpent did to Eve, that we shall not surely die; that we shall have time to repent by and by; that God will not be so strict a judge as to condemn us for such a little; that by some means or other, we shall escape? But then they come, also, in their bolder form: What do I or any man know about another world, or God's judgments? may it not be all a fiction, so that I have, in reality, nothing to fear? In short, under one form or another, is it not true, that our hearts have sometimes displayed actually hardness towards God; that the thought of God has been actually presented to our minds, but that we have turned it aside, and have not suffered it to make any impression upon us? And thus, we have not only not watched with Christ according to his command, but have actually told him that we would not. But this has been in our worst temper, certainly; it may not have happened,--I trust that it has not happened often. More commonly, I dare say, the fault has been carelessness. We have gone out of this place; sacred names have ceased to sound in our ears; sights in any degree connected with, holy things have been all withdrawn from us. Other sounds and other sights have been before us, and our minds have yielded to them altogether. There are minds, indeed, which have no spring of thought in themselves; which are quiet, and in truth empty, till some outward objects come to engage them. Take them at a moment when they are alone, or when there is no very interesting object before them, and ask them of what they are thinking. If the answer were truly given, such a mind would say, "Of nothing." Certain images may be faintly presented to it; it may be that it is not altogether a blank; yet it could not name anything distinctly. No form had been vivid enough to produce any corresponding resolution in us; we were, as it were, in a state between sleeping and waking, with neither thoughts nor dreams definite enough to affect us. This state finds exactly all that it desires in the presence or the near hope of outward objects; the mind lives in its daily pursuits, and companions, and amusements. What impressions have been once produced are soon worn away; and in a soil so shallow nothing makes a durable impression: everything can, as it were, scratch upon its surface, while nothing can strike deeply down within.

Or, again, take the rarer case of those who are over-busy. There are minds, undoubtedly, which are as incapable of rest as those of the generality of men are prone to it; there are minds which enter keenly into everything presented to them by their outward senses, and which, when their senses cease to supply them, have an inexhaustible source of thought within, which furnishes them with abundant matter of reflection or of speculation.

To such a mind, doing is most delightful; whether it be outward doing, or the mere exercise of thought, either supplies alike the consciousness of power. Where, then, is there room for the less obtruding things of God? Into that restless water, another and another image is for ever stepping down, pushing aside and keeping at a distance the sobering reflections of God and of Christ. Alas! the thorns grow so vigorously in such a soil, that they altogether choke and kill the seed of God's word.

So, then, we are either asleep, or, if we are awake, we are not waking with Christ. On one side, in that garden of Gethsemane were the disciples sleeping; below, and fast ascending the hill,--not sleeping, certainly, but with lanterns and torches and weapons,--were those whose waking was for evil. Where were they who watched with Christ one hour then,--or where are those who watch with him now?

HOW gently, yet how earnestly, does he call upon us to "watch and pray, lest we enter into temptation." To watch and to pray: for of all those around him some were sleeping, and none were praying; so that they who watched were not watching with him, but against him. In our careless state of mind the call to us is to watch; in our over-busy state the call to us is to pray; in our hard state there is equal need for both. And even in our best moods, when we are not hard, nor careless, nor over-busy, when we are at once sober and earnest and gentle, then not least does Christ call upon us to watch and to pray, that we may retain that than which else no gleam of April sunshine was ever more fleeting; that we may perfect that which else is of the earth, earthly, and when we lie down in the dust will wither and come to dust also.

Jesus Christ brought life and immortality, it is said, to light through the gospel. He brought life and immortality to light:--is this indeed true as far as we are concerned? What do we think would be the difference in this point between many of us--who will dare say how many?--and a school, I will not say of Jewish, but even of Greek or Roman or Egyptian boys, eighteen hundred, or twenty-four hundred, or three or four thousand years ago? Compare us at our worship with them, and then, I grant, the difference would appear enormous. We have no images, making the glory of the incorruptible God like to corruptible man; we have no vain stream of incense; no shedding of the blood of bulls and calves in sacrifice: the hymns which are sung here are not vain repetitions or impious fables, which gave no word of answer to those questions which it most concerns mankind to know. Here, indeed, Jesus Christ is truly set forth, crucified among us; here life and immortality are brought to light. But follow us out of this place,--to our respective pursuits and amusements, to our social meetings, or our times of solitary thought,--and wherein do we seem to see life and immortality more brightly revealed than to those heathen schools of old? Do we enjoy any worldly good less keenly, or less shrink from any worldly evil? Death, which to the heathen view was the end of all things, is to us (so our language goes) the gate of life. Do we think of it with more hope and less fear than the heathen did? Christ has risen, and has reconciled us to God. Is God more to us?--God now revealed to us as our reconciled Father--do we oftener think of him, do we love him better, than he was thought of and loved in those heathen schools, which had Homer's poetry for their only gospel? We talk of light, of revelation, of the knowledge of God, while verily and really we are walking, not in light, but in darkness: not in knowledge of God, but in blindness and hardness of heart.

"The spirit indeed is willing, but the flesh is weak." How great is the loving-kindness of these words,--how gently does Christ bear with the weakness of his disciples! But this thought may be the most blessed or the most dangerous thought in the world; the most blessed if it touches us with love, the most dangerous if it emboldens us in sin. He is full of loving-kindness, full of long-suffering; for days, and weeks, and months, and years he bears with us: we grieve him, and he entreats; we crucify him afresh, yet he will not come down from the cross in power and majesty; he endures and spares. So it is for days, and months, and years; for some years it may be to most of us,--for many years to some of the youngest. There may be some here who may go on grieving Christ, and crucifying him afresh, for as much as seventy years; and he will bear with them all that time, and his sun will daily shine upon them, and his creatures and his word will minister to their pleasure; and he himself will say nothing to them but to entreat them to turn and be saved. This may last, I say, to some amongst us for seventy years; to others it may last fifty; to many of us it may last for forty, or for thirty; none of us, perhaps, are so old but that it may last with us twenty, or at the least ten. Such is the prospect before us, if we like it: not to be depended upon with certainty, it is true, but yet to be regarded as probable. But as these ten, or twenty, or fifty, or seventy years pass on, Christ will still spare us, but his voice of entreaty will be less often heard; the distance between him and us will be consciously wider. From one place after another where we once used sometimes to see him, he will have departed; year after year some object which used once to catch the light from heaven, will have become overgrown, and will lie constantly in gloom; year after year the world will become to us more entirely devoid of God. If sorrow, or some softening joy ever turns our minds towards Christ, we shall be startled at perceiving there is something which keeps us from him, that we cannot earnestly believe in him; that if we speak of loving him, our hearts, which can still love earthly things, feel that the words are but mockery. Alas, alas! the increased weakness of our flesh, has destroyed all the power of our spirit, and almost all its willingness: it is bound with chains which it cannot break, and, indeed, scarcely desires to break. Redemption, Salvation, Victory,--what words are these when applied to that enslaved, that lost, that utterly overthrown and vanquished soul, which sin is leading in triumph now, and which will speedily be given over to walk for ever as a captive in the eternal triumph of death!

Not one word of what I have said is raised beyond the simplest expression of truth; this is our portion if we will not watch with Christ. We know how often we have failed to do so, either sleeping in carelessness, or being busy and wakeful, but not with him or for him. Still he calls us to watch and pray, lest we enter into temptation; to mark our lives and actions; to mark them often; to see whether we have done well or ill in the month past, or in the week past, or in the day past; to consider whether we are better than we were, or worse; whether we think Christ loves us better, or worse; whether we are more or less cold towards him. I know not what else can be called watching with Christ than such a looking into ourselves as we are in his sight. It is very hard to be done;--yes, it is hard--harder than anything probably which we ever attempted before; and, therefore, we must pray withal for his help, whose strength is perfected in our weakness. And if it be so hard, and we have need so greatly to pray for God's help, should we not all also be anxious to help one another? And knowing, as we do from our own consciences, how difficult it is to watch with Christ, and how thankful we should be to any one who were to make it easier to us, should we not be sure that our neighbour is in like case with ourselves; that our help may be as useful to him as we feel that his would be to us? This is our bounden duty of love towards one another; what then should be said of us if we not only neglect this duty, but do the very contrary to it; if we actually help the evil in our brother's heart to destroy him more entirely; if we will not watch with Christ ourselves, and strive to prevent others from doing so?

LECTURE XXIV.

GOOD FRIDAY.

ROMANS v. 8.

God commendeth his love towards us, in that, while we were yet sinners, Christ died for us.

We all remember the story in the Gospel, of the different treatment which our Lord met with in the same house, from the Pharisee, who had invited him into it, and from the woman who came in and knelt at his feet, and kissed them, and bathed them with her tears. Our Lord accounted for the difference in these words, "To whom little is forgiven, the same loveth little;" which means to speak of the sense or feeling in the person's own mind, "He who feels that little is or needs to be forgiven him, he also loves little." And this same difference which existed toward him when he was present on earth, exists no less now, whenever he is brought before our thoughts. The same sort of persons who saw him with indifference, think of him also with indifference; they who saw him with love, think of him also with love. There is no art, no power in the world, which can give an interest to words spoken concerning him, for those who feel that little is and that little needs to be forgiven them, or to those who never consider about their being forgiven at all. To such, this day, with its services, what they hear from the Scriptures, or what they hear from men, must be alike a matter of indifference: it is not possible that it should be otherwise. Yet, God forbid that we should design what we are saying this day only for a certain few of our congregation, as if the rest neither would nor could be interested in it. So long as any one is careless, he cannot, it is true, be interested about the things of Christ; but who can say at what moment, through God's grace, he may cease to be careless? Is it too much to say, that scarcely a service is performed in any congregation in the land, which does not awaken an interest in some one who before was indifferent? I do rot say a deep interest, nor a lasting one, but an interest; there is a thought, a heeding, an inclination of the mind to listen, created probably by the Church services in some one or other, every time that they are performed. As we never can know in whom this may be so created, as all have great need that it should be created, as all are deeply concerned whether they feel that they are so or no, so we speak to all alike; and if the language does pass over their ears like an unknown or indistinct sound, the fault and the loss are theirs; but the Church has borne her witness, and has so far done her duty.

But again, for ears not careless, but most interested; for hearts to whom Christ is more than all in the world besides; for minds, before whom the wisdom of the gospel is ever growing, rising to a loftier height, and striking downwards to a depth more profound,--yet without end in its height or its depth; is there not, also, a difficulty in speaking to them of that great thing which the Church celebrates to-day? Is there no difficulty in awakening their interest, or rather how can we escape even from wearying or repelling them, when their own affections and deep thoughts must find all words of man, whether of themselves or others, infinitely unworthy to express either the one or the other? To such, then, the words of the preacher may be no more than music without any words at all; which does but serve to lead and accompany our own thoughts, without distinctly suggesting any thoughts of another to interrupt the workings of our own minds. We would speak of Christ's death; most good it is for us and for you to think upon it; so far as our words suit the current of your own thoughts, use them and listen to them; so far as they are a too unworthy expression of what we ought to think and feel, follow your own reflections, and let the words neither offend you nor distract you.

I would endeavour just to touch, upon some of the purposes for which the Scripture tells us that Christ died, and for which his death was declared to be the great object of our faith. This done in the simplest and fewest words will best show the infinite greatness of the subject; and how truly it is, so to speak, the central point of Christianity.

First of all, Christ died as a proper sacrifice for sin; as a sacrifice, the virtue of which, is altogether distinct from our knowledge of it, or from any effect which it has a tendency to produce on our own minds. We are forgiven for his sake; we are acquitted through his death, and through faith in his blood. What a view does this open, partially, indeed,--for what mortal eye can reach to the end of it?--of the evil of sin, and of God's love! of what God's justice required, and of what God's love fulfilled! This great sacrifice was made once, but it will not be made again; for those who despise this there remains no more offering for sin, but their sin abideth with them for ever.

Secondly, Christ's death is revealed to us as a motive capable of overcoming all temptations to evil. "How much more shall the blood of Christ purge your conscience from dead works to serve the living God?" "He suffered for sins, the just for the unjust, that he might bring us to God;" that is, that a consideration of what Christ's death declares to us should have power to melt the hardest heart, and to sober the lightest: that, when we think of Christ dying, dying for us, and so purchasing for us the forgiveness of sins, and everlasting life, such a love, and such a prospect of peace with God, and of glory, should in the highest degree soften and enkindle us; and from love for him, and confidence of hope through the prospect which he has given us, we should be able to overcome all temptations. "I am persuaded," says St. Paul, "that neither death, nor life, nor angels, nor principalities, nor powers, nor things present, nor things to come, nor height, nor depth, nor any other creature, shall be able to separate us from the love of God, which is in Christ Jesus our Lord."

Thirdly, Christ suffered for as, leaving us an example that we should follow his steps. He left us an example of all meekness, and patience, and humility; he left us an example of perfect submission to God's will; he left us an infinite comfort by letting us feel when we are in any trouble, or pain, or affliction, that he was troubled too; that he knew pain, and endured affliction. Above all, in that hour which must come to all of us, he has left us the greatest of all supports;--for he endured to die; and we may enter with less fear into the darkness of the grave, for even there Christ has been for our sakes, and arose from out of it a conqueror.

Fourthly, Christ died that he might gather together in one the children of God that were scattered abroad; he died to purchase to himself his universal Church. So it is said in the Scriptures: and on this particular purpose of his death, it may not be amiss to dwell, for none so needs to be held in remembrance. Many there are, and ever have been, who have rested their whole hope towards God on his sacrifice; many who have learnt from his cross to overcome sin; from his resurrection to overcome the world; many who, amidst all the troubles of life, and in the hour of death, have been supported by the thought of his example. But where is his universal Church? where the company of God's children gathered together into one? where is the city set upon the hill, that cannot be hid? where is the visible kingdom of God, where all its people are striving under one Divine Head, against sin, the world, and the devil? This is the sign which we look for and cannot find; this is the fulfilment of the prophecies for which we seem destined to wait in vain.

And what if, on the contrary, that which is called the Church act rather the part of the world; if our worst foes be truly those of our own household: if they who should have been for our help, be rather an occasion of falling: if one of our greatest difficulties in following Christ steadily, arise from the total want of encouragement, yea, often from the direct opposition of those who are themselves pledged to follow him to the death; if that Church, which was to have been the clearest sign to the world of the truth of Christ's gospel, be now, in many respects, rather a stumbling-block to the adversary and unbeliever, so that the name of God is through us blasphemed among the heathen, rather than glorified; may we not humble ourselves before God in sorrow and in shame? and must we not confess, that through our sin, and the sin of our fathers, Christ, in respect of this one purpose of his death, has as yet died in vain?

Israel after the flesh, lamenting their Jerusalem which is now not theirs, and mourning over their ruined temple, in all their synagogues repeat constantly the prayer, O Lord, build thou the walls of Jerusalem! O Lord, build! O Lord, build! O Lord, build! is the solemn chorus, marking by its repetition the earnestness of their desire. And should not this be the prayer of the Israel of God, scattered now as they are into their thousand divided and corrupted synagogues, and no token to be seen of the pure and universal Church, the living temple of the Spirit of God; should not we too, privately and publicly, join in the prayer of the earthly Israel, and pray that Christ would build for us the walls of our true Jerusalem? For only think what it would be, if Christ's Church existed more than in name; consider what it would be if baptism were a real bond; if we looked on one another as brethren, redeemed by one ransom, pledged to one service; if we bore with one another's weaknesses; if we helped one another's endeavours; if each saw and heard, in the words and life of his neighbour, an image of Christ, and a pledge of the truth of his promises. Consider what it would be, if, with no quarrels, with no jealousies, with no unkindness, we sought not every man his own, but every man also another's welfare; as true members one of another,--of one body, of which Christ is the head. Consider what it would be, if our judgments of men and things were like Christ's judgments; neither strengthening the heart of the careless and sinful by our laxity, nor making sad the heart of God's true servant by our uncharitableness; not putting little things in the place of great, nor great things in the place of little; not neglecting the unity of the Spirit; not stickling for a sameness in the form. Or, if we carry our views a little wider; if we look out upon the world at large, and hear of rumours of wars, and see the signs of internal disorders, and perhaps may think that the clouds are gathering which, herald one of the comings of the Son of man to judgment, whether the last of all or not it were vain to ask; how blessed would it be, if we could see such an ark of Christ's Church as should float visibly upon, the stormy waters; gathering within it, in peace and safety, men of various dispositions and conditions, and opinions; those who held much of truth, and those who had mixed with it much of error: those whom Christ would call clean, and those, too, whom some of their brethren call unclean, but whom Christ has redeemed, and will save no less than their despisers; all, in short, who fled from sin and from the world to Christ, and to the company of Christ's people! O if we could but see such an ark preparing while God's long-suffering yet withholds the flood! O that all God's scattered and divided children would join together in one earnest prayer, O Lord, build thou the walls of Jerusalem! O Lord, build! O Lord, build! O Lord, build!

Yet, for this, among other purposes of mercy, did the Son of God, as on this day, suffer death upon the cross: he died that we might be one in him. Let us turn, then, from the thought of the general temple in ruins, and let us see whether we cannot, at any rate, within the walls of our own little particular congregation, fulfil also this object of Christ's death, and be one in him. Let us consider one another, to provoke unto love and to good works: we too often consider one another for the very contrary purpose, to provoke to contempt or ill-will. True it is, that if we look for it we can find much of evil in our brethren, and they can find much also in us; and we might become all haters of one another, all in some sort deserving to be hated. But where is he who is entitled to hate another's evil when he has evil in himself; and when Christ, who had none, did not hate the evil of us all, but rather died to save it? And is it not true also, that, if we look for it, we can also find in every one something to love? something, undoubtedly, even in him who has in himself least: but much, infinitely much in all, when we look upon them as Christ's redeemed. Not more beautifully than truly has it been said, that Christian souls--

"Though worn and soiled by sinful clay,
Are yet, to eyes that see them true,
All glistening with baptismal dew."

They have the seal of belonging to Christ; they are his and our brethren. And, as his latest command, and his beloved Apostle's also, was that we should love one another; so, if we would bring all our solemn thoughts of Christ's death to one point, and endeavour to derive from it some one particular lesson for our daily lives, I know not that any would be more needed or better for us, than that we should especially apply the thought of Christ dying on the cross for us to soften our angry, and proud, and selfish feelings; to restrain us from angry or sneering words; from unkind, offensive, rude, or insulting actions; to excite us to gentleness, courtesy, kindness; remembering that he, be he who he may, whom we allow ourselves to despise, or to dislike, or to annoy, or to neglect, was one so precious in Christ's sight, that he laid down his life for his sake, and invites him to be for ever with, him and with his Father.

LECTURE XXV.

EASTER DAY.

JOHN xx. 20.

91

Then the disciples went away again unto their own home.

With this verse ends the portion of the scripture chosen for the gospel in this morning's service. It finishes the account of the visit of Peter and John to the sepulchre; and, therefore, the close of the extract at this point is sufficiently natural. Yet the effect of the quiet tone of these words, just following the account of the greatest event which earth has ever witnessed, is, I think, singularly impressive; the more so when we remember that they were written by one of the very persons, whose visit had been just described; and that the writer, therefore, could tell full well, to how intense an interest there had succeeded that solemn calm. They went away from the very sight, if I may so speak, of Christ risen, to their own homes. And what thoughts do we suppose that they carried with them? Let us endeavour to recall them, for our benefit, also, who, like them, are going, as it were, to the ordinary tenure of our daily lives from this day's high solemnity.

The disciples went away to their own homes; and there they waited, either in Jerusalem or in Galilee, pursuing, as we find from the last chapter of St. John, their common occupations, till, after their Lord's ascension, power was given them from on high, and the great work of their apostleship began. During this period, Christ appeared to them several times: he conversed with them, he ate and drank with them: but he did not live continually with them, as he had done before his crucifixion: he did not take them about with him as before, while he was performing the part of the great prophet of the house of Israel. They were now at their own homes waiting for his call to more active duties. They had seen him dead, and they had seen, him risen, and they were receiving into their souls all the lessons of his life and death and resurrection, brought before them, and impressed upon them by that Holy Spirit, who, according to Christ's promise, was to take of the things which are Christ's, and to show them to Christ's disciples.

It is true that there came upon them, after this, an especial visitation of the Spirit of power, to fit them for their particular work of apostles or messengers to mankind. Having been converted themselves, they were to strengthen their brethren. And as this especial visitation of the Holy Spirit was given to them only, and to those on whom they themselves laid their hands, so none have ever since been called to that particular work to which they were called, in any thing of the same degree of fulness. What is peculiar to them as apostles is not applicable exactly to us; but we are all concerned in what belongs to them as Christians: in this respect, their case is ours; and they, when at their own homes, and engaged in their own callings, stand in the same situation as we all.

We may, however, still make a two-fold division; we may regard the apostles going away to their own homes, as a temporary thing, as a mere term of preparation for the duties which they were afterwards called to; or we may look upon it as complete so far as earth is concerned, since, taking them as Christians only and not as apostles, they might have so lived on to the end of their lives, having received all those helps which were needed for their own personal salvation, and having only to use them daily for their soul's benefit. This same distinction we may apply to ourselves. We may consider ourselves as going to our own homes for a time only, awaiting our call to active life; or we may consider ourselves as withdrawing, after every celebration of Christ's resurrection, to that round of daily duties which on earth shall never alter; and to which all the helps derived from our communion with Christ are to be applied, with nothing future, so for as earth is concerned, for which we may need them. So then, of whatever age we may be, what is said of the apostles in the text may apply to us also: after having witnessed, as it were, Christ's resurrection, we go away to our own homes. Let us first take that part of the text which is common to us all, though not in the same degree--the having been witnesses of Christ's resurrection. John and Peter found him not in the sepulchre; they found the linen clothes and the napkin lying there, but he was gone. And upon this, as John assures us, both for himself and his companion, "they believed." They believed, we should observe, when as yet they had no more seen Jesus himself after his resurrection, than we Lave now. They only knew that he had been dead, and that he was not in the sepulchre. And this we know also; we have not seen him, indeed, since his resurrection: but we are sure he is not in the sepulchre. We are sure that the malice of his enemies did not do its work: we are sure, for we are ourselves witnesses of it, that that name, and that word, which they hoped would have been destroyed for ever, like the names of many, not only of false prophets and deceivers, but even of good men and of wise, have not perished, but have brought forth fruit more abundantly, from the very cause that was intended to put them out. Christ's gospel, assuredly, is a living thing, full of vigour and full of power; it has worked mightily for good, and is working; it is so full of blessing, it tends so largely towards the happiness that is enjoyed upon earth, that we are quite sure it is not lying still buried in Christ's sepulchre.

They (the two disciples) then went away believing, because they found that he was not in the sepulchre. But Mary Magdalene came and told them, that she had seen him risen, and had heard his voice with her ears. What she told Peter and John, Peter and John are now telling to us. They tell us that they have heard him, have seen him with their eyes, have looked upon him, yea, that their hands have handled him. They tell us even more than Mary Magdalene told them; for she had not been allowed to touch him. We may well trust their testimony, as they trusted hers, being quite ready indeed to believe that he was alive, because they had found that he was not amongst the dead. And so we, finding that he is not amongst the dead, seeing and knowing the fruits of his gospel, the living and ever increasing fruits of it, may well believe that its author is risen, and that the pains of death were loosed from off him, because it was not possible that he should be holden by them.

In this way, we, like the two disciples, may be all said to be witnesses of Christ's resurrection. May it not be said still more of those amongst us who assembled this morning round Christ's table, to keep alive the memory of his death; when we partook of that bread, and drank of that cup, of which so many thousands and millions, in every age and in every land, have eaten and drunken, all receiving them, with nearly the same words,--the body that was given for us, the blood that was shed for us,--all, making allowances for human weakness, finding in that communion the peace and the strength of God; all alike receiving it with penitent hearts, and with faith, and purposes of good for the time to come? Did we not then witness that Christ is not perished? that he has been ever, and still is, mighty to save? That command given to twelve persons, in an obscure chamber in Jerusalem, by one who, the next day, was to die as a malefactor, has been, and is obeyed from one end of the world to another; and wherever it has been obeyed, there, in proportion to the sincerity of the obedience, has been the fulness of the blessing.

But this is now past, as with the two disciples, and we are going again to our own homes. There, neither the empty sepulchre nor the risen Saviour are present before us, but common scenes and familiar occupations, which, in themselves have nothing in them of Christ. So it must be; we cannot be always within these walls; we cannot always be engaged in public prayer; we cannot always be hearing Christ's word, nor partaking of his communion; we must be going about our several works, and must be busied in them; some of us in preparation for other work to come, others to go on till the end of their lives with this only. May we not hope that Christ, and Christ's Spirit, will visit us the while in these our daily callings, as he came to his disciples Peter and John, when following their business as fishers on the lake of Gennesareth?

How can we get him to visit us? There is one answer--by prayer and by watchfulness. By prayer, whether we are in our preparatory state, or our fixed one; by prayer, and I think I may add, by praying in our own words. Of course, when we pray together, some of us must join in the words of others; and it makes little difference, whether those words be spoken or read. But when we pray alone, some, perhaps, may still use none but prayers made by others, especially the Lord's prayer. We should remember, however, that the Lord's prayer was given for this very purpose, to teach us how to pray for ourselves. But it does not do this, if we use it alone, and still more, if we use it without understanding it. If we do understand it, and study it, it will indeed teach us to pray; it will show us what we most need in prayer, and what are our greatest evils; but surely it may be said, that no man ever learnt this lesson well without wishing to practise it; no man ever used the Lord's prayer with understanding and with earnestness, without adding to it others of his own. And this is not a trifling matter. We know the difficulty of attending in prayer; and if we use the words of others only, which we must, therefore, repeat from memory, it is perfectly possible to say them over without really joining with them in our minds: we may say them over to ourselves, and be actually thinking of other things the while. And the same thing holds good, of course, even with prayers that we have made ourselves, if we accustom ourselves to repeat them without alteration; they then become, in fact, the work of another than our actual mind, and may be repeated by memory alone. Therefore, it seems to be of consequence to vary the words, and even the matter of our private prayers, that so we may not deceive ourselves, by repeating merely, when we fancy that we are praying. Ten words actually made by ourselves at the moment, and not remembered, are a real prayer; for it is not hypocrisy that is the most common danger; our temper, when we are on our knees, is apt indeed to be careless, but not, I hope and believe, deceitful. This, of course, must be well known to a very large proportion of us; but, perhaps, there are some to whom it may be useful; some to whom the advice may not yet have suggested itself, that they should make their own prayers, in part, at least, whenever they kneel down to their private devotions.

And this sort of prayer, with God's blessing, is likely to make us watchful. We rise in the morning: we say some prayers of our own; we hear others read to us; and yet it is possible that we may not have really prayed ourselves in either case; we may not have brought ourselves truly into the presence of God. Hence our true condition, with all its dangers, has not been brought before our minds; the need of watchfulness has not been shown to us. But with real prayer of our own hearts' making it is different; God is then present to us, and sin and righteousness: our dream of carelessness is, for a moment at least, broken. No doubt it is but too easy to dream again; yet still an opportunity of exerting ourselves to keep awake is given us; we are roused to consciousness of our situation; and that, at any rate, renders exertion possible. There is no doubt that souls are most commonly lost by this continued dreaming, till at length, when seemingly awake (they are not so really), they are like men who answer to the call that would arouse them, but they answer, in fact, unconsciously. We cannot tell for ourselves or others any way by which our souls shall certainly be saved, in spite of carelessness; or any way by which, carelessness shall be overcome necessarily; all that can be done is, to point out how it may be overcome, by what means the soul may be helped in its endeavours; not how those endeavours and holy desires may be rendered needless.

Thus, then, we may gain Christ to visit us at our own homes and in our common callings, when we are returned to them. And that difference which I spoke of as existing between us, that some of us are waiting for Christ's call to a higher field of action, while others are engaged in that sort of duty which will last their lives, I know not that this-- though it be often important, and though I am often obliged to dwell on it--need enter into our considerations to-day. Rather, perhaps, may we overlook this difference, and feel that all of us here assembled--those in their state of earliest preparation for after duties; those to whom that earliest state is passed away, and who are entered into another state, in part preparatory, in part partaking of the character of actual life; and those also whose preparation, speaking of earth, only, is completed altogether, who must be doing, and whose time even of doing is far advanced--that all of us have in truth one great call yet before us: and that, with respect to that, we are all, as it were, preparing still. And for that great call, common to all of us, we need all the same common readiness; and that readiness will be effected in us only by the same means,--if now, before it come, Christ and Christ's Spirit shall, in our homes and daily callings, be persuaded to visit us.

LECTURE XXVI.

WHITSUNDAY.

94

Have you received the Holy Ghost since ye believed?

It appears, by what follows these words, that the question here related especially to those gifts of the Holy Ghost which were given, in the first age of the church, as a sign of God's power, and a witness that the work of the gospel was from God. Yet although this be so, and therefore the words, in this particular sense, cannot to any good purpose be asked now; yet there is another sense, and that not a lower but a far higher one, in which we may ask them, and in which it concerns us in the highest degree, what sort of answer we can give to them, I say, "what sort of answer;" for I think it is true of all Christians that, in a certain measure, they have received the Holy Ghost. Not only does the doctrine of our own, and I believe every other, church, concerning baptism, show this: but it seems also necessarily to follow, from those words of St. Paul, that "No man can say that Jesus is the Lord but by the Holy Ghost." And yet the Scripture and common experience alike show us, that a man may call Jesus Lord, and yet not be really his, nor one who will be owned by Him at the last day. So that what is of real importance to us is, the degree of fulness and force with which we could give the answer to the words of the text; not simply saying that we have received the Holy Ghost, which would be true, but might be far from sufficient; but saying that we have received Him and are receiving Him more and more, so that our hearts and lives are showing the impression of his heavenly seal daily more and more clearly and completely.

And this must really have been the answer which it concerned every Christian to be able to make; although it has been in various instances, and by very opposite parties, tried to be evaded. It is evaded alike by those who set too highly the grace given in baptism, and by those who, setting this too low, direct our attention to another point in a man's life, which they call his justification or conversion. For both alike would give an exaggerated importance to one particular moment of our lives, and to the grace then given. Now, the importance of particular moments in men's lives differs exceedingly in different persons; but yet in all may be exaggerated. I suppose that if ever in any man's life a particular point was of immense importance, it was the point of his conversion in the case of St. Paul. There were here united all that grace which according to one view accompanies baptism especially, and all which according to the other view accompanies conversion and justification. Here was a point which separated St. Paul's later life from his earlier with a broader line of separation than can possibly be the case in general. There can be no doubt that he, if ever man did, received at that particular time the Holy Ghost. But if, ten or twenty years afterwards, St. Paul had been asked concerning what the Holy Ghost had done for him, he would not certainly have confined himself in his answer to the grace once given him at his conversion and baptism, but would have spoken of that which he had been receiving since every hour and every day, carrying forward and completing that work of God which had been begun at the time of his journey to Damascus. And as he had received more and more grace, so was his confidence in his acceptance with God at the last day more and more assured. For he writes to the Corinthians, many years after his conversion and baptism, that he kept under his body, and was bringing it into subjection, lest that by any means, after having preached to others, he should be himself a castaway. And some years later still, though he does not use so strong an expression as that of becoming a castaway, yet he still says, even when writing to the Philippians from Rome, that he counted not himself to have apprehended, nor to have attained his object fully; but forgetting what was behind, even the grace of his conversion and baptism, he pressed on to the things which were before, even that continued and increasing grace which was required to bring him in safety to his heavenly crown. But if we go on some years yet farther, when his labours were ended, and the sure prospect of speedy death was before him; when the past grace was everything, and what he could expect yet to come was scarcely any other than that particular aid which we need in our struggle with the last enemy--death; then, his language is free from all uncertainty; then, in the full sense of the words, he could say that he had received the Holy Ghost, that his spirit had been fully born again for its eternal being, and that there only remained the raising up also of his mortal body, to complete that new creation of body and soul which Christ's Spirit works in Christ's redeemed. "I have fought the good fight, I have finished my course, I have kept the faith. Henceforth there is laid up for me my crown of righteousness, which the Lord, the righteous judge, will give me at that day."

It seems, then, that the great question which we should be anxious to be able to answer in the affirmative, is this, "*Are we receiving* the Holy Ghost since we believed?" "Since we believed," whether we choose to carry back the date of our first belief to the very time of our baptism, when grace was given to us,--we know not to what degree nor how,--yet given to us, as being then received into Christ's flock; or whether we go back only to that time when we can ourselves remember ourselves to have believed, and so can remember that God's grace was given to us. Have we been ever since, and are we still, receiving the Holy Ghost? O blessed above all blessedness, if we can say that this is true of us! O blessed with a blessedness most complete, if we only do not too entirely abandon ourselves to enjoy it! Elect of God; holy and beloved; justified and sanctified; there is nothing in all the world that could impair or destroy such happiness, except we ourselves, in evil hour, believed it to be out of the reach of danger.

But if the witness of memory and conscience be less favourable; if we can remember long seasons of our lives during which we were not receiving the Holy Ghost; long seasons of a cold and hard state, in which there was, as it were, neither rain nor dew, nor yet sun to ripen what had grown before; but all was so ungenial that no new thing grew; and what had grown was withering and almost dying; what shall be said, then, and how can the time be made up which was so wasted? But we remember, it may be, that this deadly season passed away: the rain fell once more, and the tender dew, and the quickening sun shone brightly: our spiritual growth began again, and is now going on healthily; we have not always been receiving the Holy Ghost since we believed, but we are receiving him now. How gracious, then, has God been to us, that he has again renewed us unto repentance; that he has shown that we have not, in the fullest sense, sinned against the Holy Ghost, seeing that the Holy Ghost still abides with us! we grieved him, and tried his long-suffering, but he has not abandoned us to our own evil hearts; we are receiving him who is the giver of life, and we still live.

But must not we speak of others? is not another case to be supposed possible? may there not be some who cannot say with truth that they are receiving the holy Ghost now? They received him once; we doubt it not; perhaps they were receiving him for some length of time; their early childhood was watched by Christian care; their youth and early manhood, when it received freshly things of this world, received also, with lively thankfulness, the grace of God; they can remember a time when they were growing in goodness; when they were being renewed after the image of God. But they can remember, also, that this time passed away; the grace of early childhood was put out by the temptations of boyhood; the grace of youth and opening manhood died away amid the hardness of this life's maturity. It is so, I believe, often; that boyhood, which is, as it were, ripened childhood, destroys the grace of our earliest years; that again, when youth offers us a second beginning of life, we are again impressed with good; but that ripened youth, which is manhood, brings with it again the reason of hardness, and again our spiritual growth, is destroyed. We can remember, I am supposing, that this fatal change did take place; but can we date it to any particular act, or month, or day, or hour? We can do so most rarely: in this respect the seed of death can even less be traced to its beginning than the seed of life. And yet there *was* a beginning, only we do not remember it. And why do we not remember it? Because the real beginning was in some act which seemed of so little consequence that it made no impression; in the altering some habit which we judged to be a mere trifle; in the indulging some temper which even at the time we hardly noticed. Some such little thing,--little in our view of it,--made the fatal turn; we received the grace of God less and less: we heeded not the change for a season; and when it was so marked that we could not but heed it, then we had ceased to regard it; and so it was that the spring of our life was dried up: and it is of no more avail to our present and future state, that we once received grace, than the rain of last winter will be sufficient to ripen the summer's harvest, if from this time forward we have nothing but drought and cold.

Some few, again, there may be, who, within their own recollection, could not say that they have received the Holy Ghost: persons who have lived among careless friends, to whom the way of life has never been steadily pointed out; while the way of death, with all its manifold paths, meeting at last in one, has been continually before them. Shall we say that these, because they have been baptized, are therefore guilty of having rejected grace given? that this sin is aggravated, because a mercy was offered them once of which they were unconscious? We would not say this; but we would say that it is impossible but that they must have received the Holy Ghost within their memory; it is impossible but that conscience must have sometimes spoken, and that they must have sometimes been enabled to obey it; it is impossible but that they must have had some notions of sin, and some desires to struggle against it; and so far as they ever felt that desire, it was the work of God's Holy Spirit. Man cannot dare to say how great the amount of their guilt may be; but guilt there certainly is; they have grieved the Holy Spirit; and, though we dare not say that they have utterly blasphemed him, yet they have a long hardness to overcome, and every hour of delayed turning to God increases it: it may be possible still to overcome it, but meanwhile it is not overcome; they are not receiving the Holy Spirit; they are not being renewed into the likeness of Christ, without which no man can see God.

Here, then, are the four cases, one of which must belong to every one of us here assembled. Either we have been always and still are receiving the Holy Ghost; or we can remember when we were not, but yet are receiving him now; or we can remember when we were, but yet now are not; or we cannot remember to have received him ever, nor are we yet receiving him. I cannot say which of the last two states is the most dreadful, nor scarcely which of the first two states is the most blessed. But yet as even those happy states admit not of over-confidence, so neither do the last two most unhappy states oblige us to despair. Not to despair; but they do urge us to every degree of fear less than despair. There is far more danger of our not fearing enough than of our being driven to despair. There is far more danger of your looking on the season of youth, of our looking on to old age; you trusting to the second freshness and tenderness of the first,--we to the calmness and necessary reflection of the last. There is far more danger of our thus hardening ourselves beyond recall; there is not only the danger, but there is the sin, the greatest sin, I suppose, of which the human mind is capable, that of deliberately choosing evil for the present rather than good, calculating that, by and by, we shall choose good rather than evil. I believe, that it is impossible to conceive of any state of mind more sinful than one which should so feel and so choose; and this is the state which we incur, and which we persist in whenever we put off the thought of repentance. Now, then, it only remains, that we apply this each to ourselves; I say all of us apply it, the young and the old alike; for there is not one here so young as not to have cause to apply it; there is not one of us who would not, I am sure, be a different person from what he now is, if he were to ask himself steadily every day, Have I been and am I receiving the Holy Ghost since I believed?

LECTURE XXVII.

TRINITY SUNDAY.

JOHN iii. 9.

How can these things be?

97

This is the second question put by Nicodemus to our Lord with regard to the truths which Jesus was declaring to him. The first was, "How can a man be born when he is old?" which was said upon our Lord's telling him that, "Except a man be born again, he cannot see the kingdom of God." Now, it will be observed, that these two questions are treated by our Lord in a different manner: to the first he, in fact, gives an answer; that is, he removes by his answer that difficulty in Nicodemus's mind which led to the question; but to the second he gives no answer, and leaves Nicodemus--and with Nicodemus, us all also--exactly in the same ignorance as he found him at the beginning.

Now, is there any difference in the nature of these two questions, which led our Lord to treat them so differently? We might suppose beforehand that there would be; and when we come to examine them, so we shall find it. The difficulty in the first question rendered true faith impossible, and, therefore, our Lord removed it; the difficulty in the second question did not properly interfere with faith at all, but might, through man's fault, be a temptation to him to refuse to believe. And as this, like other temptations, must be overcome by us, and not taken away from our path before we encounter it, so our Lord did not think proper to remove it or to lessen it.

We must now unfold this difference more clearly. When Christ said, "Except a man be born again, he cannot see the kingdom of God," Nicodemus could not possibly believe what our Lord said, because he did not understand his meaning. He did not know what he meant by "a man's being born again," and, therefore, he could not believe, as he did not know what he was to believe. Words which we do not understand, are like words spoken in an unknown language; we can neither believe them nor disbelieve them, because we do not know what they say. For instance, I repeat these words, [Greek: tous pantas haemas phanerothaenai dei emprosaen tou baematos tou Christou.] Now, if I were to ask, Do you believe these words? is it not manifest that all of you who know Greek enough, to understand them may also believe them; but of those who do not know Greek, not a single person can yet believe them? They are as yet words spoken as to the air. But when I add, that these words mean, "We must all stand before the judgment-seat of Christ;" now we can all believe them because we can all understand them.

It is, then, perfectly impossible for any man to believe a statement except in proportion as he understands its meaning. And, therefore, our Lord explained what he meant to Nicodemus, and told him that, by being born again, he did not mean the natural birth of the body; but a birth caused by the Spirit, and therefore itself a birth of a spirit: for, as that which is born from a body is itself also a body, so that which is born of a spirit is itself also a spirit. So that Christ's words now are seen to have this meaning,--No man can enter into the kingdom of God except God's Spirit creates in him a spirit or mind like unto himself, and like unto Christ, and like unto the Father. Nicodemus, then, could now understand what was meant, and might have believed it. But he asks rather another question, "How can these things be?" How can God's Spirit create within me a spirit like himself, while I continue a man as before? Many persons since have asked similar questions; but to none of them is an answer given. How God's Spirit works within us I cannot tell; but if we take the appointed means of procuring his aid, we shall surely find that he has worked and does work in us to life eternal.

We must, then, in order to believe, understand what it is that is told us; but it is by no means necessary that we should understand how it is to happen. It is not necessary, and in a thousand instances we do not know. "If we take poison, we shall die:" there is a statement which we can understand, and therefore believe. But do we understand how it is that poison kills us? Does every one here know how poisons act upon the human frame, and what is the different operation of different poisons,--how laudanum kills, for instance, and how arsenic? Surely there are very few of us, at most, who do understand this: and yet would it not be exceedingly unreasonable to refuse to believe that poison will kill us, because we do not understand the manner *how*?

Thus far, I think, the question is perfectly plain, so soon as it is once laid before us. But the real point of perplexity is to be found a step further. In almost all propositions there is something about the terms which we do understand, and something which we do not. For instance, let me say these few words:--"A frigate was lost amidst the breakers." These words would be understood in a certain degree, by all who hear me: and so far as all understand them, all can believe them. All would understand that a ship had sunk in the water, or been dashed to pieces; that it would be useful no more for the purposes for which it had been made. But what is meant by the words "frigate" and "breakers" all would not understand, and many would understand very differently: that is to say, those who had happened to have known most about the sea and sea affairs would understand most about them, while those who knew less would understand less; but probably none of us would understand their meaning so fully, or would have so distinct and lively an image of the things, as would be enjoyed by an actual seaman; and even amongst seamen themselves, there would again be different degrees of understanding, according to their different degrees of experience, or knowledge of ships, or powers of mind.

I have taken the instance at random, and any other proposition might have served my purpose as well. But men do not speak to one another at random; when they say anything to their neighbour, they mean it to produce on his mind a certain effect. Suppose that we were living near the sea-coast, and any one were suddenly to come in, and to utter the words which I have taken as my example: should we not know that what the man meant by these words was, that there was a danger at hand for which our help was needed? It matters not that we have no distinct ideas of the terms "frigate" or "breakers;" we understand enough for our belief and practice, and we should hasten to the sea-shore accordingly. Or suppose that the same words were told us of a frigate in which we had some near relation: should we not see at once that what we were meant to understand and to believe in the words was, that we had lost a relation? That is the truth with which we are concerned; and this we can understand and feel, although we may be able to understand nothing more of the words in which that truth is conveyed to us. Now, in like manner, in whatever God says to us there is a purpose: it is intended to produce on our minds a certain impression, and so far it must be understood. But when God speaks to us of heavenly things, the terms employed can only be understood in part, and so far as God's purpose with regard to our minds reaches; but there must be a great deal in them which we can no more understand than one who had never seen a ship, or a picture of one, could understand the word "frigate." Our business is to consider what impression or what actions the words are intended to produce in us. Up to this point we can and must understand them: beyond this they may be wholly above the reach of our faculties, and we can form of them no ideas at all.

It is clear that this will be the case most especially whenever God reveals to us anything concerning himself. Take these few words, for example, "God is a spirit;" take them as a mere abstract truth, and how little can we understand about them! Who will dare to say that he understands all that is contained in the words "God" and "spirit?" We might weary ourselves for ever in attempting so to search out either. But God said these words to us: and the point is, What impression did he mean them to have upon us? how far can we understand them? This he has not by any means left doubtful, for it follows immediately, "They who worship him should worship Him in spirit and in truth." For this end the words were spoken, and thus far they are clear to us. God lives not on Mount Gerizim or at Jerusalem: but in every place he hears the prayers of the sincere and contrite heart, in no place will he regard the offerings of the proud and evil.

Or again, "God so loved the world that he gave his only-begotten Son, to the end that all who believe in him should not perish, but have eternal life." Here are words in themselves, as abstract truths, perfectly overwhelming; "God," "God's only-begotten Son," "Eternity." Who shall understand these things, when it is said, that "none knoweth the Son, save the Father; that none knoweth the Father, save the Son?" But did God tell us the words for nothing? can we understand nothing from them? believe nothing? feel nothing? Nay, they were spoken that we might both understand, and believe, and feel. How must He love us, who gives for us his only-begotten Son! how surely may we believe in Him who is an only-begotten Son to his Father,--so equal in nature, so entire in union!--What must that happiness be, which reaches beyond our powers of counting! Would we go further?--then the veil is drawn before us; other truths there are, no doubt, contained in the words; truths which the angels might desire to look into; truths which even they may be unable to understand. But these are the secret things which belong unto our God; the things which are revealed they are what belong to us and to our children, that we may understand, and believe, and do them.

Again, "the Comforter, whom Christ will send unto us from the Father, even the Spirit of Truth, which proceedeth from the Father, he shall testify of Christ." What words are here! "The Spirit of Truth," "the Spirit proceeding from the Father;" the Spirit "whom Christ will send," and "send from the Father." Can any created being understand, to the full, such "heavenly things" as these? But would Christ have uttered to his disciples mere unintelligible words, which could tell them nothing, and excite in them no feeling but mere wonder? Not so; but the words told them that Christ was not to be lost to them after he had left them on earth; that every gift of God was his: that even that Spirit of God, in which is contained all the fulness of the Godhead, is the Spirit of Christ also; that that mighty power which should work in them so abundantly, was of no other or lower origin than God himself; as entirely God, as the spirit of man is man. But can we therefore understand the Spirit of God, or conceive of him? How should we, when we cannot understand our own? This, and this only, we understand and believe, that without him our spirits cannot be quickened; that unless we pray daily for his aid, and listen to his calls within us, our spirit will never be created after his image, and we cannot enter into the kingdom of God.

It is thus, and thus only, that the revelations of God's word are beyond our understandings: that in them, beings and things are spoken of, which, taken generally, and in themselves, we should in vain endeavour to comprehend. But what God means us to know, or feel, or do, respecting them, that we can understand; and beyond this we have no concern. It is, in fact, a contradiction to speak of revealing what is unintelligible; for so far as it is a revealed truth it is intelligible; so far as it is unintelligible, it is not revealed. But though a thing revealed must be intelligible in itself, yet it by no means follows that we can understand *how* it happens. When we are told that the dead shall rise again, we can understand quite well what is meant; that we beings who feel happiness and misery, shall feel them again, either the one or the other, after we seemingly have done with them for ever in the grave. But "How are the dead raised up, and with what body do they come?" are questions to which, whether asked scoffingly or sincerely, we can give no answers; here our understanding fails, and here the truth is not revealed to us.

How, then, has Christianity no mysteries? In one sense, blessed be God for it, it has many. Using mysteries in St. Paul's sense of great revelations of things which were and must be unknown to all, except God had revealed them: then, indeed, they are many; the pillar and ground of truth, great without controversy, and full of salvation. But take mysteries in our more common sense of the word,--as things which are revealed to none, and can be understood by none,--then it is true that Christianity leaves many such in existence; that many such she has done away; that none has she created. She leaves many mysteries with respect to God, and with respect to ourselves; God is still incomprehensible; life and death have many things in them beyond our questioning; we may still look around us, above us, and within us, and wonder, and be ignorant. But if she still leaves the veil drawn over much in heaven and in earth, yet from how much has she removed it! Life and death are still in many respects dark; but she has brought to light immortality. God is still in himself incomprehensible; but all his glory, and all his perfections, are revealed to us in his only-begotten Son Christ Jesus. God's Spirit who can search out in his own proper essence? yet Christianity has taught us how we may have him to dwell with us for ever, and taste the fulness of his blessings. Yea, thanks be to God for the great Christian mystery which we this day celebrate; that he has revealed himself to us as our Saviour and our Comforter; that he has revealed to us his infinite love, in that he has given us his only-begotten Son to die for us, and his own Eternal Spirit to make our hearts his temple.

LECTURE XXVIII.

EXODUS iii. 6.

And Moses hid his face, for he was afraid to look upon God.

LUKE xxiii. 30.

Then shall they begin to say to the mountains.
Fall on us; and to the hills, Cover us.

These two passages occur, the one in the first lesson of this morning's service, the other in the second. One or other of them must have been, or must be, the case of you, of me, of every soul of man that lives or has lived since the world began. There must be a time in the existence of every human being when he will fear God. But the great, the infinite difference is, whether we fear him at the beginning of our relations to him, or at the end.

The fear of Moses was felt at the beginning of his knowledge of God. When God revealed himself to him at the bush, it was, so far as we are told, the first time that Moses learnt to know him. The fear of those who say to the mountains, "Fall on us," is felt at the very end of their knowledge of God; for to those who are punished with everlasting destruction from the presence of the Lord, God is not. So that the two cases in the text are exact instances of the difference of which I spoke, in the most extreme degree. Moses, the greatest of the prophets, fears God at first; those who are cast into hell, fear him at last.

The appearance of God, as described in this passage of Scripture, is an image also of his dealings with us at the beginning of our course, when we fear him with a saving fear. "The bush burned with fire, but the bush was not consumed." God shows his terrors, but he does not, as yet, destroy with them. It is the very opposite to this at last, for then he is expressly said to be a consuming fire.

Moses turned aside to see this great sight, why the bush was not burnt. That sight is the very same which the world has been offering for so many hundreds of years: God's terrors are around it, but, as yet, it is not consumed, because he wills that we should fear him before it is too late.

There is, indeed, this great difference;--that the signs of God's presence do not now force themselves upon our eyes; so that we may, if we choose, walk on our own way, without turning aside to see and observe them. And thus we do not see God, and do not, therefore, hide our faces for fear of him, but go on, and feel no fear, till the time when we cannot help seeing him. And it may be, that this time will never come till our life, and with it our space of trial, is gone for ever.

Here, then, is our state, that God will manifest himself no more to us in such a way as that we cannot help seeing him. The burning bush will be no more given us as a sign; Christ will no more manifest himself unto the world. And yet, unless we do see him, unless we learn to fear him while he is yet an unconsuming fire, unless we know that he is near, and that the place whereon we stand is holy ground, we shall most certainly see him when he will be a consuming fire, and when we shall join in crying to the mountains, to fall on us, and to the hills, to cover us.

Every person who thinks at all, must, I am sure, be satisfied, that our great want, the great need of our condition, is this one thing--to realize to ourselves the presence of God. It is a want not at all peculiar to the young. Thoughtfulness, in one sense, is indeed likely to come with advancing years: we are more apt to think at forty than at fifteen; but it by no

101

means follows that we are more apt to think about God. In this matter we are nearly at a level at all times of our life: it is with all of us our one great want, to bring the idea of God, with a living and abiding power, home to our minds.

This is illustrated by a wish ascribed to a great and good man--Johnson, and which has been noticed with a sneer by unbelievers, a wish that he might see a spirit from the other world, to testify to him of the truth of the resurrection. This has been sneered at, as if it were a confession of the unsatisfactory nature of the evidence which we actually possess: but, in truth, it is a confession only of the weakness which clings to us all, that things unseen, which our reason only assures us to be real, are continually overpowered by things affecting our senses; and, therefore, it was a natural wish that sight might, in a manner, come to the aid of reason; that the eye might see, and the ear might hear, a form and words which belonged to another world. And this wish might arise (I do not say wisely, or that his deliberate judgment would sanction it, but it might arise) in the breast of a good man, and one who would be willing to lay down his life in proof of his belief in Christ's promises. It might arise, not because he felt any doubt, when his mind turned calmly to the subject; not because he was hesitating what should be the main principle of his life; but because his experience had told him, that there are many times in the life of man when the mind does not fully exert itself; when habit and impressions rule us, in a manner, in its stead. And when so many of our impressions must be earthly, and as our impressions colour our habits, is it not natural (I do not say wise, but is it not natural) to desire some one forcible unearthly impression, which might, on the other side, colour our habits, and so influence us at those times when the mind, almost by the necessity of our condition, cannot directly interpose its own deliberate decision as our authority?

No doubt the wish to which I have been alluding is not one which our reason would sanction; but it expresses in a very lively and striking manner a want which is most true and real, although it proposes an impossible remedy. But the question cannot but occur to us, Can it be that our heavenly Father, who knows whereof we are made, should have intended us to live wholly by faith in this world? That is, Can it have been his will that all visible signs of himself should be withdrawn from us; and that we should be left only with the record and the evidence of his mighty works done in our behalf in past times; and with that other evidence of his wisdom and power which is afforded by the wonders of his creation?

We look into the Scriptures and we learn that such was not his will. We were to live by faith, indeed, with, respect to the unseen world, there the sign given was to be for ever only the sign of Christ's resurrection. But yet it was not designed that the evidence of Christ's having redeemed us should be sought for only in the records of the past; he purposed that there should be a living record, a record that might speak to our senses as well as to our reason; that should continually present us with impressions of the reality of Christ's salvation; and so might work upon the habits of our life, as insensibly as the air we breathe. This living witness, which should last till Christ came again, was to be no other than his own body instinct with his own Spirit--his people, the temple of the Holy Ghost, his holy universal Church.

If we consider for a moment, this would entirely meet the want of which I have been speaking. It is possible, certainly, to look upon the face of nature without being reminded of God; yet it is surely true, that in the outward creation, in the order of the seasons, the laws of the heavenly bodies, the wonderful wisdom and goodness displayed in the constitution of every living thing in its order, there is a tendency at least to impress us with, the thought of God, if nothing else obstructed it. But there is a constant obstruction in the state of man. Looking at men, hearing them, considering them, it is not only possible not to be reminded of God; but their very tendency is to exclude him from our minds, because the moral workmanship which is so predominant in them has assuredly not had God for its author. We all in our dealings with one another, lead each other away from God. We present to each other's view what seems to be a complete world of our own, in which God is not. We see a beginning, a middle, and an end; we see faculties for acquiring knowledge, and for receiving enjoyment; and earth furnishes knowledge to the one and enjoyment to the other. We see desires, and we see the objects to which they are limited; we see that death removes men from all these objects, and consistently with this, we observe, that death is generally regarded as the greatest of all evils. Man's witness, then, as far as it goes, is against the reality of God and of eternity. His life, his language, his desires, his understanding appear, when we look over the world, to refer to no being higher than himself, to no other state of things than that of which sight testifies.

Now, Christ's Church, the living temple of the Holy Ghost, puts in the place of this natural and corrupt man, whose witness is against God, another sort of man, redeemed and regenerate, whose whole being breathes a perpetual witness of God. Consider, again, what we should see in such a Church. We should see a beginning, a middle, but the end is not yet visible; we should see, besides the faculties for knowledge and enjoyment which were receiving their gratification daily, other faculties of both kinds, whose gratification was as yet withheld; we should see desires not limited to any object now visible or attainable. We should see death looked to as the gate by which these hitherto unobtained objects were to be sought for; and we should hear it spoken of, not as the greatest of evils, but as an event solemn, indeed, and painful to nature, but full of blessing and of happiness. We should see love, joy, peace, long-suffering, gentleness, goodness, faith, meekness, temperance; a constitution of nature as manifestly proclaiming its author to be the God of all holiness and loving-kindness, as the wonderful structure of our eyes or hands declares them to be the work of the God of all wisdom and power. We should thus see in all our fellow-men, not only as much, but far more than in the constitution of the lower animals, or of the plants, or of the heavenly bodies, a witness of God and of eternity. Their whole lives would be a witness; their whole conversation would be a witness; their outward and more peculiar acts of worship would then bear their part in harmony with all the rest. Every day would the voices of the Church be heard in its services of prayer and thanksgiving; every day would its members renew their pledges of faithfulness to Christ, and to one another, upon partaking together the memorials of his sacrifice.

What could we desire more than such a living witness as this? What sign in the sky, what momentary appearance of a spirit from the unseen world, could so impress us with the reality of God, as this daily worshipping in his living temple; this daily sight, of more than the Shechinah of old, even of his most Holy Spirit, diffusing on every side light and blessing? And what is now become of this witness? can names, and forms, and ordinances, supply its place? can our unfrequent worship, our most seldom communion, impress on us an image of men living altogether in the presence of God, and in communion with Christ? But before we dwell on this, we may, while considering the design of the true Church of Christ, well understand how such excellent things should be spoken of it, and how it should have been introduced into the Creed itself, following immediately after the mention of the Holy Ghost. That holy universal Church was to be the abiding witness of Christ's love and of Christ's promises; not in its outward forms only, for they by themselves are not a living witness; they cannot meet our want--to have God and heavenly things made real to us; but in its whole spirit, by which renewed man was to bear as visibly the image of God, as corrupted man had lost it. This was the sure sign that Christ had appointed to abide until his coming again; this sign, as striking as the burning bush, would compel us to observe; would make us sure that the place whereon we stand is holy ground.

Then follows the question: With this sign lost in its most essential points, how can we supply its place? and how can we best avail ourselves of those parts of it which still remain? and how can we each endeavour to build up a partial and most imperfect imitation of it, which may yet, in some sort, serve to supply our great want, and remind us daily of God? This opens a wide field for thought, to those who are willing to follow it; but much of it belongs to other occasions rather than this: the practical part of it,--the means of most imperfectly supplying the want of God's own appointed sign, a true and living universal Church, shall be the subject of my next Lecture.

LECTURE XXIX.

PSALM cxxxvii. 4.

How shall we sing the Lord's song in a strange land?

This was said by the exiles of Jerusalem, when they were in the land of their captivity in Babylon. There is no reason to suppose that their condition was one of bondage, as it had been in Egypt: the nations removed by conquest, under the Persian kings, from their own country to another land, were no otherwise ill-treated; they had new homes given them in which they lived unmolested; only they were torn away from their own land, and were as sojourners in a land of strangers. But the peculiar evil of this state was, that they were torn away from the proper seat of their worship. The Jew in Babylon might have his own home, and his own land to cultivate, as he had in Judæa; but nothing could replace to him the loss of the temple at Jerusalem: there alone could the morning and evening sacrifices be offered; there alone could the sin-offering for the people be duly made. Banished from the temple, therefore, he was deprived also of the most solemn part of his religion; he was, as it were, exiled from God; and the worship of God, as it was now left to him,--that is, the offering up of prayers and praises,--was almost painful to him, as it reminded him so forcibly of his changed condition.

Such also, in some respects, was to be the state of the Christian Church after our Lord's ascension. The only acceptable sacrifice was now that of their great High Priest interceding for them in the presence of the Father: heaven was their temple, and they were far removed from it upon earth: they, too, like the Jews in Babylon, were a little society by themselves living in the midst of strangers. "Our citizenship," says St. Paul to the Philippians, "is in heaven:" here they were not citizens, but sojourners. Why, then, should not the early Christians have joined altogether in the feeling of the Jews at Babylon? why should not they, too, have felt and said, "How can we sing the Lord's song in a strange land?"

The answer is contained in what I said last Sunday; because Christ had not left them comfortless or forsaken, but was come again to them by his Holy Spirit; because God was dwelling in the midst of them; because they were not exiles from the temple of God, but were themselves become God's temple; because through the virtue of the one offering for sin once made, but for ever presented before God by their High Priest in heaven, they, in God's temple on earth, were presenting also their daily and acceptable sacrifice, the sacrifice of themselves; because also, though as yet they were a small society in a land of strangers, yet the stone formed without hands was to become a mighty mountain, and cover the whole earth: what was now the land of strangers was to become theirs; the whole earth should be full of the knowledge of the Lord; the kingdoms of the world were to become his kingdom; and thus earth, redeemed from the curse of sin, was again to be so blessed that God's servants living upon it should find it no place of exile.

But if this, in its reality, does not now exist; if, although God's temple be on earth, the appointed sacrifice in it is not offered, the living sacrifice of ourselves; if the society has, by spreading, become weak, and the kingdoms of the earth are Christ's kingdoms in name alone; are we, then, come back once more to the condition of the Jews in Babylon? are we exiles from God, living amongst strangers? and must we, too, say, with the prophet, "How can we sing the Lord's song in a strange land?"

This was the question which I proposed to answer: What can we do to make our condition unlike that of exiles from God: to restore that true sign of his presence amongst us, the living fire of his Holy Spirit pervading every part of his temple? I mean, what can we do as individuals? for the question in any other sense is not to be asked or answered here. But we, each of us, must have felt, at some time or other, our distance from God. Put the idea in what form or what words we will, we must--every one of us who has ever thought seriously at all--we must regret that there is not a stronger and more abiding influence over us, to keep us from evil, and to turn us to good.

Now, the vestiges of Christ's church left among us are chiefly these: our prayers together, whether in our families or in this place; our reading of the Scriptures together; our communion, rare as it is, in the memorials of the body and blood of Christ our Saviour. These are the vestiges of that which was designed to be with us always, and in every part of our lives, the holy temple of God, his living church; but which now presents itself to us only at particular times, and places, and actions; in our worship and in our joint reading of the Scriptures, and in our communion.

It will be understood at once why I have not spoken here of prayer and reading the Scriptures by ourselves alone. Most necessary as these are to us, yet they do not belong to the helps ministered to us by the church; they belong to us each as individuals, and in these respects we must be in the same state everywhere: these were enjoyed by the Jews even in their exile in Babylon. But the church acts upon us through one another, and therefore the vestiges of the church can only be sought for in what we do, not alone, but together. I, therefore, noticed only that prayer, and that reading of the Scriptures, in which many of us took part in common.

Such common prayer takes place amongst us every morning and evening, as well as on Sundays within these walls. Whenever we meet on those occasions, we meet as Christ's church. Now, conceive how the effect of such meeting depends on the conduct of each of us. It is not necessary to notice behaviour openly profane and disorderly: this does not occur amongst us. We see, however, that if it did occur in any meeting for the purposes of religious worship, such a meeting would do us harm rather than good: its witness to us would not be in favour of God, but against him. But take another case: when we are assembled for prayers, suppose our behaviour, without being disorderly, was yet so manifestly indifferent as to be really indecent; that is, suppose every countenance showed such manifest signs of weariness, and impatience, and want of interest in what was going forward, that it was evident there was no general sympathy with any feeling of devotion. Would not the effect here also be injurious? would not such a meeting also shock and check our approaches towards God? would it not rather convince us that God was really far distant from us, instead of showing that he was in the midst of us?

Ascend one step higher. Our behaviour is neither disorderly, nor manifestly indifferent: it is decent, serious, respectful. What is the effect in this case? Not absolutely unfavourable certainly; but yet far from being much help towards good. We bear our witness that we are engaged in a matter that should be treated with reverence: this is very right; but do we more than this? Do we show that we are engaged in a matter that commands our interest also, as well as our respect? If not, our witness is not the witness of Christ's church: it does not go to declare that God is in us of a truth.

Let us go on one step more. We meet together to pray: we are orderly, we are quiet, we are serious; but the countenance shows that we are something more than these. There is on it the expression, never to be mistaken, of real interest. Remember I am speaking of meetings for prayer, where the words are perfectly familiar to us, and where the interest therefore cannot be the mere interest of novelty. Say, then, that our countenances express interest: I do not mean strong and excited feeling; but interest, which may be very real yet very quiet also. We look as if we thought of what we were engaged in, of what we are ourselves, and of what God is to us. We are joined in one common feeling of thankfulness to him for mercies past, of wishing for his help and love for the time to come. Now, think what would be the effect of such a meeting. Would it not be, clearly, positively good! Would not every individual's earnestness be confirmed by the manifest earnestness of others? Would not his own sense of God's reality be rendered stronger, by seeing that others felt it just as he did? Then, here would be the church of God rendering her appointed witness: she would be giving her sure sign that God is not far from any one of us.

Now, then, observe what we may lose or gain by our different behaviour, whenever we meet together in prayer; what we lose, nay, what positive mischief we do, by any visible impatience or indifference; what we should gain by really joining in our hearts in the meaning of what was uttered. It is a solemn thing for the consciences of us all; but surely it must be true, that, whenever we are careless or indifferent in our public prayers, we are actually injuring our neighbours, and are, so far as in us lies, destroying the witness which the church of Christ should render to the truth of God her Saviour.

I do not know that there is anything more impressive than the sight of a congregation evidently in earnest in the service in which they are engaged. We then feel how different is our own lonely prayer from the united voice of many hearts; each cheering, strengthening, enkindling the other. We then consider one another to provoke unto love and good works. How different are the feelings with which we regard a number of persons met for any common purpose, and the same persons engaged together in serious prayer or praise! Then Christ seems to appear to us in each of them; we are all one in him. How little do all earthly unkindnesses, dislikes, prejudices, become in our eyes, when the real bond of our common faith is discerned clearly! There is indeed neither Greek nor Jew, circumcision nor uncircumcision, Barbarian, Scythian, bond nor free, but Christ is all, and in all. And to look at our brethren, once or twice in every day, with these Christian eyes, would it not also, by degrees, impress us at other times, and begin to form something of our habitual temper and regard towards them?

Thus much of our meetings for prayer. One word only on those in which we meet to read the Scriptures. Here I know, that difference of age, and our peculiar relations to each other, make us very apt to lose the religious character of our readings of the Scriptures, and to regard them merely as lessons. No doubt, the object here is instruction; it is not so much in itself a religious exercise, as a means to enable you to perform religious exercises with understanding and sincerity. Still there is a peculiar character attached even to lessons, when they are taken out of the Scriptures: and the duty of attention and interest in the work becomes even stronger than under other circumstances. But with those of a more advanced age, I think there is more than this; I think it must be our own fault, if, whilst engaged together in reading the Scriptures, which we only read because we are Christians, we do not feel that there also we are employed on a duty belonging to the Church of Christ.

Lastly, there is our joint communion in the bread, and in the cup, of the Lord's Supper. Here there is seriousness; here there is always, I trust and believe, something of real interest; and, therefore, we never, I think, meet together at the Lord's table, without feeling a true effect of Christ's gifts to and in his Church; we are strengthened and brought nearer to one another, and to him. But this most precious pledge of Christ's Church we too often forfeit for ourselves. That we have lost so much of the help which the Church was designed to give, is not our fault individually; but it is our fault that we neglect this means of strength, so great in bearing witness to Christ, and in kindling love towards one another. What can be said of us, if, with so many helps lost, we throw away that which still remains? if, of the great treasure which the Church yet keeps, we are wilfully ignorant? How much good might we do, both to ourselves and to each other, by joining in that communion! How surely should we be strengthened in all that is good, and have a help from each other, through his Spirit working in us all, to struggle against our evil!

LECTURE XXX.

1 CORINTHIANS xi. 26.

For as often as ye eat this bread and drink this cup, ye do show the Lord's death till he come.

When I spoke last Sunday of the benefits yet to be derived from Christ's Church, I spoke of them, as being, for the most part, three in number--our communion in prayer, our communion in reading the Scriptures, and our communion in the Lord's Supper; and, after having spoken of the first two of these, I proposed to leave the third for our consideration to-day.

The words of the text are enough to show how closely this subject is connected with that event which we celebrate to-day[13]: "As often as ye eat this bread, and drink this cup, ye do show the Lord's death till he come." The communion, then, with one another in the Lord's Supper is doing that which this day was also designed to do; it is showing forth, or declaring, the Lord's death; it is declaring, in the face of all the world, that we partake of the Lord's Supper because we believe that Christ our Passover was sacrificed for us.

[13] Good Friday.

God might, no doubt, if it had so pleased him, have made all spiritual blessing come to us immediately from himself. Without ascending any higher with the idea, it is plain that Christianity might have been made a thing wholly between each individual man and Christ; all our worship might have been the secret worship of our own hearts; and in eating the bread, and drinking the cup, to show forth the Lord's death, each one of us might have done this singly, holding communion with Christ alone. I mean, that it is quite conceivable that we should have had Christianity, and a great number of Christians spread all over the world, but yet no Christian Church. But, although this is conceivable, and, in fact, is practically the case in some particular instances where individual Christians happen to be quite cut off from all other Christians,--as has been known sometimes in foreign and remote countries; and although, through various evil causes, it has become, in many respects, too much the case with us all; for our religion is with all of us, I am inclined to think, too much a matter between God and ourselves alone; yet still it is not the design of Christ that it should be so: his people were not only to be good men, redeemed from sin and death and brought to know and love the truth, in which relation Christianity would appear like a divine philosophy only, working not only upon individuals, but through their individual minds, and as individuals; but they were to be the Christian Church, helping one another in things pertaining to God, and making their mutual brotherhood to one another an essential part of what are called peculiarly their acts of religion. So that the Church of England seems to have well borne in mind this character of Christianity, namely, that it presents us not each, but all together, before God; and therefore it is ordered that even in very small parishes, where "there are not more than twenty persons in the parish of discretion to receive the communion, yet there shall be no communion, except four, or three at the least, out of these twenty communicate together with the priest." Nay, even in the Communion of the Sick, under circumstances which seem to make religion particularly an individual matter between Christ and our own single selves; when the expected approach of death seems to separate, in the most marked manner, according to human judgment, him who is going hence from his brethren still in the world; even then it is ordered that two other persons, at the least, shall communicate along with the sick man and the minister. Nor is this ever relaxed except in times of pestilence; when it is provided, that if no other person can be persuaded to join from their fear of infection, then, and then only upon special request of the diseased, the minister may alone communicate with them. So faithfully does our Church adhere to this true Christian notion, that at the Lord's Supper we are not to communicate with Christ alone, but with him in and together with our brethren; so that I was justified in regarding the Holy Communion as one of those helps and blessings which we still derive from the Christian Church--from Christ's mystical body.

It is the natural process of all false and corrupt religions, on the contrary, to destroy this notion of Christ's Church, and to lead away our thoughts from our brethren in matters of religion, and to fix them merely upon God as known to us through a priest. The great evil in this is, (if there is any one evil greater than another in a system so wholly made up of falsehood, and so leading to all wickedness; but, at any rate, one great evil of it is,) that whereas the greatest part of all our lives is engaged in our relations towards our brethren, that there lie most of our temptations to evil, as well as of our opportunities of good, if our brethren do not form an essential part of our religions views, it follows, and always has followed, that our behaviour and feelings towards them are guided by views and principles not religious; and that by this fatal separation of what God has joined together, our worship and religious services become superstitious, while our life and actions become worldly, in the bad sense of the term, low principled, and profane.

If this is not so clear when put into a general form, it will be plain enough when I show it in that particular example which we are concerned with here. Nowhere, I believe, is the temptation stronger to lose sight of one another in our religious exercises, and especially in our Communion. Our serious thoughts in turning to God, turn away almost instinctively from our companions about us. Practically, as far as the heart is concerned, we are a great deal too apt to go to the Lord's table each alone. But consider how much we lose by this. We are necessarily in constant relations with one another; some of those relations are formal, others are trivial; we connect each other every day with a great many thoughts, I do not say of unkindness, but yet of that indifferent character which is no hindrance to any unkindness when the temptation to it happens to arise. This must always be the case in life; business, neighbourhood, pleasure,--the occasions of most of our intercourse with one another,--have in them nothing solemn or softening: they have in themselves but little tendency to lead us to the love of one another. Now, if this be so in the world, it is even more so here; your intercourse with one another is much closer and more constant than what can exist in after life with any but the members of your own family; and yet the various relations which this intercourse has to do with, are even less serious and less softening than those of ordinary life in manhood. The kindliness of feeling which is awakened in after years between two men, by the remembrance of having been at school together, even without any particular acquaintance with each other, is a very different thing from the feeling of being at school with each other now. I do not wonder, then, that any one of you, when he resolves to come to the Holy Communion, should rather try to turn away his thoughts from his companions, and to think of himself alone as being concerned in what he is going to do. I do not wonder at it; but, then, neither do I wonder that, when the Communion is over, and thoughts of his companions must return, they receive little or no colour from his religious act so lately performed; that they are as indifferent as they were before, as little furnishing a security against neglect, or positive unkindness, or encouragement of others to evil. Depend upon it, unless your common life is made a part of your religion, your religion will never sanctify your common life.

Now consider, on the one hand, what might be the effect of going to the Holy Communion with a direct feeling that, in that Communion, we, though many, were all brought together in Christ Jesus. And first, I will speak of our thoughts of those who are partakers of the Communion with us, then of those who are not. When others are gone out, and we who are to communicate are left alone with each other, then, if we perceive that there are many of us, the first natural feeling is one of joy, that we are so many; that our party,--that only true and good party to which we may belong with all our hearts,--that our party,--that Christ's party, seems so considerable. Then there comes the thought, that we are all met together freely, willingly, not as a matter of form, to receive the pledges of Christ's love to us, to pledge ourselves to him in return. If we are serious, those around us may be supposed to be serious too; if we wish to have help from God to lead a holier life, they surely wish the same; if the thought of past sin is humbling us, the same shame is working in our brethren's bosoms; if we are secretly resolving, by God's grace, to serve him in earnest, the hearts around us are, no doubt, resolving the same. There is the consciousness, (when and where else can we enjoy it?) that we are in sympathy with all present; that, coloured merely by the lesser distinctions of individual character, one and the same current of feeling is working within us all. And, if feeling this of our sympathy with one another, how strongly is it heightened by the thought of what Christ has done for us all! We are all loving him, because he loved us all; we are going together to celebrate his death, because he died for us all; we are resolving all to serve him, because his Holy Spirit is given to us all, and we are all brought to drink of the same Spirit. Then let us boldly carry our thoughts a little forward to that time, only a short hour hence, when we shall again be meeting one another, in very different relations; even in those common indifferent relations of ordinary life which are connected so little with Christ. Is it impossible to think, that, although we shall meet without these walls in very different circumstances, yet that we have seen each other pledging ourselves to serve Christ together? if the recollection of this lives in us, why should it not live in our neighbour? If we are labouring to keep alive our good resolutions made at Christ's table, why should we think that others have forgotten them? We do not talk of them openly, yet still they exist within us. May not our neighbour's silence also conceal within his breast the same good purposes? At any rate, we may and ought to regard him as ranged on our side in the great struggle of life; and if outward circumstances do not so bring us together as to allow of our openly declaring our sympathy, yet we may presume that it still exists; and this consciousness may communicate to the ordinary relations of life that very softness which they need, in order to make them Christian.

Again, with regard to those who go out, and do not approach to the Lord's table. With some it is owing to their youth; with others to a mistaken notion of their youth; with others to some less excusable reason, perhaps, but yet to such as cannot yet exclude kindness and hope. But having once felt what it is to be only with those who are met really as Christians, our sense of what it is to want this feeling is proportionably raised. Is it sad to us to think that our neighbour does not look upon us as fellow Christians? is it something cold to feel that he regards us only in those common worldly relations which leave men in heart so far asunder? Then let us take heed that we do not ourselves feel so towards him. We have learnt to judge more truly, to feel more justly, of our relations to every one who bears Christ's name: if we forget this, we have no excuse; for we have been at Christ's table, and have been taught what Christians are to one another. And let our neighbour be ever so careless, yet we know that Christ cares for him; that his Spirit has not yet forsaken him, but is still striving with him. And if God vouchsafes so much to him, how can we look upon him as though he were no way connected with us? how can we be as careless of his welfare, as apt either to annoy him, or to lead him into evil, or to take no pains to rescue him from it, as if he were no more to us than the accidental inhabitant of the same place, who was going on his way as we may be on ours, neither having any concern with the other?

And, now, is it nothing to learn so to feel towards those around us; to have thus gained what will add kindness and interest to all our relations with others; and, in the case of many, will give an abiding sense of the truest sympathy, and consequently greater confidence and encouragement to ourselves? Be sure that this is not to profane the Lord's Supper, but to use it according to Christ's own ordinance. For though the thoughts of which I have been speaking, have, in one sense, man and not God for their object, yet as they do not begin in man but in Christ, and in his love to us all, so neither do they, properly speaking, rest in man as such, but convert him, as it were, into an image of Christ: so that their end, as well as their beginning, is with Him. I do earnestly desire that you would come to Christ's table, in order to learn a Christian's feelings towards one another. This is what you want every day; and the absence of which leads to more and worse faults than, perhaps, any other single cause. But, then, this Christian feeling towards one another, how is it to be gained but by a Christian feeling towards Christ? and where are we to learn brotherly love in all our common dealings, but from a grateful thought of that Divine love towards us all which is shown forth in the sacrament of the Lord's Supper; inasmuch as, so often as we eat that bread and drink that cup, we do show the Lord's death till He come.

LECTURE XXXI.

LUKE i. 3, 4.

It seemed good to me also, having had perfect understanding of all things from the very first, to write unto thee in order, most excellent Theophilus, that thou mightest know the certainty of those things wherein thou hast been instructed.

These words, from the preface to St. Luke's Gospel, contain in them one or two points on which it may be of use to dwell; and not least so at the present time, when they are more frequently brought under our notice than was the case a few years ago. On a subject which we never, or very rarely hear mentioned, it may be difficult to excite attention; and, as a general rule, there is little use in making the attempt. But when names and notions are very frequently brought to our ears, and in a degree to our minds, then it becomes important that we should comprehend the matter to which they relate clearly and correctly; and a previous interest respecting it may be supposed to exist, which make further explanation acceptable.

St. Luke tells Theophilus that it seemed good to him to write in order an account of our Lord's life and death, that Theophilus might know the certainty of those things in which he had been instructed; and this, as a general rule, might well describe one great use of the Scripture to each of us, as individual members of Christ's Church--it enables us to know the certainty of the things in which we have been instructed. We do not, in the first instance, get our knowledge of Christ from the Scriptures,--we, each of us, I mean as individuals,--but from the teaching of our parents first; then of our instructors, and from books fitted for the instruction of children; whether it be the Catechism of the Church, or books written by private persons, of which we know that there are many. But as our minds open, and our opportunities of judging for ourselves increase, then the Scripture presents itself to acquaint us with the certainty of what we had heard already; to show us the original and perfect truth, of which we have received impressions before, but such as were not original nor perfect; to confirm and enforce all that was good and true in our early teaching; and if it should so happen that it contained any thing of grave error mixed with truth, then to enable us to discover and reject it.

It is apparent, then, that the Scripture, to do this, must have an authority distinct from, and higher than, that of our early teaching; but yet it is no less true that it comes to us individually recommended, in the first instance, by the authority of our early teaching, and received by us, not for its own sake, but for the sake of those who put it into our hands. What child can, by possibility, go into the evidence which makes it reasonable to believe the Bible, and to reject the authority of the Koran? Our children believe the Bible for our sakes; they look at it with respect, because we tell them that it ought to be respected; they read it, and learn it, because we desire them; they acquire a habit of veneration for it long before they could give any other reason for venerating it than their parents' authority. And blessed be God that they do; for, as it has been well said, if we their parents do not endeavour to give our children habits of love and respect for what is good and true, Satan will give them habits of love for what is evil: for the child must receive impressions from without; and it is God's wisdom that he should receive these impressions from his parents, who have the strongest interest in his welfare, and who have besides that instinctive parental love which, more surely, as well as more purely, than any possible sense of interest, makes them earnestly desire their child's good.

But when our children are old enough to understand and to inquire, do we then content ourselves with saying that they must take our word for it; that the Bible is true because we tell them so? Where is the father who does not feel, first, that he himself is not fitted to be an infallible authority; and, secondly, that if he were, he should be thwarting the providence of God, who has willed not simply that we should believe with understanding. He gladly therefore observes the beginnings of a spirit of inquiry in his son's mind, knowing that it is not inconsistent with a belief in truth, but is a necessary step to that which alone in a man deserves the name of belief--a belief, namely, sanctioned by reason. With what pleasure does he point out to his son the grounds of his own faith! how gladly does he introduce him to the critical and historical evidence for the truth of the Scriptures, that he may complete the work which he had long since begun, and deliver over the faith which had been so long nursed under the shade of parental authority, to the care of his son's own conscience and reason!

We see clearly that our individual faith, although grounded in the first instance on parental authority, yet rests afterwards on wholly different grounds; namely, on the direct evidence in confirmation of it which is presented to our own minds. But with regard to those who are called the Fathers of the Church, it is contended sometimes that we do receive the Scriptures, in the end, upon their authority: and it is argued, that if their authority is sufficient for so great a thing as this, it must be sufficient for every thing else; that if, in short, we believe the Scriptures for their sake, then we ought also to believe other things which they may tell us, for their sake, even though they are not to be found in Scripture.

In the argument there is this great fault, that it misstates the question at the outset. The authority of the Fathers, as they are called, is never to any sound mind the only reason for believing in the Scriptures; I think it is by no means so much as the principle reason. It is one reason, amongst many; but not the strongest. And, in like manner, their authority in other points, if there were other and stronger reasons which confirmed it,--as in many cases there are,--is and ought to be respected. But, because we lay a certain stress upon it, it does not follow that we should do well to make it bear the whole weight of the building. Because we believe the Scriptures, partly on the authority of the Fathers, as they are called, but more for other reasons, does it follow that we should equally respect the authority of the Fathers when there are no other reasons in support of it, but many which make against it?

In truth, however, the internal evidence in favour of the authenticity and genuineness of the Scriptures is that on which the mind can rest with far greater satisfaction than on any external testimonies, however valuable. On one point, which might seem most to require other evidence--the age, namely, and origin of the writings of the New Testament--it has been wonderfully ordered that the books, generally speaking, are their own witness. I mean that their peculiar language proves them to have been written by persons such as the apostles were, and such as the Christian writers immediately following them were not; persons, namely, whose original language and habits of thinking were those of Jews, and to whom the Greek in which they wrote was, in its language and associations, essentially foreign. I do not dwell on the many other points of internal evidence: it is sufficient to say that those who are most familar with such inquiries, and who best know how little any external testimony can avail in favour of a book where the internal evidence is against it, are most satisfied that the principal writings of the New Testament do contain abundantly in themselves, for competent judges, the evidence of their own genuineness and authenticity.

That the testimony of the early Christian writers goes along with this evidence and confirms it, is matter indeed of sincere thankfulness; because more minds, perhaps, are able to believe on external evidence than on internal. But of this testimony of the Christian writers it is essential to observe, that two very important points are such as do indeed affect this particular question much, but yet do not confer any value on the judgment of the witness in other matters. When a very early Christian writer quotes a passage from the New Testament, such as we find it now in our Bibles, it is indeed an argument, which all can understand, that he had before him the same Bible which we have, and that though he lived so near to the beginning of the gospel, yet that some parts of the New Testament must have been written still nearer to it. This is an evidence to the age of the New Testament, valuable indeed to us, but implying in the writer who gives it no qualities which confer authority; it merely shows that the book which he read must have existed before he could quote it. A second point of evidence is, when a very early Christian writer quotes any part of the New Testament as being considered by those to whom he was writing as an authority. This, again, is a valuable piece of testimony; but neither does it imply any general wisdom or authority in the writer who gives it: its value is derived merely from the age at which he lived, and not from his personal character. And with regard to the general reception of the New Testament by the Christians of his time, which, in the case supposed, he states as a fact, no doubt that the general opinion of the early Christians, where, as in this case, we can be sure that it is reported correctly, is an authority, and a great authority, in favour of the Scriptures: combined, as it is, with the still stronger internal evidence of the books themselves, it is irresistible. But it were too much to argue that, therefore, it was alone sufficient, not only when destitute of other evidence, but if opposed to it; and especially if it should happen to be opposed to that very Scripture which we know they acknowledged to be above themselves, but which we do not know that they were enabled in all cases either rightly to interpret or faithfully to follow.

When, therefore, we are told that, as we believe the Scriptures themselves upon tradition, so we should believe other things also, the answer is, that we do not believe the Scriptures either entirely or principally, upon what is called tradition; but for their own internal evidence; and that the opinions of the early Christians, like those of other men, may be very good in certain points, and to a certain degree, without being good in all points, and absolutely; that many a man's judgment would justly weigh with us, in addition to other strong reasons in the case itself, when we should by no means follow it where we were clear that there were strong reasons against it. This, indeed, is so obvious, that it seems almost foolish to be at the trouble of stating it; but what is so absurd in common life, that the contrary to it is a mere truism, is, unfortunately, when applied to a subject with which we are not familiar, often considered as an unanswerable argument, if it happen to suit our disposition or our prejudices.

But, although the Scripture is to the Church, and to the individual, too, who is able to judge for himself, the only decisive authority in matters of faith, yet we must not forget that it comes to us as it did to Theophilus, to persuade us of the certainty of things in which we have been already instructed; not to instruct from the beginning, by itself alone, those to whom its subject is entirely strange: in other words, it is and ought to be the general rule, that the Church teaches, and the Scripture confirms that teaching: or, if it be in any part erroneous, reproves it. For some appear to think, that by calling the Scripture the sole authority in matters of faith, we mean to exclude the Church altogether; and to call upon every man,--nay, upon every child,--to make out his own religion for himself from the volume of the Scriptures. The explanation briefly given is this; that while the Scripture alone teaches the Church, the Church teaches individuals; and that the authority of her teaching, like that of all human teaching, whether of individuals or societies, varies justly according to circumstances; being received, as it ought to be, almost implicitly by some, as a parent's is by a child, and by others listened to with respect, as that which is in the main agreeable to the truth, but still not considered to be, nor really claiming to be received as, infallible. But this part of the subject will require to be considered by itself on another occasion.

LECTURE XXXII.

LUKE i. 3,4.

It seemed good to me also, having had perfect understanding of all things from the very first, to write unto thee in order, most excellent Theophilus, that than mightest know the certainty of those things in which thou hast been instructed.

I said at the conclusion of my lecture, last Sunday, that when we of the Church of England assert that the Scripture is the sole authority in matters of faith, we by no means mean to exclude the office of the Church, nor to assert any thing so extravagant, as that it is the duty of every person to sit down with the volume of the Scriptures in his hand, and to make out from that alone, without listening to any human authority, what is the revelation made by God to man. But I know that many are led to adopt notions no less extravagant of the authority of the Church and of tradition,--even to the full extent maintained by the Church of Rome,--because they see no other refuge from what appears to them, and not unreasonably, so miserable and so extreme a folly; for an extreme and a most miserable folly doubtless it would be, in any one, to throw aside all human aid except his own; to disregard alike the wisdom of individuals, and the agreeing decisions of bodies of men; to act as if none but himself had ever loved truth, or had been able to discover it; and as if he himself did possess both the will and the power to do so.

This is so foolish, that I doubt whether any one ever held such notions, and, much more, whether be acted upon them. But is it more wise to run from one form of error into its opposite, which, generally speaking, is no less foolish and extravagant? What should we say of a man who could see no middle course between never asking for advice, and always blindly following it; between never accepting instruction upon any subject, and believing his instructors infallible? And this last comparison, with our particular situation here, will enable us, I think, by referring to our own daily experience, to understand the present question sufficiently. The whole system of education supposes, undoubtedly, that the teacher, in those matters which he teaches, should be an authority to the taught: a learner in any matter must rely on the books, and on the living instructors, out of which and from whom he is to learn. There are difficulties, certainly, in all learning; but we do not commonly see them increased by a disposition on the part of the learner to question and dispute every thing that is told him. There is a feeling rather of receiving what he is told implicitly; and, by so doing, he learns: but does it ever enter into his head that his teacher is infallible? or does any teacher of sane mind wish him to think so? And observe, now, what is the actual process: the mind of the learner is generally docile, trustful, respectful towards his teacher; aware, also, of his own comparative ignorance. It is certainly most right that it should be so. But this really teachable and humble learner finds a false spelling in one of his books; or hears his teacher, from oversight, say one word in his explanation instead of another: does he cease to be teachable and humble,--is it really a want of childlike faith, and an indulgence of the pride of reason, if he decides that the false spelling was an error of the press; that the word which his teacher used was a mistake? Yet errors, mistakes, of how trifling a kind soever, are inconsistent with infallibility; and the perceiving that they are errors is an exercise of our individual judgment upon our instructors. To hear some men talk, we should think that no boy could do so without losing all humility and all teachableness; without forthwith supposing that he was able to be his own instructor.

I have begun on purpose with an elementary case, in which a very young boy might perceive an error in his books, or in his instructors, without, in any degree, forfeiting his true humility. But we will now go somewhat farther: we will take a more advanced student, such as the oldest of those among you, who are still learners, and who know that they have much to learn, but who, having been learners for some time past, have also acquired some knowledge. In the books which they refer to, and from which they are constantly deriving assistance, do they never observe any errors in the printing? do they never find explanations given, which they perceive to be imperfect, nay, which they often feel to be actually wrong? And, passing from books to living instructors, should we blame a thoughtful, attentive, and well-informed pupil, because his mind did not at once acquiesce in our interpretation of some difficult passage; because he consulted other authorities on the subject, and was unsatisfied in his judgment; the reason of his hesitation being, that our interpretation appeared to him to give an unsatisfactory sense, or to be obtained by violating the rules of language? Is he proud, rebellious, puffed up, wanting in a teachable spirit, without faith, without humility, because he so ventures to judge for himself of what his teacher tells him? Does such a judging for himself interfere, in the slightest degree, with the relation between us and him? Does it make him really cease to respect us? or dispose him to believe that he is altogether beyond the reach of our instruction? Or are we so mad as to regard our authority as wholly set at nought, because it is not allowed to be infallible? Doubtless, it would be wholly set at nought, if we had presumed to be infallible. Then it would not be merely that, in some one particular point, our decision had been doubted, but that one point would involve our authority in all; because it would prove, that we had set up beforehand a false claim: and he who does so is either foolish, or a deceiver; there is apparent a flaw either in his understanding, or in his principles, which undoubtedly does repel respect.

Let me go on a step farther still. It has been my happiness to retain, in after years, my intercourse with many of those who were formerly my pupils; to know them when their minds have been matured, and their education, in the ordinary sense of the term, completed. Is not the relation between us altered then still more? Is it incompatible with true respect and regard, that they should now judge still more freely, in those very points, I mean, in which heretofore they had received my instructions all but implicitly? that on points of scholarship and criticism, they should entirely think for themselves? Or does this thinking for themselve mean, that they will begin to question all they had ever learnt? or sit down to forget purposely all their school instructions, and make out a new knowledge of the ancient languages for themselves? Who does not know, that they whose minds are most eager to discern truth, are the very persons who prize their early instruction most, and confess how much they are indebted to it; and that the exercise of their judgments loads them to go on freely in the same path in which they have walked so long, here and there it may be departing from it where they find a better line, but going on towards the same object, and generally in the same direction?

What has been the experience of my life,--the constantly observing the natural union between sense and modesty; the perfect compatibility of respect for instruction with freedom of judgment; the seeing how Nature herself teaches us to proportion the implicitness of our belief to our consciousness of ignorance: to rise gradually and gently from a state of passively leaning, as it were, on the arm of another, to resting more and more of our weight on our own limbs, and, at last, to standing alone, this has perpetually exemplified our relations, as individuals, to the Church. Taught by her, in our childhood and youth, under all circumstances; taught by her, in the great majority of instances, through our whole lives; never, in any case, becoming so independent of her as we do in riper years, of the individual instructor of our youth; she has an abiding claim on our respect, on our deference, on our regard: but if it should be, that her teaching contained any thing at variance with God's word, we should perceive it more or less clearly, according to our degrees of knowledge; we should trust or mistrust our judgment, according to our degree of knowledge; but in the last resort, as we suppose that even a young boy might be sure that his book was in error, in the case of a manifest false print, so there may be things so certainly inconsistent with Scripture, that a common Christian may be able to judge of them, and to say that they are like false prints in his lesson, they are manifest errors, not to be followed, but avoided. So far he may be said to judge of his teacher; but not the less will he respect and listen to her authority in general, unless she has herself made the slightest error ruinous to her authority by claiming to be in all points, great or small, alike infallible.

Men crave a general rule for their guidance at all times, and under all circumstances; whereas life is a constant call upon us to consider how far one general rule, in the particular case before us, is modified by another, or where one rule should be applied, and where another. To separate humility from idolatry, conscience from presumption, is often an arduous task: to different persons there is a different besetting danger; so it is under different circumstances, and at different times. Every day does the seaman, on a voyage, take his observations, to know whereabouts he is; he compares his position with his charts; he considers the direction of the wind, and the set of the current, or tide; and from all these together, he judges on which side his danger lies, on what course he should steer, or how much sail he may venture to carry. This is an image of our own condition: we cannot have a general rule to tell us where we should follow others, and where we must differ from them; to say what is modesty, and what is indolence; what is a proper deference to others, and what is a trusting in man so far, that it becomes a want of trust in God. Only, we are sure that these are points which we must decide for ourselves; the human will must be free, so far as other men are concerned. If we say, that we will implicitly trust others, then there is our decision, which no one could have made for us, and which is our own choice as to the principle of our lives; for which choice, we each of us, and no one else in all the world, must answer at the judgment-seat of God. Only, in that word there is our comfort, that, for our conduct in so doubtful a voyage as that of life, amidst so many conflicting opinions, each courting our adherence to it,--amidst such a variety of circumstances without, and of feelings within, and on which, notwithstanding, our condition for all eternity must depend,--we shall be judged, not by erring man, not by our own fallible conscience, but by the all-wise, and all-righteous God. With him, after all, even in the very courts of his holy Church, we yet, in one sense, must each of us live alone. On his gracious aid, given to our own individual souls, and determining our own individual wills, depends the character of our life here and for ever.

114

Trusting to him, praying to him, we shall then make use of all the means that his goodness has provided for us; we shall ask counsel of friends; we shall listen to teachers; we shall delight to be in the company of God's people, of one mind, and of one voice, with the good and wise of every generation; we shall be afraid of leaning too much to our own understanding, knowing how it is encompassed with error; but knowing that other men are encompassed with error also, and that we, and not they, must answer for our choice before Christ's judgment, we must, in the last resort, if our conscience and sense of truth cannot be persuaded that other men speak according to God's will,--we must follow our own inward convictions, though all the world were to follow the contrary.

LECTURE XXXIII.

JOHN ix. 29.

We know that God spake unto Moses; as for this fellow, we know not from whence he is.

The questions involved in the conversations recorded in this chapter, are of great practical importance. Not perhaps of immediate practical importance to all in this present congregation; but yet sure to be of importance to all hereafter, and of importance to many at this actual moment. Nay, they are of importance to those who, from their youth, might be thought to have little to do with them, either where the mind is already anxious and inquiring beyond its years, or where it happens to be exposed to strong party influences, or that its passions are likely to be engaged on a particular side, however little the understanding may be interested in the matter. In fact, in religious knowledge, as in other things, the omissions of youth are hard to make up in manhood; they who grow up with a very small knowledge of the Scriptures, and with no understanding of any of the questions connected with them, can with difficulty make up for this defect in after years; they become, according to the influences to which they may happen to be subjected, either unbelieving or fanatical.

If we were to question the youngest boy about the language held in this chapter by the Pharisees, and by the man who had been born blind, we should, no doubt, be answered, that what the Pharisees said, was wrong; and what the man born blind said, was right. This would be the answer which it would be thought proper to give; because it would be perceived that the Pharisees' language expressed unbelief in Christ; and that the man born blind was expressing gratitude and faith towards him. Nor, indeed, should we expect a young boy to go much farther than this; for such general impressions are, at his age, as much many times as can be looked for. But it is strange to observe how much this want of understanding outlasts the age of boyhood; how apt men are to judge according to names, and to see no farther: to say, that the language of the Pharisees was wrong, because they find it employed against Christ; but yet to use the very same language themselves, whilst they think that they are all the while speaking for Christ.

But in this conversation between the Pharisees and the blind man, there are, indeed, as I said, points involved of very great importance; it contains the question as to the degree of weight to be attached to miracles; and the question, no less grave, with what degree of tenacity we should reject what claims to be a new truth, because it seems to be at a variance with supposed old truths to which we have been long accustomed to cling with undoubting affection.

The question as to the weight of miracles is contained in the sixteenth verse. Some of the Pharisees said, This man is not of God, because he keepeth not the Sabbath day. Others said, How can a man that is a sinner do such miracles? That is to say, the first party rejected

115

the miracles because they seemed to be wrought in favour of a supposed false doctrine; the other accepted the doctrine, because it seemed warranted to their belief by the miracles.

The second question is contained in the words of the text, "We know that God spake to Moses; as for this fellow, we know not from whence he is." We have been taught from our childhood, and have the belief associated with every good and pious thought in us, that God spake to Moses, and gave him the law as our rule of life; but as for this fellow, we know not from whence he is. His works may be wonderful, his words may be specious; but we never heard of him before, and we cannot tear up all the holiest feelings of our nature to receive a new doctrine. We will hold to the old way in which, we were taught by our fathers to walk, and in which they walked before us.

This last question is one which, as we well know, is continually presented to our minds. No one says, that the Pharisees were right, any more than those very Pharisees thought that their fathers were right who had killed the prophets. But as our Lord told them, that they were in truth the children in spirit of those who had killed the prophets; because, although they had been taught to condemn the outward form of their fathers' action, they were repeating it themselves in its principles and spirit; so many of those who condemn the Pharisees are really their exact image, repeating now against the truths of their own days the very same arguments which the Pharisees used against the truths of theirs.

For the arguments of these Pharisees, both as regards miracles, and as regards the suspicion with which we should look on a doctrine opposed to the settled opinions of our lives, have in fact, in both cases, a great mixture of justice in them; and it is this very mixture which we may hope beguiled them; and also beguiles those, who in our own days repeat their language.

For most certain it is that the Scripture itself supposes the possibility of false miracles. The case is especially provided against in Deuteronomy. It there says, "If there arise among you a prophet or a dreamer of dreams, and giveth thee a sign or a wonder, and the sign or the wonder come to pass whereof he spake unto thee, saying, Let us go after other gods which thou hast not known, and let us serve them: thou shalt not hearken unto the words of that prophet or that dreamer of dreams, for the Lord your God proveth you, to know whether ye love the Lord your God with all your heart and with all your soul." Observe how nearly this comes to the language of the Pharisees, "This man is not of God, because he keepeth not the Sabbath day." "Here," they might have said, "is the very case foreseen in the Scriptures: a prophet has wrought a sign and a wonder, which is at the same time a breach of God's commandments. God has told us that such signs are not to be heeded, that he does but prove us with them to see whether we love him truly: knowing that where there is a love of him, the heart will heed no sign or wonder, how great soever, which would tempt it to think lightly of his commandments." Shall we say that this is not a just interpretation of the passage in Deuteronomy? shall we say that this is the language of unbelief or of sin? or, rather, shall we not confess that it is in accordance with God's word, and holy, and faithful, and true? And yet this most just language led those who used it to reject one of Christ's greatest miracles, and to refuse the salvation of the Holy One of God. Can God's truth be contrary to itself? or can truth and goodness lead so directly to error and to evil?

Now, then, where is the solution to be found? for some solution there must be, unless we will either condemn a most true principle, or defend a most false conclusion. The error lies in confounding God's moral law with his law of ordinances; precisely the same error which led the Jews to stone Stephen. The law had undoubtedly commanded that he who blasphemed God should be stoned; the Jews called Stephen's speaking against the holy place and against the law blasphemy against God, and they murdered God's faithful servant and Christ's blessed martyr. Even so the law had said, Let no miracle be so great as to tempt you to forsake God: the Jews considered the forsaking the law of the Sabbath to be a forsaking of God, and they said that Christ's miracle was a work of Satan. There is no blasphemy into which we may not fall, no crime from which we shall be safe, if we do not separate in our minds most clearly such laws as relate to moral and eternal duties, and such as relate to outward or positive ordinances, even when commanded or instituted by God himself. It is most false to say that the fact of their being commanded sets them on a level with each other. So long as they are commanded to us, it is no doubt our duty to obey them equally: but the difference between them is this, that whereas the first are commanded to us and to our children for ever, and no possible evidence can be so great as to persuade us that God has repealed them; (for the utmost conceivable amount of external testimony, such as that of miracles, could only lead to madness;--the human mind might, conceivably, be overwhelmed by the conflict, but should never and could never be tempted to renounce its very being, and lie against its Maker;) the others, that is, the commands to observe certain forms and ordinances, are in their nature essentially temporary and changeable: we have no right to assume that they will be continued, and therefore a miracle at any time might justly require us to forsake them; and not only an outward miracle, but the changed circumstances of the times may speak God's will no less clearly than a miracle, and may absolutely make it our duty to lay aside those ordinances, which to us hitherto, and to our fathers before us, were indeed the commands of God.

Now let us take the other question,--which may indeed be called a question as to the allowableness of resting confidently in truth already gained, without consenting to examine the claims of something asserting itself to be a new truth, yet which seems to interfere with the old. Is nothing within us to be safe from possible doubt, or is everything? Or is it here, as in the former case, that there are truths so tried and so sacred that it were blasphemy to question them; while there are others, often closely intermixed with these, which are not so sacred, because they are not eternal; which may and ought to be examined when occasion requires; and which may be laid aside, or exchanged rather, for some higher truth, if it shall reasonably appear that their work is done, and that if we retain them longer they will change their character, and become no longer true but false. "David having served his own generation by the will of God, fell asleep, and was gathered unto his fathers, and saw corruption; but He whom God raised again saw no corruption." This is the difference between positive ordinances and moral: the first serve their appointed number of generations by the will of God, and then are gathered to their fathers, and perish; the latter are by the right hand of God exalted, the same yesterday, to-day, and forever.

"We know," said the Jews, "that God spake to Moses; but for this fellow, we know not from whence he is." There was a time when their fathers had held almost the very same language to Moses: "they refused him, saying Who made thee a ruler and a judge over us?" But now they knew that God had spoken to Moses, but were refusing Him who was sent unto them after Moses. God had spoken unto Moses, it was most true: he had spoken to him and given him commandments which were to last for ever; and which Christ, so far from undoing, was sent to confirm and to perfect; he had spoken to him other things, which were not to last for ever, but yet which were not to be cast away with dishonour; but having, in the fulness of time, done their work, were then, like David, to fall asleep. All that was required of the Jews, was not to reject as blasphemy a doctrine which should distinguish between these two sorts of truths: which in no way requires to believe that God had not spoken to Moses,--which, on the contrary, maintained that he had so spoken,--but only contended that he has also, in these last days, spoken unto us by his Son; and that his Son, bearing the full image of Divine authority, might well be believed if he spoke of some parts of Moses's law as having now fulfilled their work, seeing that they were such parts only as, by their very nature, were not eternal: they had not been from the beginning, and therefore they would not live on to the end.

The practical conclusion is, that, whilst we hold fast, with an undoubting and unwavering faith, all truths which, by their very nature, are eternal, and to deny which is no other than to speak against the Holy Ghost, we should listen patiently to, and pass no harsh judgment on, those who question other truths not necessarily eternal, while they declare that they are, to the best of their consciences, seeking to obey God and Christ. When I say, that we should listen patiently, and not pass harsh judgments upon those who question such points, I say it without at all meaning that we should agree with them. It would be monstrous indeed, to suppose that old opinions are never combated wrongly; that old institutions are never pronounced to have lived out their appointed time, when, in fact, they are still in their full vigour. But the language of those who defend the doctrines and the ordinances of the Church may, and often does, partake of the sin of that of the Pharisees, even when those against whom they are contending, are not, like Christ, bringing in a new

117

and higher truth, but an actual error. To point out that it is an error, to defend ourselves and the Church from it, is most right, and most highly our duty; but it is neither right, nor our duty, but the very sin of the Pharisees, to put it down merely by saying, "As for this fellow, we know not from whence he is;" to treat the whole question as an impiety, and to deny the virtues and the holiness of those who maintain it, because they are, as we call it, "speaking blasphemous things against the holy place and against the law." The mischief of this to ourselves is infinite; nay, in its extreme, it leads to language which is fearfully resembling the very blasphemy against the Holy Ghost; for, when we say, as has been said, that where men's lives are apparently good and holy, and their doctrines are against those of the Church, the holiness is an unreal holiness, and that we cannot see into their hearts, this is, in fact, denying the Holy Spirit's most infallible sign--the fruits of righteousness; and being positive rather of the truth of the Church, than of the truth of God. There is nothing so certain as that goodness is from God; nothing so certain as that sin is not from God; nothing so certain as that sin is not from him. To deny, or doubt this, is to dispute the greatest assurance of truth that God has ever been pleased to give to us. It does not, by any means, follow, that all good men are free from error, nor that error is less error because good men hold it; but to make the error which is less certain, a reason for disputing the goodness which is more certain, is the spirit, not of God, nor of the Church of God, but of those false zealots who put an idol in God's place; of such as rejected Christ and murdered Stephen.

LECTURE XXXIV.

1 CORINTHIANS xiv, 20.

Brethren, be not children in understanding: howbeit,
in malice be ye children, but in understanding be men.

It would be going a great deal too far to say, that they who fulfilled the latter part of this command, were sure also to fulfil the former; that they who were men in understanding, were, therefore, likely to be children in malice. But the converse holds good, with remarkable certainty, that they who are children in understanding, are proportionally apt to be men in malice: that is, in proportion as men neglect that which should be the guide of their lives, so are they left to the mastery of their passions; and as nature and outward circumstances do not allow these passions to remain as quiet and as little grown as they are in childhood,--for they are sure to ripen without any trouble of ours,--so men are left with nothing but the evils of both ages, the vices of the man, and the unripeness and ignorance of the child.

It is indeed a strange and almost incredible thing, that any should ever have united in their minds the notions of innocence and ignorance as applied to any but literal children: nor is it less strange, that any should ever have been afraid of their understanding, and should have sought goodness through prejudice, and blindness, and folly. Compared with this, their conduct was infinitely reasonable who weakened and tormented their bodies in order to strengthen, as they thought, their spiritual nature. Such conduct was, by comparison, reasonable because there is a great deal of bodily weakness and discomfort, which really does not interfere with the strength and purity of our character in itself, although, by abridging our activity, it may lessen our means of usefulness. But what should we say of a man who directed his ill usage of his body to that part of our system which is most closely connected with the brain; who were purposely to impair his nervous system, and subject himself to those delusions and diseased views of things which are the well-known result of any disorder there? Yet this is precisely what they do who seek to mortify and lower their understanding.

It is as impossible that they should become better men by such a process, as if they were literally to take medicines to affect their nerves or their brain, in the hope of becoming idiotic or delirious. It is, in fact, the worst kind of self-murder; for it is a presumptuous destroying of that which is our best life, because we dread to undergo those trials which God has appointed for the perfecting both of it and of us.

But from the wilful blindness of these men, let us turn to the Christian wisdom of the Apostle: "In malice be ye children, but in understanding be men." Let us turn to what is recorded of our Lord in his early life, at that age when, as man, the cultivation of his understanding was his particular duty--that he was found in the temple, sitting in the midst of the doctors, both hearing them and asking them questions: not asking questions only, as one too impatient or too vain to wait for an answer, or to consider it when he had received it; not hearing only, as one careless and passive, who thinks that the words of wisdom can improve his mind by being indolently admitted through the ears, with no more effort than his body uses when it is refreshed by a cooling air, or when it is laid down in running water; but both hearing and asking questions; docile and patient, yet active and intelligent; knowing that the wisdom was to be communicated from without, but that it belongs to the vigorous exercise of the power within, to apprehend it, and to convert it to nourishment.

Now, what is recorded of our Lord for our example, as to the manner in which he received instruction when delivered by word of mouth, this same thing should we do with that instruction, which, as is the case with most of ours, we derive from reading. Put the Scriptures in the place of those living teachers whom Christ was so eager to hear; the words of Christ, and of his Spirit, instead of those far inferior guides from whom, notwithstanding, he, for our sakes, once submitted to learn; and what can be more exact than the application of the example? Let us be found in God's true temple, in the communion of his faithful people,--his universal Church, sitting down as it were, surrounded by the voices of the oracles of God--prophets, apostles, and Jesus Christ himself: let us be found with the record of these oracles in our hands, both reading them and asking them questions.

It is quite clear that what hinders a true understanding of anything is vagueness; and it is by this process of asking questions that vagueness is to be dispelled: for, in the first place, it removes one great vagueness, or indistinctness, which is very apt to beset the minds of many; namely, the not clearly seeing whether they understand a thing or no; and much more, the not seeing what it is that they do understand, and what it is which they do not. Take any one of our Lord's parables, and read it even to a young child: there will be something of an impression conveyed, and some feelings awakened; but all will be indistinct; the child will not know whether he understands or no, but will soon gain the habit of supposing that he does, as that is at once the least troublesome, and the least unpleasant to our vanity. And this same vague impression is often received by uneducated persons from reading or hearing either the Scriptures or sermons; it is by no means the same as if they had read or heard something in an unknown language; but yet they can give no distinct account of what they have heard or read; they do not know how far they understand it, and how far they do not. Here, then, is the use of "asking questions,"--asking questions of ourselves or of our book, I mean, for I am supposing the case of our reading, when it can rarely happen that we have any living person at hand to give us an answer. Now, taking the earliest and simplest state of knowledge, it is plain that the first question to put to ourselves will be, "Do I understand the meaning of all the words and expressions in what I have been reading?" I know that this is taking things at their very beginning, but it is my wish to do so. Now, so plain and forcible is the English of our Bible, generally speaking, that the words difficult to be understood will probably not be many; yet some such do occur, owing, in some instances, to a change of the language; as in the words "let," and "prevent," which now signify, the one, "to allow, or suffer to be done," and the other "to stop, or hinder," but which signified, when our translation was made, the first, "to stop or hinder," and the second, "to be beforehand with us;" as in the prayer, "Prevent us, O Lord, in all our doings, with thy most gracious favour;" the meaning is, "Let thy favour be with us beforehand, O Lord, in whatever we are going to do." In other instances the words are difficult because they are used in a particular sense, such as we do not learn from our common language; of which kind are the words "elect," "saints," "justification," "righteousness," and many others. Now, if we ask ourselves "whether we understand these words or no," our common sense, when thus questioned, will readily tell us, whether we do or not; although if we had not directly asked the question, it might never have thought about it. Of course, our common sense cannot tell us what the true meaning is; that is a matter of information, and our means of gaining information may be more or less; but still, a great step is gained, the mist is partly cleared away; we can say to ourselves, "Here is something which I do understand, and here is something which I do not; I must keep the two distinct, for the first I may use, the second I cannot; I will mark it down as a thing about which I may get explanation at another time; but at present it is a blank in the picture, it is the same as if it were not there." This, then, is the first process of self-questioning, adapted, as I have already said, to those whose knowledge is most elementary.

Suppose, however, that we are got beyond difficulties of this sort--that the words and particular expressions of the Scriptures are mostly clear to us. Now, take again one of our Lord's parables; say, for instance, that of the labourers in the vineyard: we read it, and find that he who went to work at the eleventh hour received as much as he who had been working all the day. This seems to say, that he who begins to serve God in his old age shall receive his crown of glory no less than he who has served him all his life. But now try the process of self-questioning: what do I think that Christ means me to learn from this? what is the lesson to me? what is it to make me feel, or think, or do? If it makes me think that I shall receive an equal crown of glory if I begin to serve God in my old age, and therefore if it leads me to live carelessly, this is clearly making Christ encourage wickedness; and such a thought is blasphemy. He cannot mean me to learn this from it: let me look at the parable again. Who is it who is reproved in those words which seem to contain its real object? It is one who complains of God for having rewarded others equally with himself. Now this I can see is not a good feeling: it is pride and jealousy. In order, then to learn what the parable means me to learn, let me put myself in the position of those reproved in it. If I complain that others are rewarded by God as much as I am, it is altogether a bad feeling, and one which I ought to check; for I have nothing to do with God's dealings to others, let me think of what concerns myself. Here I have the lesson of the parable complete: and here I find it is useful for me. But if I take it for a different object, and suppose that it means to encourage waiting till the eleventh hour--waiting till we are old before we repent--we find that we make it only actually to be mischievous to us. And thus we gain a great piece of knowledge: namely, that the parables of our Lord are mostly designed to teach, some one particular lesson, with respect to some one particular fault: and that if we take them generally, as if all in them was applicable to all persons, whether exposed to that particular fault or not, we shall absolutely be in danger of deriving mischief from them instead of good. It is true, that in this particular parable, the gross wickedness of such an interpretation as I have mentioned is guarded against even in the story itself; because those who worked only at the eleventh hour are expressly said to have stood idle so long only because no man had hired them; their delay, therefore, was no fault of their own. But even if this circumstance had been left out, it would have been just the same; because the general rule is, that we apply to a parable only for its particular lesson, and do not strain it to any thing else. Had this been well understood, no one would have ever found so much difficulty in understanding the parable of the unjust steward.

This is another great step towards the dispelling vagueness, to apply the particular lesson of each part of Scripture to that state of knowledge, or feeling, or practice in ourselves, which it was intended to benefit; to apply it as a lesson to ourselves, not as a general truth for our neighbours. And the very desire to do this, makes us naturally look with care to the object of every passage--to see to whom it was addressed, and on what occasion; for this will often surely guide us to the point that we want. But in order to do this, we must strive to clothe the whole in our own common language; to get rid of those expressions which to us convey the meaning faintly; and to put it into such others as shall come most strongly home to us. This I have spoken of on other occasions; and I have so often witnessed the bad effects of not doing so, that I am sure it may well bear to be noticed again; I mean the putting such words as "persecution," "the cares and riches of the world," "the kingdom of God," "confessing Christ," "denying Christ," and many others, into a language which to us has more lively reality, which makes us manifestly see that it is of us, and of our common life, and of our dangers, that the scripture is speaking, and not only of things in a remote time and country, and under circumstances quite unlike our own. Therefore I have a strong objection to the use of what is called peculiarly religious language, because I am sure that it hinders us from bringing the matter of that language thoroughly home to us; our minds do not entirely assimilate with, it; or if they fancy that they do, it is only by their becoming themselves affected, and losing their sense of the reality of things around them. For our language is fixed for us, and we cannot alter it; and into that common language in which we think and feel, all truth must be translated, if we would think and feel respecting it at once rightly, clearly, and vividly. Happy is he, who, by practising this early, has imbued his own natural language with the spirit of God's wisdom and holiness; and who can see, and understand, and feel them the better, because they are so put into a form with which he is perfectly familiar.

More might be said, very much more, but here I will now pause. In this world, wherein heavenly things are, after all, hard to seize and fix upon, we have great need that no mists of imperfect understanding darken them, over and above those of the corrupt will. To see them clearly, to understand them distinctly and vividly, may, indeed, after all be vain: a thicker veil may yet remain behind, and we may see and understand, and yet perish. Only the clear sight of God in Christ can be no light blessing; and there may be a hope, that understanding and approving with all our minds his excellent wisdom, the light may warm us as well as assist our sight; that we may see, and not in our vague and empty sense, but in the force of the scriptural meaning of the word,--may see, and so believe.

LECTURE XXXV.

MATTHEW xxvi. 45, 46.

Sleep on now and take your rest; behold, the hour is at hand, and the Son of Man is betrayed into the hands of sinners. Rise, let us be. going; behold, he is at hand that doth betray me.

I take these verses for my text, in the first place, because some have fancied a difficulty in them, and have even proposed to alter the translation, and read the first words as a question, "Do ye still sleep and take your rest?" and because they are really a very good illustration of our Lord's manner of speaking, a manner which it is of the highest importance to us fully to understand. And, secondly, I take them as a text for the general lesson which they convey to us; their mixture of condemnation and mercy; their view, at once looking backwards and forwards, not losing sight of irreparable evils of a neglected past, nor yet making those evils worse by so dwelling upon them as to forget the still available future; not concealing from us the solemn truth, that what is done cannot be undone, yet warning us also not to undo by a vain despair that future which may yet be done to our soul's health.

First, a difficulty has been fancied to exist in the words, as if our Lord had bade his disciples to do two contradictory things: telling them, first, to sleep on and take their rest, and then saying, "Rise, let us be going." And because in St. Luke's account, when our Lord comes to his disciples the last time, his words are given thus, "Why sleep ye? rise and pray, that ye enter not into temptation:" therefore, as I have said, his words in the text have been translated, "Are ye sleeping and resting for the remainder of the time?" Now, I should not take up your time with things of this sort, where I believe our common translation to be most certainly right, were it not for the sake of one or two general remarks, which I think may not be out of place. It is a general rule, that in passages not obscure, but appearing to contain some moral difficulty, if I may so speak; that is, something which seems inconsistent with our notions of God's holiness, or wisdom, or justice; something, in short, of a stumbling-block, which we fear may occasion a triumph to unbelievers; it is a rule, I say, that in passages of this kind the difficulty is not to be met by departing from the common-received translation. And the reason of this is plain; that had not the commonly received translation in such cases been clearly the right one, it would never have come to be commonly received. Amongst the thousands of interpreters of Scripture, all, from the earliest time, anxious to remove grounds of cavil from the adversaries of their faith, a passage would never have been translated so as to afford such a ground, if the right translation of it could have been different. Such places are especially those in which the common translation needs not to be suspected; and it is merely leading us astray from the true explanation of the apparent difficulty, when we thus attempt to evade it by tampering with the translation. A notable instance of this was afforded some few years since in a new translation of some of the books of the Old Testament; in which it was pretended that most of those points which had been most attacked by unbelievers were, in fact, mere mistranslations, and that the real meaning of the original was something totally different; and, in order to show the necessity of his alterations, the writer entirely allowed the objections of unbelievers to the common reading; and said that no sufficient answer had been or could be made to them. This was an extreme case, and probably imposed only on a very few: but less instances of the same thing are common: St. Paul's words about being baptized for the dead, have been twisted to all sorts of senses, from their natural and only possible meaning, because men could not bear to believe that the superstition of being baptized as proxies for another could have existed at a period which they were resolved to consider so pure: and so in the text, a force has been put upon the words which they cannot bear, in order to remove a supposed contradiction: and all that would have been gained by the change would be, to have one instructive illustration the less of our Lord's peculiar manner of discourse, and one instance the less of the inimitable way in which his language, addressed directly to the circumstances before him, contains, at the same time, a general lesson, for the use of all his disciples in all ages.

Our Lord's habitual language was parabolical; I use the word in a wide sense, to include all language which is not meant to be taken according to the letter. Observe his conversation with the Samaritan woman; it begins at once with parable, "If thou hadst known who it was that asked of thee, saying, Give me to drink, thou wouldst have asked of him, and he would have given thee living water." And again, "Whoso drinketh of the water that I shall give him shall never thirst, but it shall be in him a well of water, springing up unto life eternal." This seems to have been, if I may venture to say so, the favourite language in which he preferred to speak; but when he found that he was not understood, then, according to the nature of the case, he went on in two or three different manners. When he, to whom all hearts were open, saw that the misunderstanding was wilful, that it arose out of a disposition glad to find an excuse, in his pretended obscurity, for not listening to him and obeying him, then, instead of explaining his language, he made it more and more figurative; more likely to be misunderstood, or to offend those whom he knew to be disposed beforehand to misunderstand and to be offended. A famous example of this may be seen in the sixth chapter of St. John; there he first calls himself the Bread of Life, and says, that whosoever should eat of that bread should live for ever: but when he found that the Jews cavilled at this language, instead of explaining it, he only added expressions yet more strongly parabolical; "Except ye eat the flesh of the Son of man, and drink his blood, ye have no life in you:" and he dwells on this image so long, that we find that many of his disciples, bent on interpreting it literally, and, in this sense, finding it utterly shocking, went back and walked no more with him. Again, when he found not a disposition to cavil, but yet a profound ignorance of his meaning, arising from a state of mind wholly unused to think of spiritual good and evil, he neither used, as to those who wilfully misunderstood him, language that would offend them still more, nor yet did he offer a direct explanation; but he broke off the conversation, and adopted another method of instruction. Thus, when the Samaritan woman, thinking only of bodily wants, answered him by saying, "Sir, give me this water, that I thirst not, neither come hither to draw," he neither goes on to speak to her in the same language, nor yet does he explain it; but at once addresses her in a different manner, saying, "Go, call thy husband, and come hither." Thirdly, when he was speaking to his own disciples, to whom it was given to know the mysteries of the kingdom of God, he generally explained his meaning,--at least so far as to prevent practical error,--when he found that they had not understood him. Thus, when he had said to them, "Beware of the leaven of the Pharisees, and of the leaven of Herod," and they thought only of leaven and of bread in the literal sense, he upbraids them, indeed, for their slowness, saying, "Are ye also yet without understanding?" but he goes on to tell them in express terms that he did not mean to speak to them of the leaven of bread. And the words of the text are an exactly similar instance: his first address is parabolical; that is, it is not meant to be taken to the letter; "Sleep on now, and take your rest," meaning, "Ye can now do me no good by watching, for the time is past, and he who betrayed me is at hand; ye might as well sleep on now and take your rest, for I need not try you any longer." But, as the time was really pressing, and there was a possibility that they might have misunderstood his words, and have really continued to sleep, he immediately added in different language, "Rise, let us be going; behold, he is at hand that doth betray me." We must be prepared, then, to find that our Lord's language, not only to the Jews at large, but even to his own disciples, is commonly parabolical; the worst interpretation which we can give to it is commonly the literal one. His conversation with his disciples, just before he went out to the garden of Gethsemane, as recorded in the thirteenth, and following chapters of St. John, is a most striking proof of this. If any one looks through them, he will find how many are the comparisons, and figurative manners of speaking, which abound in them, and how often his disciples were at a loss to understand his meaning, And he himself declares this, for, at the end of the sixteenth chapter, he says expressly, "These things I have spoken unto you in proverbs;"--that is, language not to be taken according to the letter;--"the time is coming when I will no more speak unto you in proverbs, but will show you plainly of the Father." And then, when he goes on to declare, what he never, it seems, had before told them in such express and literal language, "I came forth from the Father, and am come into the world: again I leave the world, and go to my Father," his disciples seem to have welcomed with joy this departure from his usual manner of speaking, and said immediately, "Lo! now speakest thou plainly, and speakest no proverb: now we know that thou knowest all things, and needest not that any man should ask thee: by this we believe that thou camest forth from God."

But let us observe what it is that he said: "A time is coming when I shall no more speak unto you in proverbs, but shall show you plainly of the Father." That time came immediately. He spoke to them after his resurrection, opening their understandings to understand the Scriptures: he spoke yet more fully, by his Spirit, after the day of Pentecost, leading them into all truth. And what they thus heard in the ear, they proclaimed, according to his bidding, upon the house-tops. When the Holy Spirit brought to their remembrance all that he had said to them, and gave their minds a spiritual judgment, to compare what they thus had brought before them, to see his words in their true light and their true bearings, comparing spiritual things with spiritual, they were no niggards of this heavenly treasure; nor did they, according to the vain heresy of the worst corrupters of Christ's gospel, imitate and surpass that sin which they had so heavily judged in Ananias. They kept back no part-of that which they professed and were commanded to lay wholly and entirely at the feet of God's church. They did not so lie to the Holy Ghost, as to erect a wicked system of priestcraft in the place of that holy gospel of which they were ministers. They had no reserve of a secret doctrine for themselves and a chosen few, keeping in their own hands the key of knowledge, and opening only half of the door; but as they had freely received, so they freely gave; all that they knew, they taught to all: and so, through their blessed teaching, we too can understand our Lord's words as they were taught to understand them: and what is parabolical, is no longer on that account obscure, but full of light and of beauty, fulfilling the end for which it was chosen, the most effective of all ways of teaching, because the liveliest.

I have left myself but little space to touch upon the second part of the subject--the general lesson conveyed in our Lord's-words to his disciples: "Sleep on now, and take your rest.--Rise; let us be going." How truly do we deserve the reproof; how thankfully may we accept the call. We have forfeited many opportunities which we would in vain recover; we have been careless when we should have been watchful; and that for which we should have watched, is now lost by our neglect; and it is no good to watch for it any more. Let us remember this, while it is called to-day; for how often is it particularly applicable to us here, from the passing nature of your stay amongst us! To both you and us too often belongs our Lord's remonstrance, "What, could ye not watch with me one hour?" So short a time as you stay here, could we not be watching with Christ that little period: from which, if well improved, there might spring forth a fruit so lasting? But, alas! we too often sleep it away: we do not all that we might do, nor do you; evil grows instead of good, till the time is past, and you leave us; and we may as well sleep on, and take our rest, so far as all that particular good was concerned--the improvement, namely, of your time at this place, for which we are alike set to watch. But are we to take the words of reproach literally? May we really sleep on, and take our rest? Oh vain and wilful folly, so to misunderstand! But, lest we should misunderstand, let us hear our Lord's next words: "Rise; let us be going," and that instantly: the time and opportunity already lost for ever is far more than enough.--"Rise; let us be going:" so Christ calls us; for he has still other work for us to do, for him, and with him. The future is yet our own, though the past be lost. We have sinned greatly and irreparably; but let us not do so yet again: other opportunities are afforded us; the disciples would not watch with him in the garden, but he calls them to go with him to his trial and his judgment; and one, we know, watched by him even on his cross:--so he calls to us; so he calls now; but he will not so call for ever. There will be a time when we might strike out the words, "Rise; let us be going;" they will concern us then no more. It is only said, "Sleep on now, and take your rest: all your watching time has been wasted, and you can now watch no more;" there remains only to sleep--to sleep that last sleep, from which we shall then never wake to God and happiness, but in which we shall be awake for ever to sin and to misery.

LECTURE XXXVI.

2 CORINTHIANS v. 17, 18.

Old things are passed away; behold, all things are become new: and
all things are of God, who hath reconciled us to himself by Jesus Christ.

I have, from time to time, spoken of that foolish misuse of the Scriptures, by which any one opening the volume of the Bible at random, and taking the first words which he finds, straightway applies them either to himself or to his neighbour; and then boasts that he has the word of God on his side, and that whosoever differs from him, is disputing and despising the word of God. The most extreme instances of this way of proceeding are so absurd, that they could not be noticed in this place becomingly; and these, of course, stand palpable to all, except to those who have allowed themselves to fall into them. But far short of these manifest follies, great errors have been maintained on general points, and great mistakes, whether of over presumption or of over fear, have been committed as to men's particular state, by quoting Scripture unadvisedly; by taking hold of its words to the neglect or actual violation of its spirit and real meaning. This is a great and a very common mischief, but yet there is a truth at the bottom of the error; it is true, that the greatest questions relating to God and to ourselves, may find their answer in the Scriptures; it is true, that if we search for this answer wisely we may surely find it.

Consider the words of the text, and see how easily they may be perverted, if with no more ado we take them, as said of ourselves, each individually, and as containing to each of us a statement positive of truth. "Old things are passed away; behold, all things are become new." If we believe that this is God's word respecting each of us, what violence must we do to our memory of the past, and our consciousness of the present, if we do try to persuade ourselves that so total a change has taken place in each of us, that what we once were, we are no longer; that what we are, we once were not; and this not in some few particular points, but in the main character of our minds. Again, "All things are of God, who hath reconciled us to himself by Jesus Christ." If we apply these words to each of us, what exceeding presumption would they breed! If all things in us and about us are now of God, what room can there be for sin? If God hath reconciled us to himself by Jesus Christ, what room can there be for fear or for danger? And thus, while we say we are quoting and believing the word of God, we do in fact turn it into a lie; we make it assert a falsehood as to our past state, and a falsehood as to our future state; we make it say, that our old nature is passed away, when it is not; that we have got a new nature when we have not; that we are reconciled to God, and therefore in safety, when we are, in fact, in the extremest danger.

But it is easy to see that we have no right to apply to ourselves words written by St. Paul eighteen hundred years ago, and applied by him to other persons. I go, then, farther; and I say, that if every member of the church of Corinth, to which they were written, had applied them to himself in the manner which I have shown above, the words would in many instances have been perverted no less, and would have been made to state what was false, and not what was true. And the same may be said of many other passages of St. Paul's Epistles, which, having been similarly misinterpreted, have furnished matter for endless controversies, and on which opposite theories of doctrine have been fondly raised, each of them alike unchristian and untrue.

Thus our present position is this:--that oftentimes by taking the representations of Scripture as true in fact, whether of ourselves or of others, we come to conclusions at once false and mischievous; being, as the case may be, either presumptuous, or fearful, or uncharitable, and claiming for each of these faults the sanction of the word of God.

A similar mistake in interpreting human compositions, has led to faults of another kind. Assuming as before, in interpreting St. Paul's words, that the language of our Liturgy is meant to describe, as a matter of fact, the actual feelings and condition of those who use it, or for whom it is used; and seeing manifestly that these feelings and condition do not agree with the words; we do not here, as with the Scripture, do violence to our common sense and conscience, by insisting upon it that we agree with the words, but we find fault with the words as being at variance with the matter of fact. Some say that the language of the General Confession is too strong a statement of sin; that the language of the Communion Service, of the Baptismal Service, and above all, of the Burial Service, is too full of encouragement and of assurance; that men are not all so bad as to require the one, 'nor so good as to deserve the other; that in both cases it should be lowered, to agree with the actual condition of those who use it.

Now it is worthy of notice, at any rate, that the self-same rule of interpretation applied to the Scripture and the Liturgy is found to suit with neither. We adhere positively to our rule: and thus, as we hold the words of Scripture sacred, we force common sense and conscience to make the facts agree with them; but not having the same respect for the words of the Liturgy, we complain of them as faulty and requiring alteration, because they do not agree with the facts.

I will not enter into the question whether the Liturgy has done wisely or not in thus imitating the Scripture; but I do contend that, in point of fact, there is this resemblance between them. St. Paul's Epistles, in particular, although it is true of other parts of the Scripture also, contain, as does the Liturgy of our Church, a great many passages which, if taken either universally or even generally as containing a matter of fact, will lead us into certain error. Is it, therefore, so very certain that we do wisely in so interpreting them?

With regard to our Liturgy I need not follow up the question now; but with regard to St. Paul, it is certain that he, in many parts of his Epistles, chooses to represent that which ought to be as that which actually was: he chooses to regard those to whom he is writing as being in all respects true Christians, as being worthy of their privileges, as answering to what God had done to them, as forming a church really inhabited by the Holy Spirit, and therefore being a true and living body of due proportions to Christ its Divine head. Nor does he trust exclusively to the common sense and conscience of those to whom he was writing to interpret his language correctly. He might have thought indeed that if he wrote to them as redeemed, justified, sanctified, as having all things new, as being the children of God, and the heirs of God, and the temples of the Holy Ghost, any individual who felt that he was none of these things, that sin was still mighty within him, and that he was sin's slave, would neither deny his own conscience, nor yet call St. Paul a deceiver; but would read in the difference between St. Paul's description of him and the reality, the exact measure of his own sin, and need of repentance and watchfulness. But he does not rely on this only: he notices sins as actually existing; he mingles the language of reproof and of anxiety, so as to make it quite clear that he did not mean his descriptions of their holiness and blessedness to apply to them all necessarily; he knew full well that they did not: but yet he knew also that, considering what God had done for them, it was monstrous that they should not be truly applicable.

But why then, you will say, did he use such language? why did he call men forgiven, redeemed, saved, justified, sanctified?--he uses all these terms often as applicable generally to those to whom he was writing;--why did he call them so, when in fact they were not so? He called them so for the same reason which, made prophecy foretell blessings upon Israel of old, and on the Christian church afterwards, which were fulfilled on neither:--in order to declare, and keep ever before us, what God has done and is willing to do for us: what he fain would do for us, if we would but suffer him; what divine powers are offered to us, and we will not use them; what divine happiness is designed for us, and we will not enter into it. Let us ponder all the magnificence of the scriptural language,--the words of the text for example, not as describing what we are when we are full of sin; nor yet as mere exaggerated language, which must be brought down to the level of our present reality. Let us consider it as containing the words of truth and soberness; not one jot or one tittle needs to be abated; it must not be lowered to us, but we rather raised to it. It is a truth, it is the word of God, it is the seal of our assurance: it is that which good men of old would have welcomed with the deepest joy; which, to good men now is a source of comfort unspeakable. For it tells us that God has done for us, is doing, will do, all that we need; it tells us that the price of our redemption has been paid, the kingdom of heaven has been set open, the power to walk as God's children has been given: that so far as God is concerned we are redeemed, we are saved, we are sanctified; it is but our own fault merely that we are not all of these actually and surely.

This is not a little matter to be persuaded of; if it be true, as I fear it is, that too many of us do not love God, is it not quite as true that we cannot believe that God loves us? Have we any thing like a distinct sense of the words of St. John, "We love God because he first loved us?" We believe in the love of our earthly friends; those who have so lately left their homes have no manner of doubt that their parents are interested in their welfare, though absent; that they will often think of them; and that, as far as it is possible at a distance from them, they are watching over their good, and anxious to promote it. The very name home implies all this; it implies that it is a place where those live who love us; and I do not question that the consciousness of possessing this love does, amidst all your faults and forgetfulnesses, rise not unfrequently within your minds, and restrain you from making yourselves altogether unworthy of it. Now, I say, that the words of the text, and hundreds of similar passages, are our assurance, if we would but believe them, that we have another home and another parent, by whom we are loved constantly and earnestly, who has done far more for us than our earthly parents can do. I grant that it is hard to believe this really; so infinite is the distance between God and us, that we cannot fancy that he cares for us; he may make laws for a world, or for a system, but what can he think or feel for us? It is, indeed, a thought absolutely overpowering to the mind; it may well seem incredible to us, judging either from our own littleness or our own forgetfulness; so hard as we find it to think enough of those to whom we are most nearly bound, how can the Most High. God think of us? But if there be any one particle of truth in Christianity, we are warranted in saying that God does love us; strange as it may seem, He, whom neither word nor thought of created being can compass; He, who made us and ten thousand worlds, loves each one of us individually; "the very hairs of our heads are all numbered." He so loved us, that he gave his only-begotten Son to die for us; and St. Paul well asks, "He that spared not his own Son, but delivered him up for us all, will he not also with him freely give us all things?"

Believe me, you could have no better charm to keep you safe through, the temptations of the coming half year, than this most true persuasion that God loves you. The oldest and the youngest of us may alike repeat to himself the blessed words, "God loves me;" "God loves me; God has redeemed me: God would dwell in my heart, that I might dwell in him: God has placed me in his church, has made me a member of Christ his own Son, has made me an inheritor of the kingdom of heaven." I might multiply words, but that one little sentence is, perhaps, more than all, "God loves me." Oh that you would believe him when he assures you of it, for then surely you would not fail to love him. But whether you believe it or not, still it is so: God loves every one of us; he loves each one of us as belonging to Christ his Son. He does love each, of us; let us not cast his love away from us, and refuse to love him in return; he does love each of us now, but there may be a time to each of us,--there will be, assuredly, if we will not believe that he loves us, when he will love us no more for ever.

LECTURE XXXVII.

EZEKIEL xx. 49.

Then said I, Ah, Lord God I they say of me, Doth he not speak parables?

Nothing is more disheartening, if we must believe it to be true, than the language in which some persons talk of the difficulty of the Scriptures, and the absolute certainty that different men will ever continue to understand them differently. It is not, we are told, with the knowledge of Scripture as with that of outward nature: in the knowledge of nature, discoveries are from time to time made which set error on the one side, and truth on the other, absolutely beyond dispute; there the ground when gained is clearly seen to be so; and as fresh sources of knowledge are continually opening to us, it is not beyond hope that we may in time arrive infinitely near to the enjoyment of truth,--truth certain in itself, and acknowledged by all unanimously. But with Scripture, it is said, the case is far otherwise; discoveries are not to be expected here, nor does a later generation derive from, its additional experience any greater insight into the things of God than was enjoyed by the generations before it. And when we see that actually the complete Scriptures have been in the world not much less than eighteen hundred years; that within that period no other book has been so much studied; and yet that differences of opinion as to the matters spoken of in it have ever existed, and exist now as much as ever, what reasonable prospect is there, it is asked, of future harmony or of clearer demonstrations of divine truth; and will not the good on these points ever continue to differ from the good, and the wise to differ from the wise?

This language, so discouraging as it is, may be heard from two very opposite parties, so that their agreement may appear to give it the more weight: it is used by men who are indifferent to religious truth, as an excuse for their taking no pains to discover what the truth really is; it is echoed back quite as strongly by another set of persons who wish to magnify the uncertainties of the Scripture in order to recommend more plausibly the guidance of some supposed authoritative interpreter of it. But yet it ought to be at any rate a painful work to any serious mind to be obliged to dwell not only on the obscurities of God's word, but on its perpetual and invincible obscurities; and, though an interpreter may be necessary if we know not the language of those with whom we are conversing, yet how much better would it be that we should ourselves know it: nay, and if we are told that we cannot know it, that our best endeavours will be unable to master it, the suspicion inevitably arises in our minds, that our pretended interpreter may be ignorant of it also; that he is not in truth better acquainted with it than we, but only more presumptuous or more dishonest.

Still a statement may be painful, but at the same time true. There is undoubtedly something in such language as I have been alluding to, which appears to be confirmed by experience. There is no denying the fact, that the Scriptures have been a long time in the world; that they have been very generally and carefully read; and yet that men do differ exceedingly as to religious truth, and these differences do not seem to be tending towards agreement. It seems to me, there fore, desirable that every student of the Scriptures should know, as well as may be, what the exact state of the question is; for if the subject of his studies is really so hopelessly uncertain, it is scarcely possible that his zeal in studying it should not be abated; nay, could we wisely encourage him to bestow his pains on a hopeless labour?

Now, in the very outset, there is this consideration which many of us here are well able to appreciate. We read many books written in dead languages, most of them more ancient than any part of the New Testament, some of them older than several of the books of the Old. We know well enough that these ancient books are not without their difficulties; that time, and thought, and knowledge are required to master them; but still we do not doubt that, with the exception of particular-passages here and there, the true meaning of these books may be discovered with undoubted certainty. We know, too, that this certainty has increased; that interpretations, which, were maintained some years ago, have been set aside by our improved knowledge of the languages and condition of the ancient world, quite as certainly as old errors in physical science have been laid to rest by later discoveries. Farther, our improved knowledge has taught us to distinguish what may be known from what may be probably concluded, and what is probable from what can merely be guessed at. When we come to points of this last sort, to passages which cannot be interpreted or understood, we leave them at once as a blank; but we enjoy no less, and understand with no less certainty, the greatest portions of the book which, contain them. And this experience, with regard to the works of heathen antiquity, makes it a startling proposition at the very outset, when we are told that with the works of Christian antiquity the case is otherwise.

We thus approach the statement as to the hopeless difficulty of Scripture, confirmed, as we are told it is, by the actual fact of the great disagreements among Christians, with a well-grounded mistrust of its soundness; we feel sure that there is something in it which is confused or sophistical. And considering the fact which appears to confirm it, I mean the actual differences between Christians and Christians, it soon appears by no means to bear out its supposed conclusion. For the differences between Christians and Christians by no means arise generally from the difficulty of understanding the Scripture aright, but from disagreement as to some other point, quite independent of the interpretation of the Scriptures. For example, the great questions at issue between us and the Roman Catholics turn upon two points,--Whether there is not another authority, in matters of Christianity, distinct from and equal to the Scriptures,--and whether certain interpretations of Scripture are not to be received as true, for the sake of the authority of the interpreter. Now, suppose for a moment, that the works of Plato or Aristotle were to us in the place of the Scriptures; and that the question was, whether these works of theirs could be understood with certainty; it would prove nothing against our being able to understand them, if, whilst we look to them alone, another man were to say, that, to his judgment, the works of other philosophers were no less authoritative; or, if he were to insist upon it, that the interpretations given by the scholiasts were always sure to be correct, because the scholiasts were the authorized interpreters of the text. No doubt our philosophical opinions and our practice might differ widely from such a man's; but the difference would prove nothing as to the obscurity of Plato's or Aristotle's text, because another standard had been brought in, distinct from their works, and from the acknowledged principles of interpretation, and thus led unavoidably to a different result.

The same also is the case as to the questions at issue between the Church of England and many of the Dissenters. In these disputes it is notorious that the practice and authority of the church are continually appealed to, or, it may be, considerations of another kind, as to the inherent reasonableness of a doctrine; all which are, again, a distinct matter from the interpretation of Scripture. One of the greatest men of our time has declared, that, in the early part of his life, he did not believe in the divinity of our Lord; but he has stated expressly, that he never for a moment persuaded himself that St. Paul or St. John did not believe it; their language he thought was clear enough, upon the point; but the notion appeared to him so unreasonable in itself, that he disbelieved it in spite of their authority. It is manifest, that, in this case, great as the difference was between this great man's early belief and his later, yet it in no way arose from the obscurity of the Scripture. The language of the Scripture was as clear to him at first as it was afterwards; but in his early life he disbelieved it, while, in his latter life, he embraced it with all his heart and soul.

It must not be denied, however, that we are here arrived at one of the causes which are likely, for a long time, to keep alive a false interpretation of Scripture, and which do not affect our interpretation of heathen writings. For most men, in such a case as I have referred to, when they do not believe the language of the Scripture, but wish to alter it, whether by omission or addition, do not deal so fairly with it as that great man did to whom I have alluded. They have neither his knowledge nor his honesty; a false interpretation is more easily disguised from them, owing to their ignorance, and they let their wishes more readily warp their judgment. Thus, they will not say as he did, "The Scripture clearly says so and so, but I cannot believe it;" they rather say, "This is very unreasonable and shocking, the Scripture cannot mean to say this;" or, "This is very pious and very ancient, the Scripture cannot but sanction this." And certainly, if men will so deal with it, there remains no certainty of interpretation then. But this is not the way that we deal with other ancient writings; and its unfairness and foolishness, if ever attempted to be practised there, are so palpable as to be ridiculous. No doubt it is difficult to convince men against their will; nevertheless, there is a good hope, that, as sound principles of interpretation are more generally known, they will put to shame a flagrant departure from them; and that those who try to make the Scripture say more or less than it has said, will be gradually driven to confess that Scripture is not their real authority; that their own notions in the one case, and the authority of the Church in the other case, have been the real grounds of their belief, to which they strove to make the Scriptures conform.

Nothing that I have said is, in any degree, meant to countenance the opinions of those who talk of the Bible,--or rather, our translation of it,--being its own interpreter; meaning, that if you give a Bible to any one who can read, he will be able to understand it rightly. Even in this extravagance, there is indeed something of a truth. If a man were so to read the Bible, much he would, unquestionably, be able to understand; enough, I well believe, if honestly and devoutly used, to give him, if living in a desert island by himself, the knowledge of salvation. But when we talk of understanding the Bible, so as to be guided by it amidst the infinite varieties of opinion and practice which beset us on every side, it is the wildest folly to talk of it as being, in this sense, its own interpreter. Our comfort is, not that it can be understood without study, but with it; that the same pains which, enable us to understand heathen writings, whose meaning is of infinitely less value to us, will enable us, with God's blessing, to understand the Scriptures also. Neither do I mean, that mere intellectual study would make them clear to the careless or the undevout; but, supposing us to seek honestly to know God's will, and to pray devoutly for his help to guide us to it, then our study is not vain nor uncertain; the mind of the Scriptures may be discovered; we may distinguish plainly between what is clear, and what is not clear; and what is not clear will be found far less in amount, and infinitely less in importance, than what is clear. I do not say, that a true understanding of the Scriptures will settle at once all religious differences;-- manifestly, it cannot; for, although I may understand them well, yet if a man maintains an opinion, or a practice, upon some other authority than theirs, we cannot agree together. Nevertheless, we may be allowed to hope and believe, that in time, if men could be hindered from misinterpreting the Scripture in behalf of their own opinions, their opinions themselves would find fewer supporters; for, as Christianity must come, after all, from our blessed Lord and his apostles, men will shrink from saying that that is no truth of Christianity which Christ and his apostles have clearly taught, or that that is a truth of Christianity, however ancient, and by whatever long line of venerable names supported, which they have as clearly, in our sole authentic records of them, not taught. It is not, therefore, without great and reasonable hope, that we may devote ourselves to the study of the Scriptures; and those habits of study which are cultivated here, and in other places of the same kind, are the best ordinary means of arriving at the truth. We are constantly engaged in extracting the meaning of those who have written in times past, and in a dead language. We do this according to certain rules, acknowledged as universally as the laws of physical science: these rules are developed gradually,--from the simple grammar which forms our earliest lessons, to the rules of higher criticism, still no less acknowledged, which are understood by those of a more advanced age. And we do this for heathen writings; but the process is exactly the same--and we continually apply it, also, for that very purpose--with what is required to interpret the Word of God. After all is done, we shall still, no doubt, find that the Scripture has its parables, its passages which cannot now be understood; but we shall find, also, that by much the larger portion of it may be clearly and certainly known; enough to be, in all points which really concern our faith and practice, a lantern to our feet, and an enlightener to our souls.

LECTURE XXXVIII.

ISAIAH v.1.

Now will I sing to my well-beloved a song of my beloved touching his vineyard.

Whatever difficulties we may find in understanding and applying many parts of the prophetical Scriptures, yet every thinking person could follow readily enough, I suppose, the chapter from which these words are taken, as it was read in the course of this morning's service; and he would feel, while understanding it as said, immediately and in the first instance, of the Jewish Church or nation, seven centuries and a half before the birth of our Lord, that it was no less applicable to this Christian church and nation at the present period. We cannot, indeed, expect to find a minute agreement in particular points between ourselves and the Jews of old; the difference of times and circumstances renders this impossible; both they and we stand, on the one hand, in so nearly the same relation to God, and we both so share, on the other hand, in the same sinful human nature, that the complaints, and remonstrances of the prophets of old may often, be repeated, even in the very same words, by the Christian preacher now.

If this be so, then the language of various parts of the service of the Church in this season of Advent ought to excite in us no small apprehension; for whilst the lessons from the Old Testament describe the evil state of the Jewish people in the eighth century before Christ, and threaten it with destruction, so the gospels for this day, and for last Sunday, speak of the evil state of the same people when our Lord was upon earth; and the chapter from which the gospel of this day is taken, contains, as we know, a full prophecy of the destruction that was, for the second time, going to overwhelm the earthly Jerusalem. We cannot but fear, therefore, that if our state now be like that of God's people of old, eight centuries before our Lord's coming, and again like their state at his coming: and if, after the first period, their city and temple were burnt, and they were carried captive to Babylon,--and again, after the second period, the city and temple were burnt again, and the people were dispersed, even to this day,--that, as the punishment has twice surely followed the sin, so it will not fail to find it out in this third case also.

And be it remembered that the people, or church of God, as such, can receive their punishment only in this world: for, taken as a body, it is an institution for this world only. We each of us, no doubt, shall have our own separate individual judgment after death; and, in the mean time, our fortunes and our character often bear no just correspondence with each other. But nations and churches have their judgments here: and although God's long-suffering so suspends it for many generations that it may seem as if it would never fall, yet does it come surely at the last; and almost always we can ourselves trace the connexion between the sin and the punishment, and can see that the one was clearly the consequence of the other. And thus our church and nation may feel their national judgments in this world quite independently of the several personal judgments which will be passed upon us each hereafter individually, when we stand before Christ's judgment seat.

I have thus ventured to bring the condition of the church as a body before our minds, although well knowing how much more we are concerned with the state of our own souls individually. Yet still the more general view is not without great use; and indeed it bears directly upon our individual state: our actions and our feelings having often a close connexion with, general church matters; and these actions and feelings being necessarily good or bad, according to the soundness of our judgment on the matter which occasions them. Besides which, it seems to me that general views, rather than what relates to particular faults, may be with most propriety dwelt on by those who have no direct connexion with the congregation which they are addressing.

In the first place, then, whenever we think of the state and prospects of Christ's church, whether for good or for evil, it is most desirable that we should rightly understand our own relations to it. "The vineyard of the Lord of hosts is the house of Israel;" or, in the language of the New Testament, "Christ is the vine, and we are the branches." Men continually seem to forget that they are members of the church; citizens, to use St. Paul's expression, of Christ's kingdom, as much as ever they are citizens of their earthly country. But they speak of the church as they might speak of any useful institution or society in their neighbourhood, whose object they approved of, and which they were glad to encourage, but without becoming members of it, or identifying themselves with its success or failure. For example, they speak of the church as they might speak of the universities, which indeed are institutions of great importance to the whole country, but yet they are manifestly distinct from the mass of the community: they have their own members, their own laws, and their own government, with which, people in general have nothing to do. And so many persons speak and feel of the church, regarding it evidently as consisting only of the clergy: our common language, no doubt, helping this confusion, because we often speak of a man's going into the church when he enters into holy orders, just as if ordination were the admission into the church, and not baptism. Now, if the clergy did indeed constitute the church, then it would very much resemble the condition of the universities: for it would then be indeed a society very important to the welfare of the whole country, but yet one that was completely distinct, and which had its members, laws, and government quite apart: for men in general do not belong to the clergy, nor are they concerned directly in such canons as relate to the peculiar business of the clergy, nor does the bishop's superintendence, as commonly exercised, extend at all to them. But God designed for his church far more than that it should contain one order of men only, or that it should comprise commonly but one single individual in a parish, preaching to and teaching the rest of the inhabitants, like a missionary amongst a population of heathens. Look at St. Paul's account of the church of Corinth, in the 12th chapter of his 1st epistle to the Corinthians, and see if any two things can be more different than his notion of a church, and that which many people seem to entertain amongst us. Compare the living body there described, made up of so many various members, each having its separate office, yet each useful to and needed by the others and by the body,--and our notion of a parish committed to the charge of a single individual: as if all the manifold gifts which the church requires could by possibility be comprised in the person of any one Christian; as if the whole burden were to rest upon his shoulders, and the other inhabitants might regard the welfare of the church as his concern only, and not theirs.

But not only is the church too often confined in men's notions to the single class or profession of the clergy, but it has been narrowed still farther by the practical extinction of one of the orders of the clergy itself. Where the laity have come to regard their own share in the concerns of the church as next to nothing, the order of deacons, forming, as it were, a link between the clergy and the laity, becomes proportionably of still greater importance.

The business of the deacons, as we well know, was in an especial manner to look after the relief of the poor; and by combining this charge with the power of baptizing, of reading the Scriptures, and of preaching also, when authorized by the bishop, they exhibited the peculiar character of Christianity, that of sanctifying the business of this world by doing everything in the name of the Lord Jesus. No church, so far as we know, certainly no church in any town, existed without its deacons: they were as essential to its completeness as its bishop and its presbyters.

Take any one of our large towns now, and what do we find? A bishop, not of that single town only, but of fifty others besides: one presbyter in each, church, and no deacons! Practically, and according to its proper character, the order of deacons is extinct; and those who now bear the name are most commonly found exercising the functions of presbyters; that is, instead of acting as the assistants of a presbyter, they are often the sole ministers of their respective parishes; they alone baptize; alone offer up the prayers of the church, alone preach the word: nothing marks their original character, except their inability to administer the communion; and thus, by a strange anomaly, the church in such parishes is actually left without any power of celebrating its highest act, that of commemorating the death, of Christ in the Lord's supper; and if it were not for another great evil, the unfrequent celebration of the Communion, the system could not go on: because the deacon would be so often obliged to apply to other ministers to perform that duty for him, that the inconvenience, as well as the unfitness, of the actual practice, would be manifest to every one.

Again, what has become of church discipline? That it has perished, we all well know: but its loss is the consequence of that fatal error which makes the clergy alone constitute the church. It is quite certain that men will not allow the members of a single profession to exercise the authority of society; to create and define offences; to determine their punishment, and to be the judges of each particular offender. As long as the clergy are supposed to constitute the whole church, church discipline would be nothing but priestly tyranny. And yet the absence of discipline is a most grievous evil; and there is no doubt that, although it must be vain when opposed to public opinion, yet, when it is the expression of that opinion, there is nothing which it cannot achieve. But public opinion cannot enforce church discipline now, because that discipline would not be now the expression of the voice of the church, but simply of a small part of the church, of the clergy only.

So deeply has this fatal error of regarding the clergy as the church extended itself, that at this moment a man's having been baptized is no security for his being so much as a believer in the truth of Christianity: no matter that he was made in his baptism a member of Christ, a child of God, and an inheritor of the kingdom of heaven; no matter that at a more advanced period of his life he was confirmed, and entered into the church by his own act and deed; still the church belongs to the clergy; they may hold such and such, language, and teach such and such doctrine; it would be very improper in them to do otherwise; and he has a great respect for the church, and would strenuously resist all its enemies, but truly, as for his own belief and his own conduct, these he will guide according to other principles, as imperative upon him as the rules of the church upon churchmen. Well indeed, do such men bear witness that they are not of the church, indeed; that their portion is not with God's people; that Christ is not their Saviour, nor the Holy Spirit their Comforter and Guide: but what blasphemy is it to call themselves friends of the church! as if Christ's church could have any friends except God and his holy angels: the church has its living and redeemed members; it may have those who are craving to be admitted within its shelter, being convinced that God is in it of a truth; but beyond these he who is not with it is against it; he who is not Christ's servant, serves his enemy.

Farther, it is this same deadly error which is the root and substance of popery. There is no one abuse of the Romish system which may not be traced to the original and very early error of drawing a wide distinction between the clergy and the laity; of investing the former in such a peculiar degree with the attributes of the church that at last they retained them almost exclusively. In other words, the great evil of popery is, that it has destroyed the Christian church, and has substituted a priesthood in its room. This is the fault of the Greek church, almost as much as of the Roman; and the peculiar tenet of the Romish church, that the supreme government is vested in one single member of this priesthood, the Bishop of

Rome, is in some respects rather an improvement of the system, than an aggravation of it. For even an absolute monarchy is a less evil than an absolute aristocracy; and an infallible Pope is no greater corruption of Christ's truth, than an infallible general council. The real evils of the system are of a far older date than the supremacy of the Bishop of Rome, and exist in places where that supremacy is resolutely denied. And if we attend to them carefully, we shall see that these evils have especially affected the Christian church as distinguished from the Christian religion. It is worth our while to attend to this distinction; for the Christian religion and the Christian church together, and neither without the other, form the perfect idea of Christianity. NOW, by the Christian religion, I mean the revelation of what God has done or will do for us in Christ; the great doctrines of the Trinity, the incarnation, the atonement, the resurrection, the presence of the Holy Spirit amongst us, and our own resurrection hereafter, to an existence of eternal happiness or misery. And these truths, if revealed to any single person living in an uninhabited island, might be abundantly sufficient for his salvation; if God disposed his heart to receive them, and to believe them earnestly, they would be the means of his overcoming his corrupt nature, and of passing from death unto life. But because men do not generally live alone, but with one another; and because they cannot but greatly hinder, or help each other by their mutual influence, therefore the Christian church was instituted for the purpose of spreading and furthering the growth of the Christian religion in men's hearts; and its various ministeries, its sacraments, its services and festivals, and its discipline were all designed with that object. And it is all these which popery has perverted; popery, whether in the Roman church or in the Greek church, or even in the Protestant church, for it has existed more or less in all. But even in the Roman church, where the perversion has been most complete, it has comparatively affected but little the truths of the Christian religion; all the great doctrines, which I mentioned, are held as by ourselves; the three creeds, the Apostles' creed, the Nicene, and the Athanasian, are used by the Roman church no less than by our own. Thus it often happens that we can read with great edification the devotional works of Roman Catholic writers, because in such works the individual stands apart from the Christian church, and is concerned only with the Christian religion: they show how one single soul, having learnt the tidings of redemption with faith, and thankfulness, improves them to its own salvation. But the moment that he goes out of his closet, and begins to speak and act amongst other men, then the corruption of popery shows itself. The Christian church was designed to help each individual towards a more perfect knowledge and love of God, by the counsel and example of his brethren, and by the practices which, he was to observe in their society. But the corrupt church exercises its influence for evil; it omits all the benefits to be derived from a living society, and puts forward, in their place, the observance of rites and ceremonies; knowledge and love are no longer looked to as the perfections of a Christian, but ignorance and blind obedience; not the mortifying all our evil passions universally, but the keeping them chained up, as it were under priestly control, to be let loose at the priest's bidding, against those whom he calls the church's enemies; that glorious church which he has destroyed and converted it into an idol temple, in that he, as God sitteth in the temple of God, showing himself that he is God.

To resist this great and monstrous evil, we must not exclaim against it under one of its forms only, even although that form exhibit it, indeed, in its most complete deformity; but we must strive against it under all its forms, remembering that its essence consists in putting the clergy in the place of the church; and taking from the great mass of the church their proper share in its government, in its offices, and therefore in its benefits, and in the sense of its solemn responsibilities. We speak often of church extension, meaning by this term the building new places of public worship, and the appointing additional ministers to preach the word and administer the sacraments. And no doubt such church extension is a good and blessed work, for it brings the knowledge of the truths of Christ's religion, and the benefit of his ordinances, the sacraments, within the reach of many who might otherwise have been without them. But it were a yet truer and more blessed church extension which should add to the building and the single minister, the real living church itself, with all its manifold offices and ministries, with its pure discipline, with its holy and loving sense of brotherhood. Without this, Christ will still, indeed, as heretofore, lay his hands on some few sick folk and heal them; his grace will convey the truths of his gospel to individual souls, and they will believe and be saved. But the fulfilment of prophecy; the triumph of Christ's kingdom; the changing an evil world into a world redeemed; this can only be done by a revival of the Christian church in its power, the living temple of the Holy Ghost, which, visibly to all mankind, in the wisdom and holiness of its members, showed that God was in the midst of it. It may be that this is a fond hope, which we may not expect to see realized; but looking on the one hand to the strong and triumphant language of prophecy, I know not how any hope of the advancement of Christ's kingdom can be more bold than God's word will warrant: and on the other, tracing the past history of the church, its gradual corruption may be deduced distinctly from one early and deadly mischief, which has destroyed its efficacy; so that, if this mischief can be removed, and the church become such as Christ designed it to be, it does not seem presumptuous to hope that his appointed instrument, working according to his will, should be enabled to obtain the full blessings of his promise.

And now, in conclusion, if we ask, what should follow from all that has been said? what it should lead us all, if it be true, to feel or to do?--the answer is, that considerations of this sort are not such as lead at once to some distinct change in our conduct; to the laying aside some favourite sin, or the practising some long neglected duty. And yet the thoughts which I have endeavoured to suggest to your minds may, if dwelt upon, lead, in the end, to a very considerable alteration, both in our feelings and in our practice. First of all, it is not a little matter to be convinced practically, that it is baptism, and not ordination, which makes us members of the church; that it is by sharing in the communion of Christ's body and blood, not by being admitted into the ministry, that the privileges and graces of Christ's church are conferred upon us. And most wisely, and most truly, does our Church separate ordination from the two Christian sacraments, as an institution far less solemn, and conferring graces far less important: for the difference between a Christian and a Christian minister is but one of office, not of moral or spiritual advancement, not of greater or less nearness to God. One is our master, even Christ; and all we are brethren. Words which certainly do not imply that all members of the church are to have the same office, or that all offices are of equal importance and dignity; but which do imply, most certainly, that any attempt to convert the ministry into a priesthoood, that is, to represent them as standing, in any matter, as mediators between Christ and his people, or as being essentially the channel through which his grace must pass to his church, is directly in opposition to him; and is no better than idolatry. It was by baptism that we have all been engrafted into Christ's body; it is by the communion of his body and blood that we continue to abide in him; it is in his whole body, in his church, and not in its ministers, as distinct from his church, that his Holy Spirit abides.

Thus feeling that we each are members of the church, that it is our highest country, to which we are bound with a far deeper love than to our earthly country, is not its welfare our welfare; its triumph our triumph; its failures our shame? We shall see, then, that church questions are not such merely, or principally, as concern the payment of the clergy, or their discipline, but all questions in which God's glory and man's sins or duties are concerned; all questions in the decision of which, there is a moral good and evil; a grieving of Christ's Spirit, or a conformity to him. And in such questions as concern the church, in the more narrow and common sense of the word, seeing that we are all members of the church, we should not neglect them, as the concern of others, but take an interest in them, and act in them, so far as we have opportunity, as in a matter which most nearly concerns ourselves. We feel that we have an interest in our country's affairs, although we are not members of the government or of the legislature; we have our part to perform, without at all overstepping the modesty of private life: and it is the constant influence of public opinion, and the active interest taken by the country at large in its own concerns, which, in spite of occasional delusion or violence, is mainly instrumental in preserving to us the combined vigour and order of our political constitution. And so, if we took an equal interest in the affairs of our divine commonwealth, our Christian church, and endeavoured as eagerly to promote every thing which tended to its welfare, and to put down and prevent every thing which might work it mischief, then the efforts of the clergy to advance Christ's kingdom would be incalculably aided, while there would then be no danger of our investing them with the duties and responsibilities which belong properly to the whole church; they could not then have dominion over our faith, nor by possibility become lords over God's heritage, but would be truly ensamples to the flock, the helpers of our joy, the glory of Christ.

LECTURE XXXIX.

COLOSSIANS iii. 17.

Whatsoever ye do in word or deed, do all in the name of the Lord Jesus, giving thanks to God and the Father by Him.

This, like the other general rules of the gospel, is familiar enough to us all in its own words; but we are very apt to forbear making the application of it. In fact, he who were to apply it perfectly would be a perfect Christian: for a life of which every word and deed were said and done in the name of the Lord Jesus, would be a life indeed worthy of the children of God, and such as they lead in heaven; it would leave no room for sin to enter. The art of our enemy has been therefore to make us leave this command of the apostle's in its general sense, and avoid exploring, so to speak, all the wisdom contained within it. Certain actions of our lives, our religious services, the more solemn transactions in which we are engaged, we are willing to do in Christ's name; but that multitude of common words and ordinary actions by which more than sixty-nine out of our seventy years are filled, we take away from our Lord's dominion, under the foolish, and hypocritical pretence that they are too trifling and too familiar to be mixed up with the thought of things so solemn.

This is one fault, and by far the most common. We make Christ's service the business only of a very small portion of our lives; we hallow only a very small part of our words and actions by doing them in his name. Unlike our Lord's own parable, where he compares Christianity to leaven hidden in the three measures of meal till the whole was leavened, the practice rather has been to keep the leaven confined to one little corner of the mass of meal; to take care that it should not spread so as to leaven the whole mass; to keep our hearts still in the state of the world when Christ visited it--"the light shineth in darkness, and the darkness comprehended it not;" that is, it did not take the light into itself so as to be wholly enlightened: the light shone, and there was a bright space immediately around it; but beyond there was a blackness of darkness into which it vainly strove to penetrate.

On the other hand there has been, though, more rarely, a fault of the opposite sort. Men have said that they were in all their actions of ordinary life doing Christ's will, that they endeavoured always to be promoting some good object; and that the peculiar services of religion, as they are called, were useless, inasmuch as in spirit they are worshipping God always. This is a great error; because, as a matter of fact, it is false. We may safely say that no man ever did keep his heart right with God in his ordinary life, that no one ever became one with Christ, and Christ with him, without seeking Christ where he reveals himself, it may not be more really, but to our weakness far more sensibly, than in the common business of daily life. We may be happy if we can find Christ there, after we have long sought him and found him in the way of his own ordinances, in prayer, and in his holy communion. Even Christ himself, when on earth, though his whole day was undeniably spent in doing the will of his heavenly father,--although to him doubtless God was ever present in the commonest acts no less than in the most solemn,--yet even he, after a day spent in all good works, desired a yet more direct intercourse with God, and was accustomed to spend a large portion of the night in retirement and prayer.

Without this, indeed, we shall most certainly not say and do all in the name of the Lord Jesus; much more shall we be in danger of forgetting him altogether. But supposing

135

that we are not neglectful of our religious duties, in the common sense of the term, that we do pray and read the Scriptures, and partake of Christ's communion, yet it will often happen that we do not connect our prayers, nor our reading, nor our communion, with many of the common portions of our lives; that there are certain things in which we take great interest, which, notwithstanding, we leave, as it were, wholly without the range of the light of Christ's Spirit. There is a story told that, in times and countries where there prevailed the deepest ignorance, some who came to be baptized into the faith of Christ, converted from their heathen state, not in reality but only in name, were accustomed to leave their right arm unbaptized, with the notion that this arm, not being pledged to Christ's service, might wreak upon their enemies those works of hatred and revenge which in baptism they had promised to renounce. It is too much to say that something like this unbaptized right arm is still to be met with amongst us--that men too often leave some of their very most important concerns, what they call by way of eminence their business--their management of their own money affairs, and their conduct in public matters--wholly out of the control of Christ's law?

Now at this very time public matters are engaging the thoughts of a great many persons all over the kingdom: and are not only engaging their thoughts, but are also become a practical matter, in which they are acting with great earnestness. Is it nothing that there should be so much, interest felt, so much pains taken, and yet that neither should be done in the name of the Lord Jesus, nor to the glory of God? It cannot be unsuited to the present season to dwell a little on this subject, which has nothing whatever to do with men's differences of opinion, but relates only to their acting, whatever be their political opinions, on Christian principles, and in a Christian spirit.

First, consider what we pray for in the prayer which we have been using every week for the high court of parliament: we pray to God, that "all things may be so ordered and settled by the endeavours of parliament, upon the best and surest foundations, that peace and happiness, truth, and justice, religion and piety, may be established among us for all generations." These great blessings we beg of God to secure to us and to our children through the endeavours of parliament; if, therefore, we are any ways concerned in fixing who the persons are to be who are to compose this parliament, it is plain that there is put into our hands a high privilege, if you will; but along with it, as with all other privileges, a most solemn responsibility.

But, if it be a solemn responsibility in the sight of God and of Christ, surely the act of voting, which many think so lightly of, and which many more consider a thing wholly political and worldly, becomes, indeed, a very important Christian duty, not to be discharged hastily or selfishly, in blind prejudice or passion, from self-interest, or in mere careless good nature and respect of persons; but deliberately, seriously, calmly, and, so far as we can judge our deceitful hearts, purely; not without prayer to Him who giveth wisdom liberally to those that ask it, that he will be pleased to guide them aright, to his own glory, and to the good of his people.

Do I say that if we were to approach this duty in this spirit, and with such prayers, we should all agree in the same opinion, and all think the same of the same men? No, by no means; we might still greatly differ; but we should, at least, have reason to respect one another, and to be in charity with one another; and if we all earnestly desired and prayed to be directed to God's glory, and the public good, God, I doubt not, would give us all those ends which we so purely desired, although in our estimate of the earthly means and instruments by which they were to be gained, we had honestly differed from one another.

Now, supposing that we had this conviction, that what we were going to do concerned the glory of God and the good of his people, and that we approached it therefore seriously as a Christian duty, yet it may be well that many men might feel themselves deficient in knowledge; they might not understand the great questions at issue; they might honestly doubt how they could best fulfil the trust committed to them. I know that the most ignorant man will feel no such hesitation if he is going to give his vote from fancy, or from prejudice, or from interest; these are motives which determine our conduct quickly and decisively. But if we regard our vote as a talent for which we must answer before God that we may well be embarrassed by a consciousness of ignorance; we may well be anxious to get some guidance from others, if we cannot find it in ourselves. Here, then, is the place for

136

authority,--for relying, that is, on the judgment of others, when we feel that we cannot judge for ourselves. But is their no room for the exercise of much good sense and fairness in ourselves as to the choice of the person by whose judgment we mean to be guided? Are we so little accustomed to estimate our neighbours' characters rightly, as to be unable to determine whom we may consult with advantage? Surely if their be any one whom we have proved, in the affairs of common life, to be at once honest and sensible, to such an one we should apply when we are at a loss as to public matters. If there is such an one amongst our own relations or personal friends, we should go to him in preference: if not, we can surely find one such amongst our neighbours: and here the authority of such of our neighbours as have a direct connexion with us, if we have had reason to respect their judgment and their principles, may be properly preferred to that of indifferent persons; the authority of a master, or an employer, or of our minister, or of our landlord, may and ought, under such circumstances, to have a great and decisive influence over us.

On the other hand, supposing again that we have this strong sense of the great responsibility in the sight of God of every man who has the privilege of a vote, we shall be exceedingly careful not to tempt him to sin by fulfilling this duty ill. Nothing can be more natural or more proper than that those who have strong impressions themselves as to the line to be followed in public matters, should be desirous of persuading others to think as they do; every man who loves truth and righteousness must wish that what he himself earnestly believes to be true and righteous, should be loved by others also; but the highest truth, if professed by one who believes it not in his heart, is to him a lie, and he sins greatly by professing it. Let us try as much as we will to convince our neighbours; but let us beware of influencing their conduct, when we fail in influencing their convictions: he who bribes or frightens his neighbour into doing an act which no good man would do for reward or from fear, is tempting his neighbour to sin; he is assisting to lower and to harden his conscience,-- to make him act for the favour or from the fear of man, instead of for the favour or from the fear of God; and if this be a sin in him, it is a double sin in us to tempt him to it. Nor let us deceive ourselves by talking of the greatness of the stake at issue; that God's glory and the public good are involved in the result of the contest, and that therefore we must do all in our power to win it. Let us by all means do all that we can do without sin; but let us not dare to do evil that good may come, for that is the part of unbelief; it becomes those who will not trust God with the government of the world, but would fain guide its course themselves. Here, indeed, our Lord's command does apply to us, that we be not anxious; "Which of you by taking thought can add to his stature one cubit?" How little can we see of the course of Providence! how little can we be sure that what we judged for the best in public affairs may not lead to mischief! But these things are in God's hand; our business is to keep ourselves and our neighbours from sin, and not to do or encourage in others any thing that is evil, however great the advantages which we may fancy likely to flow from that evil to the cause even of the highest good.

There is no immediate prospect, indeed, that we in this particular congregation shall be called upon to practise the duty of which I have been now speaking; and, indeed, it is for that very reason that I could dwell on the subject more freely. But what is going on all around us, what we hear of, read of, and talk of so much as we are many of us likely to do in the next week or two about political matters, *that* we should be accustomed to look upon as Christians: we should by that standard try our common views and language about it, and, if it may be, correct them: that so hereafter, if we be called upon to act, we may act, according to the Apostle's teaching, in the name of our Lord Jesus. And I am quite sure if we do so think and so act, although our differences of opinion might remain just the same, yet the change in ourselves, and I verily believe in the blessings which God would give us, would be more than we can well believe; and a general election, instead of calling forth, as it now does, a host of unchristian passions and practices, would be rather an exercise of Christian judgment, and forbearance, and faith, and charity; promoting, whatever was the mere political result, the glory of God, advancing Christ's kingdom, and the good of this, as it would be then truly called, Christian nation.

NOTES.

NOTE A. P. 5.

"*But our path is not backwards but onwards*"--This thought is expressed very beautifully in lines as wise and true as they are poetical:

"Grieve not for these: nor dare lament
That thus from childhood's thoughts we roam:
Not backward are our glances bent,
But forward to our Father's home.
Eternal growth has no such fears,
But freshening still with seasons past,
The old man clogs its earlier years,
And simple childhood comes the last."
Burbridge's Poems, p. 309.

NOTE B. P. 102.

"*Some may know the story of that German nobleman,*" &c.--The Baron von Canitz. He lived in the latter half of the seventeenth century, and was engaged in the service of the electors of Brandenburg, both of the great elector and his successor. He was the author of several hymns, one of which is of remarkable beauty, as may be seen in the following translation, for the greatest part of which I am indebted to the kindness of a friend: but the language of the original, in several places, cannot be adequately translated in English.

Come, my soul, thou must be waking--
Now is breaking
O'er the earth another day.
Come to Him who made this splendour
See thou render
All thy feeble powers can pay.
From the stars thy course be learning:
Dimly burning
'Neath the sun their light grows pale:
So let all that sense delighted
While benighted
From God's presence fade and fail.
Lo! how all of breath partaking,
Gladly waking,
Hail the sun's enlivening light!
Plants, whose life mere sap doth nourish,
Rise and flourish,
When he breaks the shades of night.
Thou too hail the light returning,--
Ready burning
Be the incense of thy powers;--
For the night is safely ended:
God hath tended
With His care thy helpless hours.

138

Pray that He may prosper ever
Each endeavour
When thine aim is good and true;
But that He may ever thwart thee,
And convert thee,
When thou evil wouldst pursue.
Think that He thy ways beholdeth--
He unfoldeth
Every fault that lurks within;
Every stain of shame gloss'd over
Can discover,
And discern each deed of sin.
Fetter'd to the fleeting hours,
All our powers,
Vain and brief, are borne away;
Time, my soul, thy ship is steering,
Onward veering,
To the gulph of death a prey.
May'st thou then on life's last morrow,
Free from sorrow,
Pass away in slumber sweet;
And released from death's dark sadness,
Rise in gladness,
That far brighter Sun to greet.
Only God's free gifts abuse not,
His light refuse not,
But still His Spirit's voice obey;
Soon shall joy thy brow be wreathing,
Splendour breathing
Fairer than the fairest day.
If aught of care this morn oppress thee,
To Him address thee,
Who, like the sun, is good to all:
He gilds the mountain tops, the while
His gracious smile
Will on the humblest valley fall.
Round the gifts His bounty show'rs,
Walls and tow'rs
Girt with flames thy God shall rear:
Angel legions to defend thee
Shall attend thee,
Hosts whom Satan's self shall fear.

NOTE C. P. 122.

"*But, once admit a single exception, and the infallible virtue of the rule ceases.*"--Thus the famous Canon of Vincentius Lirinensis is like tradition itself, always either superfluous or insufficient. Taken literally, it is true and worthless;--because what *all* have asserted,*always*, and in *all places*, supposing of course that the means of judging were in their power, may be assumed to be some indisputable axiom, such as never will be disputed any more than it has been disputed hitherto. But take it with any allowance, and then it is of no use in settling a question: for what *most* men have asserted, *most commonly*, and in *most places*, has a certain *à priori* probability, it is true, but by no means such as may not be outweighed by probabilities on the other side; for the extreme improbability consists not in the prevalence of error amongst millions, or for centuries, or over whole continents,--but in its being absolutely universal, so universal, that truth could not find a single witness at any time or in any country. But the single witness is enough to "justify the ways of God," and reduces what otherwise would have been a monstrous triumph of evil to the character of a severe trial of our faith, severe indeed as the trials of an evil world will be, but no more than a trial such as, with God's grace, may be overcome.

NOTE D. P. 189.

"*It was an admirable definition of that which excites laughter,*" &c.--[Greek: To geloion apurtaepa ti chai aiochos auodnnoy chai on phthartichon oion enthus to geloion prosopon aischron ti chai dieotruppenon anen odunaes]--*Aristotle, Poetic,* ii.

NOTE E. P. 245.

"*I would endeavour just to touch upon some of the purposes for which the Scripture tells us that Christ died.*"--The Collects for Easter Sunday and the Sundays just before it and after it, illustrate the enumeration here given. The Collect for the Sunday next before Easter speaks of Christ's death only as an "example of his great humility." The Collect for Easter-day speaks of the resurrection, and connects it with our spiritual resurrection, as does also the Collect for the first Sunday after Easter. But the collect for the Second Sunday after Easter speaks of Christ as being at once our sacrifice for sin and our example of godly life,--a sacrifice to be regarded with entire thankfulness, and an example to be daily followed.

NOTE F. P. 282.

"*Such also was to be the state of the Christian Church after our Lord's ascension.*"--And therefore, as I think, St. Peter applies to the Christians of Asia Minor the very terms applied to the Jews living in Assyria or in Egypt; he addresses them as [Greek: parepidaemois diasporas], (1 Peter i. 1,) that is, as strangers and sojourners, scattered up and down in a country that was not properly their own, and living in a sort of banishment from their true home. That the words are not addressed to Jewish Christians, and therefore are not to be understood in their simple historical sense, seems evident from the second chapter of the Epistle, verses 9, 10, and iv. 2,3.

NOTE G. P. 315.

"*Not only an outward miracle, but the changed circumstances of the times may speak God's will no less clearly than a miracle,*" &c.--What I have here said does not at all go beyond what has been said on the same subject by Hooker: "Laws, though both ordained of God himself, and the end for which they were ordained continuing, may, notwithstanding, cease, if by alteration of persons or times they be found insufficient to attain unto that end. In which respect why may we not presume that God doth even call for such change or alteration as the very condition of things themselves doth make necessary?... In this case, therefore, men do not presume to change God's ordinance, but they yield thereunto, requiring itself to be changed."--*Ecclesiastical Polity,* b. iii. § 10.

NOTE H. P. 320.

"Nor is it less strange that any should ever have been afraid of their understandings, and should have sought goodness through prejudice, and blindness, and folly."--For some time past the words "Rationalism" and "Rationalistic" have been freely used as terms of reproach by writers on religious subjects; the 73d No. of the "Tracts for the Times" is entitled, "On the introduction of Rationalistic Principles into Religion," and a whole chapter in Mr. Gladstone's late work on Church Principles is headed "Rationalism." Yet we still want a clear definition of the thing signified by this name. The Tract for the Times says, "To rationalize, is to ask for *reasons* out of place; to ask improperly how we are to *account* for certain things; to be unwilling to believe them unless they can be accounted for, i.e. referred to something else as a cause, to some existing system, as harmonizing with them, or taking them up into itself.... It is characterised by two peculiarities;--its love of systematizing, and its basing its system upon personal experience, on the evidence of sense."--P. 2. Mr. Gladstone says more generally, "Rationalism is commonly, at least in this country, taken to be the reduction of Christian *doctrine* to the standard and measure of the human understanding."--P. 37. But neither of these definitions will include all the arguments and statements which have been called by various writers "rationalistic;" and while the terms used are thus vague, they are often applied very indiscriminately, and the tendency of this use of them is to depreciate the exercise of the intellectual faculties generally. The subject seems to deserve fuller consideration than it has yet received; there is a real evil which the term Rationalism is meant to denounce; but it has not been clearly apprehended, and what is good has sometimes been confounded with it, and denounced under the same name.

I cannot pretend to discuss the subject fully in a mere note, even if I were otherwise competent to do it. But one or two points may be noticed, as likely to assist the inquiry, wherever it is worthily entered on.

1st. It is important to bear in mind the distinction which Coleridge enforces so earnestly between the understanding and the reason. I do not know whether Mr. Gladstone, in the passage quoted above, uses the word "understanding" as synonymous with reason, or in that stricter sense in which Coleridge employs it. But the writer of the Tract seems to allude to the stricter sense, when he calls it a characteristic of rationalism "to base its system upon personal experience, on the evidence of sense." If this be the case, then it would seem that rationalism is the appealing to the decision of the understanding in points where the decision properly belongs not to the understanding, but to the reason. This is a great fault, and one to which all persons who belong to the sensualist school in philosophy, as opposed to the idealist school, would be more or less addicted. But then, this fault consists not in an over-estimating of man's intellectual nature generally, but in the exalting one part of it unduly, to the injury of another part; in deferring to the understanding, rather than to the reason.

2d. Faith and reason are often invidiously contrasted with each other, as if they were commonly described in Scripture as antagonists; whereas faith is more properly opposed to sight, or to lust, being, in fact, a very high exercise of the pure reason; inasmuch as we believe truths which our senses do not teach us, and which our passions would have us, therefore, reject, because those truths are taught by Him in whom reason recognises its own author, and the infallible source of all truth.

3d. It were better to oppose reason to passion than to faith; for it may be safely said, that he who neglects his reason, so far as he does neglect it, does not lead a life of faith afterwards, but a life of passion. He does not draw nearer to God, but to the brutes, or rather to the devils; for his passions cannot be the mere instinctive appetites of the brute, but derive from the wreck of his intellectual powers, which he cannot utterly destroy, just so much of a higher nature that they are sins, and not instincts, belonging to the malignity of diabolic nature, rather than to the mere negative evil of the nature of brutes.

4th. Faith may be described as reason leaning upon God. Without God, reason is either overpowered by sense and understanding, and, in a manner, overgrown, so that it

141

cannot comprehend its proper truths; or, being infinite, it cannot discover all the truths which concern it, and therefore needs a farther revelation to enlighten it. But with God's grace strengthening it to assert its supremacy over sense and understanding, and communicating to it what of itself it could not have discovered, it then having gained strength and light not its own, and doing and seeing consciously by God's help, becomes properly faith.

5th. Faith without reason, is not properly faith, but mere power worship; and power worship may be devil worship; for it is reason which entertains the idea of God--an idea essentially made up of truth and goodness, no less than of power. A sign of power exhibited to the senses might, through them, dispose the whole man to acknowledge it as divine; yet power in itself is not divine, it may be devilish. But when reason recognises that, along with this power, there exist also wisdom and goodness, then it perceives that here is God; and the worship which, without reason, might have been idolatry, being now according to reason is faith.

6th. If this were considered, men would be more careful of speaking disparagingly of reason, seeing that it is the necessary condition of the existence of faith. It is quite true, that when we have attained to faith, it supersedes reason; we walk by sunlight, rather than by moonlight; following the guidance of infinite reason, instead of finite. But how are we to attain to faith? in other words, how can we distinguish God's voice from the voice of evil? for we must distinguish it to be God's voice before we can have faith in it. We distinguish it, and can distinguish it no otherwise, by comparing it with that idea of God which reason intuitively enjoins, the gift of reason being God's original revelation of himself to man. Now, if the voice which comes to us from the unseen world agree not with this idea, we have no choice but to pronounce it not to be God's voice; for no signs of power, in confirmation of it, can alone prove it to be God. God is not power only, but power, and truth, and holiness; and the existence of even infinite power, does not necessarily involve in it truth and holiness also; else the notion of the world being governed by an evil being would be no more than a contradiction in terms; and the horrible strife of the two principles of Manicheism would be a mere matter of indifference; for if power alone constitutes God, whichever principle triumphed over the other, would become God by the very fact of its victory; and thus triumphant evil would be good.

7th. Reason, then, is the mean whereby we attain to faith, and escape the devil worship of idolatry; but the understanding is not a necessary condition of faith, and very often impedes it; for the understanding having for its basis the reports of sense and experience, has no direct way of arriving at things invisible, and rather shrinks back from that world with which it is in no way familiar. It has a work to do in regard to revelation, and an important work; but divine things not being its proper matter, its work concerning them must be subordinate, and its tendency is always to fall back from the invisible to the visible,-- from matters of faith to matters of experience. Its work, with respect to revelation, is this-- that it should inquire into the truth of the outward signs of it; which outward signs being necessarily things visible and sensible, fall within its province of judgment. Thus understanding judges the external witnesses of a revelation: if miracles be alleged, it is the business of understanding to ascertain the fact of their occurrence; if a book claim to be the record of a revelation, it belongs to the understanding to make out the origin of this book, the time when it was written, who were its authors, and what is the first and grammatical meaning of its language. Or, again, if any men profess to be the depositaries of divine truth, by an extraordinary commission from God, the understanding, being familiar with man's nature and motives, can judge of their credibility--can see whether there are any marks of folly in them, or of dishonesty, or whether they are at once sensible and honest. And in all such matters, the prerogative of the understanding to judge is not to be questioned; for all such points are strictly within its dominion; and our Lord's words are of universal application, that we should render to Cæsar the things which are Cæsar's, no less than we should render to God the things that are God's.

Faith may exist, as I said, without the action of the understanding, but never without that of the reason. It may exist independent of the understanding, because faith in God is the natural result of the idea of God: and that idea belongs to the reason, and the understanding is not concerned with it. But when a special revelation has been given us, through human instruments; when the understanding is called in to certify the particular fact, that in such and such particular persons, writings, or events, God has made himself manifest in an extraordinary manner; it is the human instrumentality which requires the judgment of the understanding; the bringing in of human characters, and sensible facts, which are matters of sense and experience; and, therefore, it is mere ignorance when Christians speak slightingly of the outward and historical evidences of Christianity, and indulge in very misplaced contempt for Paley and others who have worked out the historical proof of it. Such persons may observe, if they will, that where the historical evidence has not been listened to, there a belief in Christianity, properly so called, is wanting. Living examples might, I think, be named of men whose reason entirely acknowledges the internal proofs of a divine origin which are contained in the Christian doctrines, but whose understandings are not satisfied as to the facts of the Christian history, and particularly as to the fact of our Lord's resurrection. Such men are a remarkable contrast to those whose understandings are fully satisfied of the historical truth of our Lord's resurrection, but who are indifferent to, or actually deny, those doctrinal truths of which another power than the understanding must be the warrant. It is important to observe, therefore, that in a revelation involving, as an essential part of it, certain historical facts, there is necessarily a call for the judgment of the understanding, although in religious faith simply the understanding may have no place.

8th. Now, then, the clearest notion which can be given of rationalism is, I think, be this: that it is the abuse of the understanding in subjects where the divine and the human, so to speak, are intermingled. Of human things the understanding can judge, of divine things it cannot;--and thus, where the two are mixed together, its inability to judge of the one part makes it derange the proportions of both, and the judgment of the whole is vitiated. For example, the understanding examines a miraculous history; it judges truly of what I may call the human part of the case; that is to say, of the rarity of miracles,--of the fallibility of human testimony,--of the proneness of most minds to exaggeration,--and of the critical arguments affecting the genuineness or the date of the narrative itself. But it forgets the divine part, namely, the power and providence of God, that He is really ever present amongst us, and that the spiritual world, which exists invisibly all around us, may conceivably, and by no means impossibly, exist, at some times and to some persons, even visibly. These considerations, which the understanding is ignorant of, would often modify our judgment as to the human parts of the case. Things not impossible in themselves are believed upon sufficient testimony; and with all the carelessness and exaggeration of historians, the mass of history is notwithstanding generally credible. Again, with regard to the history of the Old Testament, our judgment of the human part in it requires to be constantly modified by our consciousness of the divine part, or otherwise it cannot fail to be rationalistic; that is, it will be the judgment of the understanding only, unchecked by the reason. Gesenius' Commentary on Isaiah is rationalistic, for it regards Isaiah merely as a Jewish writer, zealously attached to the religion of his country, and lamenting the decay of his nation, and anxiously looking for its future restoration. No doubt Isaiah was all this, and therefore Gesenius' Commentary is critically and historically very valuable; the human part of Isaiah is nowhere better illustrated; but the divine part of the prophecy of Isaiah is no less real, and the consciousness of its existence should actually qualify our feelings and language even with reference to the human part.

9th. The fault, then, of rationalism appears to me to consist not so much in what it has as in what it has not. The understanding has its proper work to do with respect to the Bible, because the Bible consists of human writings and contains a human history. Critical and historical inquiries respecting it are, therefore, perfectly legitimate; it contains matter which is within the province of the understanding, and the understanding has God's warrant for doing that work which he appointed it to do; only, let us remember, that the understanding cannot ascend to things divine; that for these another faculty is necessary,-- reason or faith. If this faculty be living in us, then there can be no rationalism; and what is called so is then no other than the voice of Christian truth. Where a man's writings show that he is keenly alive to the divine part of Scripture, that he sees God ever in it, and regards it truly as his word, his judgments of the human part in it are not likely to be rationalistic;

and if his understanding decides according to its own laws, upon points within its own province, while his faith duly tempers it, and restrains it from venturing upon another's dominion, the result will, in all probability, be such as commonly attends the use of God's manifold gifts in their just proportions,--it will image, after our imperfect measure, the holiness of God and the truth of God.

It is very true, and should be acknowledged in the fullest manner, that for the study of the highest moral and spiritual questions another faculty than the understanding is wanting; and that without this faculty the understanding alone cannot arrive at truth. But it is no less true, that while there is, on the one side, a faculty higher than the understanding, which is entitled to pronounce upon its defects; "for he that is spiritual judgeth all things," ([Greek: auachriuei];) so there is a clamour often raised against it, not from above, but from below,--the clamour of mere shallowness and ignorance, and passion. Of this sort is some of the outcry which is raised against rationalism. Men do not leap, *per saltum mortalem*, from ordinary folly to divine wisdom: and the foolish have no right to think that they are angels, because they are not humanly wise. There is a deep and universal truth in St. Paul's words, where he says, that Christians wish "not to be unclothed but clothed upon, that mortality may be swallowed up of life." Wisdom is gained, not by renouncing or despising the understanding, but by adding to its perfect work the perfect work of reason, and of reason's perfection, faith.

NOTE I. P. 331.

"*A famous example of this may be seen in the sixth chapter of St. John,*" &c.--The interpretation of this chapter, and particularly of the part alluded to in the text, is of no small importance; for it is remarkable, that the highest notions with respect to the presence of our Lord in the Holy Communion are often grounded upon this passage in St. John's Gospel, which yet, in the judgment of others, most decisively repels them.

The whole question resolves itself into this--Are our Lord's words in this place co-ordinate with the Holy Communion, or subordinate to it? That is, do they and the communion alike point to some great truth superior to them both: or do our Lord's words, in St. John, point to the communion itself as their highest meaning?

The communion itself expresses a truth above itself by a symbolical action; the words of our Lord, in St. John, are exactly the same with that symbolic action; it is natural, therefore, to understand them not as referring to it, but to the same[14] higher truth to which it refers also: and the more so as the communion is not once mentioned by St. John either in his Gospel or in his Epistles; but the idea which the communion expresses appears to have been familiar to his mind; at least, if we suppose that his mention of the blood and water flowing from our Lord's side in his Gospel, and his allusion again to the same fact in his Epistle, have reference in any degree to it, which seems to me most probable.

[14] The common tendency to make the Christian sacraments an ultimate end rather than a mean, is exhibited in the heading of the tenth chapter of the 1st Epistle to the Corinthians, in our authorized version, where we find the first verses described as stating, that "the Jews' sacraments were types of ours." Whereas, so far is it from the apostle's argument to represent our sacraments as the reality of which the Jews' sacraments were the type, that he is describing theirs and ours as co-ordinate with each other, and both alike subordinate to the same truth; and he argues, that if the Jews, with their sacraments, did notwithstanding lose the reality which those sacraments typified, so we should take heed lest we, with our sacraments, should lose it also. The erroneous heading is not given in the Geneva Bible, where we have, on the contrary, the true observation; "the sacraments of the old fathers were all one with ours, for they respected Christ only." It is true that if no more were meant than that "the Jews' sacraments were like ours," there would be no reason to object to the expression; but apparently more is meant, as the word type seems to imply that what it is compared with is the reality, of which it is itself only the image; and one thing cannot properly be called the type of another, when both are but types of the same third

thing. But the divines of James the First's reign and of his son's, were to the reformers exactly what the so-called fathers were to the apostles: the very same tendencies, growing up even in Elizabeth's reign, becoming strengthened under the Stuart kings, and fully developed in the nonjurors, which distinguish the divines of the seventeenth century from those of the sixteenth, distinguish also the church system from the gospel. There are many who readily acknowledge this difference in the English church, while they would deny it in the case of the ancient church. Indeed, it is not yet deemed prudent to avow openly that they prefer the so-called fathers to the apostles, and therefore they try to persuade themselves that both speak the same language. And doubtless, if the Scriptures are to be interpreted according to the rule of the writers of the third, and fourth, and fifth centuries, the thing can easily be effected; as, by a similar process, the Articles of the Church of England, if interpreted according to the rule of the nonjurors and their successors, might be made to speak the very sentiments which their authors designed to condemn.

Our Lord repels the notion of a literal acceptation of his words, where he says,--"It is the Spirit which profiteth, the flesh profiteth nothing; the words which I speak unto you, they are Spirit and they are life." It seems impossible, therefore, to refer these words, which he tells us expressly are Spirit and life, to any outward act of eating and drinking as their highest truth and object.

But the words in the sixth chapter of St. John do highly illustrate the institution and purpose of the communion, and especially the remarkable words which our Lord used in instituting it. They show what infinite importance he attached to that truth which he expressed both in symbolical words and action under the same figure, of eating His body and drinking His blood. But to suppose that that truth can only be realized by one particular ritual action, so that the one great work of a Christian is to receive the Lord's supper,--which it must be, if our Lord's words in the sixth chapter of St. John refer to the communion,--is so contrary to the whole character of our Lord's teaching, and not least so in the very words so misinterpreted, that to maintain such a doctrine, leading, as it does, to such manifold superstitions, is actually to preach another Gospel than Christ's--to bring in a mystical religion instead of a spiritual one,--to do worse than to Judaize.

NOTE K. P. 345.

"A set of persons, who wish to magnify the uncertainties of the Scripture in order to recommend more plausibly the guidance of some supposed authoritative interpreter of it."--"The high church party," we have been lately told, "take Holy Scripture for their guide, and, in the interpretation of it, defer to the authority of primitive antiquity: the low church party contend for the sufficiency of private judgment." It is become of the greatest importance to see clearly, not what one party, or another, may contend for, but what is the real truth, and what, accordingly, is the duty of every Christian man to do in this matter. The sermon to which this note refers, is an attempt to show that Scripture is not hopelessly obscure or ambiguous; but it may not be inexpedient here to consider a little, what are the objections to the principle of the high church party; to clear away certain difficulties which are supposed to beset the opposite principle; and to state, if possible, what the truth of the whole question is.

I. The objections to the principle of the high church party are these: 1st. Its extreme vagueness. What is primitive antiquity? and where is its authority to be found? Does "primitive antiquity" mean the first three centuries? or the first two? or the first five? or the first seven? Does it include any of the general councils? or one of them? or four? or six? Are Irenæus and Tertullian the latest writers of "primitive antiquity?" or does it end with Augustine? or does it comprehend the venerable Bede? One writer has lately told us, that our Reformers wished the people to be taught, "that, for almost seven hundred years, the church was most pure." Are we, then, to hold that "primitive antiquity" embraces a period of nearly seven centuries? Seven centuries are considerably more than a third part of the whole duration of the church, from its foundation to this hour: can the third part of a nation's history be called its primitive antiquity? Is a tenet, or a practice taught when Christianity had been more than six hundred years in the world, to be called primitive? We know not, then, in the first place, what length of time is signified by "primitive antiquity."

But let it signify any length of time we choose, I ask, next, where is its authority to be found? In the decisions of the general councils? But if we call the first four centuries "primitive antiquity," we find in this period only two general councils; if we include the fifth century, we get four; if we take in the sixth and seventh centuries, we have then, in all, six general councils. Will the decisions of any, or all, of these six councils furnish us with an authoritative interpretation of Scripture? They give us the Nicene and the Constantinopolitan creeds; they condemn various notions with respect to the person of our Lord, and to some other points of belief; and they contain a variety of regulations for the discipline and order of the church; but, with the exception of some particular passages, there is no authority in the creeds, or canons, or anathemas of those councils, for the interpretation of Scripture; they leave its difficulties just where they were before. It is but little then, which the first six general councils will do towards providing the student of Scripture with an infallible standard of interpretation.

Where, however, except in the councils, can we find any thing claiming to be the voice of the church? Neither individual writers, nor yet all the writers of the first seven centuries together, can properly be called the church. They form, even altogether, but a limited number of individuals, who, in different countries, and at different periods, expressed, in writing, their own sentiments, but without any public authority. Origen, one of the ablest and most learned of them all, was anathematized by the second council of Constantinople; Tertullian was heretical during a part of his life; Lactantius was taxed with heterodoxy. How are we to know who were sound? And if sound generally, that is to say, if they stand charged with no heretical error, yet it does not follow that a man is infallible because he is not heretical; and none of these writers have been distinguished like the five great Roman lawyers whom the edict of Theodosius[15] selected from the mass, and gave to their decisions a legal authority. Or again, if it be said that the agreement of the great majority of them is to be regarded as decisive, we answer, that as no individual amongst them is in himself an authority legally, so neither can any number of them be so; and if a moral authority only be meant, such as we naturally ascribe to the concurring judgment of many eminent men, then this is a totally different question, and is open to inquiry in every separate case; for as, on the one hand, no one denies that such a concurring judgment is *an*authority, yet, on the other hand, it may be outweighed, either by the worth of the few who differ from the judgment, or by the reason of the case itself; and the concurring judgment of the majority may show no more than the force of a general prejudice, which only a very few individuals were sensible enough to resist.

[15] Cod. Theodos. lib. i. tit. iv. The edict is issued in the name of the emperors Theodosius (the younger) and Valentinian (the younger), in the year A.D. 426.

In fact, it would greatly help to clear this question if we understand what we mean by allowing, or denying, the authority of the so-called fathers. The term *authority* is ambiguous, and according to the sense in which I use it, I should either acknowledge it or deny it.--The writers of the first four, or of the first seven centuries, have *an* authority, just as the scholiasts and ancient commentators have: some of them, and in some points, are of weight singly; the agreement of many of them has much weight; the agreement of almost all of them would have great weight. In this sense, I acknowledge their authority; and it would be against all sound principles of criticism to deny it. But if, by authority, is meant a *decisive* authority, a judgment which may not be questioned, then the claim of authority in such a case, for any man, or set of men, is either a folly or a revelation. Such an authority is not human, but divine: if any man pretends to possess it, let him show God's clear warrant for his pretension, or he must be regarded as a deceiver or a madman.

But it may be said, that an authority not to be questioned was conferred, by the Roman law, on the opinions of a certain number of great lawyers: if a judge believed that their interpretation of the law was erroneous, he yet was not at liberty to follow his own private judgment in departing from it. Why may not the same thing be allowed in the church? and why may not the interpretations of Cyprian, or Athanasius, or Augustine, or Chrysostom, be as decisive, with respect to the true sense of the Scripture, as those of Gaius,

146

Paulus, Modestinus, Ulpian, and Papinian, were acknowledged to be with respect to the sense of the Roman law?

The answer is, that the emperor's edict could absolve the judge from following his own convictions about the sense of the law, because it gave to the authorized interpretation the force of law. The text, as the judge interpreted it, was a law repealed; the comment of the great lawyers was now the law in its room. As a mere literary composition, he might interpret it rightly, and Gaius, or Papinian, might be wrong; but if his interpretation was ever so right grammatically or critically, yet, legally it was nothing to the purpose;--Gaius's interpretation had superseded it, and was not the law which he was bound to obey. But, in the church, the only point to be aimed at is the discovery of the true meaning of the text of the divine law: no human power can invest the comment with equal authority. The emperor said, and might say to his judges, "You need not consider what was the meaning of the decemvirs, when they wrote the twelve tables, or, of Aquillius, when he drew up the Aquillian law. The law for you is not what the decemvirs may have meant, but what their interpreters may have meant: the decemvirs' meaning, if it was their meaning, is no longer the law of Rome." But who can dare to say to a Christian, "You need not consider what was the meaning of our Lord and his apostles; the law for you now is the meaning of Cyprian, or Ambrose, or Chrysostom;--that meaning has superseded the meaning of Christ." A Christian must find out Christ's meaning, and believe that he has found it, or else he must still seek for it. It is a matter, not of outward submission, but of inward faith; and if in our inward mind we are persuaded that the interpreter has mistaken our Lord's meaning, how can we by possibility adopt that interpretation in faith?

Here we come to a grave consideration--that this doctrine of an infallible rule of interpretation may suit ignorance or scepticism: it is death to a sincere and reasonable and earnest faith. It is not hard for a sceptical mind to deceive itself by saying, that it receives whatever the church declares to be true: it may receive any number of doctrines, but it will not really believe them. We may restrain our tongues from disputing them, we may watch every restless thought that would question them, and instantly, by main force, as it were, put it down; but all this time our minds do not assimilate to them; they do not take them up into their own nature, so as to make them a part of themselves, freshening and supplying the life-blood of their very being. Truth must be believed by the mind's own act; our souls must be drawn towards it with a reasonable love; some affinity there must be between it and them, or else they can never really comprehend it. The sceptic may desperately become a fanatic also, but he is not become, therefore, a believer.

Authority cannot compel belief; the sceptic who knows not what it is to grasp anything with the firm grasp of faith, may mistake his acquiescence in a doctrine for belief in it; the ignorant and careless, who believe only what their senses tell them, may lay up the words of divine truth in their memory, may repeat them loudly, and be vehement against all who question them. But minds to which faith is a necessity, which cannot be contented to stand by the side of truth, but must become altogether one with it,--minds which know full well the difference between opinion and conviction, between not questioning and believing,--they, when their own action is superseded by an authority foreign to themselves, are in a condition which they find intolerable. Told to believe what they cannot believe; told that they ought not to believe what they feel most disposed to believe; they retire altogether from the region of divine truth, as from a spot tainted with moral death, and devote themselves to other subjects: to physical science, it may be, or to political; where the inherent craving of their nature may yet be gratified, where, however insignificant the truth may be, they may yet find some truth to believe. This has been the condition of too many great men in the church of Rome; and it accounts for that bitterness of feeling with which Machiavelli, and others like him, appear to have regarded the whole subject of Christianity.

The system, then, of deferring to the authority of what is called the ancient church in the interpretation of Scripture, is impracticable, inasmuch as, with regard to the greatest part of the Scripture, the church, properly speaking, has said nothing at all; and if it were practicable, it would be untenable, because neither the old councils, nor individual writers, could give any sign that they had a divine gift of interpretation; and if such a gift had been given to them, it would have been equivalent to a new revelation, the sense of the comment

147

being thus preferred to what we could not but believe to be the sense of the text. Above all, the system is destructive of faith, having a tendency to substitute passive acquiescence for real conviction; and therefore I should not say that the excess of it was popery, but that it had once and actually those characters of evil which we sometimes express by the term popery, but which may be better signified by the term idolatry; a reverence for that which ought not to be reverenced, leading to a want of faith in that which is really deserving of all adoration and love.

II. But it is said that the system of relying on private judgment is beset by no less evils: that it is itself inconsistent, and leads to Socinianism and Rationalism, and, in the end, to utter unbelief; so that, the choice being only between two evils, men may choose the system of church authority as being the less evil of the two. If this were so, I see not how faith could be attained at all, or what place would be left for Christian truth. But the system of the Church of England[16] is, I am persuaded, fully consistent, and has no tendency either to Socinianism or Rationalism. Let us see first what that system is.

[16] Much has been lately written to show that the Church of England allows the authority of the ancient councils and writers, and does not allow the right of private judgment. But it is perfectly clear, from the 21st Article, that it does not allow the authority of councils; that is to say, it holds that a council's exposition of doctrine may be false, and that such an exposition is of no force "unless it may be declared that it be taken out of Holy Scripture." Who, then, is to declare this? for to suppose that the declaration of the council itself is meant is absurd: the answer, I imagine, would be, according to the mind of the Reformers, "Every particular or national church," and especially the King as the head of the church. They would not have allowed private judgment, because they conceived that a private person had nothing to do but to obey the government; and it was for the government to determine what the truth of Scripture was. The Church of England, then, expressly disclaims the authority of councils, and, in its official instruments, it neither allows nor condemns private judgment; but the opinions of the Reformers, and the constitution of the church in the 16th century, were certainly against private judgment: their authority for the interpretation of Scripture was undoubtedly the supreme government of the church, i.e. not the bishops, but the King and parliament. But then this had respect not to the power of discerning truth, but to the right of publishing it, which is an wholly different question. That an individual was not bound *in foro conscientiæ* to admit the truth of any interpretation of Scripture which did not approve itself to his own mind, was no less the judgment of the Church of England than that if he publicly disputed the interpretation of the church, he might be punished as unruly and a despiser of government. But then it should ever be remembered that the church, with the Reformers, was not the clergy. And now that the right of publication is conceded by the church, it is quite just to say that the Church of England allows private judgment; and if that judgment differ from her own, she condemns not the act of judging at all, but the having come to a false conclusion.

It is urged that the act of I Elizabeth, c. 1, allows that to be heresy which the first four councils determined to be so. This is true; but it also adjudges to be heresy whatever shall be hereafter declared to be so by "the high court of parliament, with the assent of the clergy in their convocation." The Church of England undoubtedly allowed the decisions of the first four councils, in matters of doctrine, to be valid, as it allowed the three creeds, because it decided that they were agreeable to Scripture; but the binding authority was that of the English Parliament, not of the councils of Nicæa or Constantinople.

As to the canon of 1571, which allows preachers to teach nothing as religious truth but what is agreeable to the Scriptures, "*and* which the catholic fathers and ancient bishops have collected from that very doctrine of Scripture," it will be observed that it is merely negative, and does not sanction the teaching of the "catholic fathers and ancient bishops," generally, or say that men shall teach what they taught; but that they shall not teach as matter of religious faith, a new deduction from Scripture of their own making, but such truths as had been actually deduced from Scripture before, namely, the great articles of the Christian faith.

Farther, the canons of 1571 are of no authority, not having received the royal assent.--*See Strype's Life of Parker*, p. 322, ed. 1711.

It is invidiously described as maintaining "the sufficiency of private judgment." Now we maintain the sufficiency of private judgment in interpreting the Scriptures in no other sense than that in which every sane man maintains its sufficiency, in interpreting Thucydides or Aristotle; we mean, that, instead of deferring always to some one interpreter, as an idle boy follows implicitly the Latin version of his Greek lesson, the true method is to consult all[17]accessible authorities, and to avail ourselves of the assistance of all. And we contend, that, by this process, as we discover, for the most part, the true meaning of Thucydides and Aristotle with undoubted certainty, so we may also discover, not, indeed, in every particular part or passage, but generally, the true meaning of the Holy Scriptures with no less certainty.

[17] Of course no reasonable man can doubt the importance of studying the early Christian writers, as illustrating not only the history of their own times, but the New Testament also. For the Old Testament, indeed, they do little or nothing, and for the New they are of much less assistance than might have been expected; but still there is no doubt that they are often useful.

But if another man maintains that a different meaning is the true one, how are we to silence him, and how are we justified in calling him a heretic? If by the term heretic we are to imply moral guilt, I am not justified in applying it to any Christian, unless his doctrines are positively sinful, or there is something wicked, either in the way of dishonesty or bitterness, in his manner of maintaining them. The guilt of any given religious error, in any particular case, belongs only to the judgment of Him who reads the heart. But if we mean by heresy "a grave error in matters of the Christian faith, overthrowing or corrupting some fundamental article of it," then we are as fully justified in calling a gross misinterpretation of Scripture "heresy," as we should be justified in calling a gross misinterpretation of a profane Greek or Latin author, ignorance, or want of scholarship. There is no infallible authority in points of grammar and criticism, yet men do speak confidently, notwithstanding, as to learning and ignorance; Porson and Herman are known to have understood their business, and a writer who were to set their decisions at defiance, and to indulge in mere extravagances of interpretation, would be set down as one who knew nothing about the matter. So we judge daily in all points of literature and science; nay, we in the same manner venture to call some persons mad, and on the strength of our conviction we deprive them of their property, and shut them up in a madhouse: yet if madmen wore to insist that they were sane, and that we were mad, I know not to what infallible authority we could appeal; and, after all, what are we to do with those who deny that authority to be infallible? we must then go to another infallible authority to guarantee the infallibility of the first, and this process will run on for ever.

But, in truth, there is more in the matter than the being justified or not justified in calling our neighbour a heretic. The real point of anxiety, I imagine, with many good and thinking men is this: whether a reasonable belief can be fairly carried through; whether the notion of the all-sufficiency of Scripture is not liable to objections no less than the system of church-authority; whether, in short, our Christian faith can be consistently maintained without a mortal leap at some part or other of the process; nay, whether, in fact, if it were otherwise, our faith would not seem to stand rather on the wisdom of man than on the power of God.

I use these words, because these and other such passages of the Scripture are often quoted as I have now quoted them, and produce a great effect on those who do not observe that they are quoted inapplicably; for the question is not between man's wisdom and God's power, but simply whether we have reason to believe that God's power has been here manifested; or, rather, to see whether we cannot give a reason for the faith which is in us, such faith resting upon God's power and wisdom as manifested in Christ Jesus; for if no reason can be rendered for our faith, then our minds, so far as they are concerned, are believing a lie; they are believing in spite of those laws by which God has determined their nature and condition.

Yet, however we believe, blindly or reasonably, (for some men, by God's mercy, are accidentally, as it were, in possession of the truth, the falsehood of their own minds in holding it not being, it is to be hoped, imputed to them as a sin;) however we believe, I never mean to say that our faith is not God's gift, to be sought for and retained by constant prayer and watchfulness, and to be forfeited by carelessness or sin. That is no true faith in which reason does not accord; yet neither can reason alone and without God ever become perfected into faith. For although intellectually, the grounds of belief may be made out satisfactorily, yet we are not able to follow our pure reason by ourselves; and no work on the evidences of Christianity can by itself give us faith; and much less can amid the manifold conflicts of life maintain it. That faith is thus the gift of God, and not our own work, I would desire to feel as keenly and continually, as with the fullest conviction I acknowledge it.

Now, to resume the consideration of that which, as I said, is the real point of anxiety with many. They doubt whether the course of a reasonable belief can be held to the end without interruptions: they say that the received notions of the inspiration, and consequently of the complete truth of the Scriptures cannot reasonably be maintained; that he who does maintain them does so by a happy inconsistency;--he is to be congratulated for not following up his own principles; but why should he then find fault with others who do that avowedly and consistently to which he is driven against his professions by the clear necessity of the case?

This argument was pressed by Mr. Newman, some time since, in one of the Tracts for the Times; and it was conducted, as may be supposed, with great ingenuity, but with a recklessness of consequences, or an ignorance of mankind, truly astonishing; for he brought forward all the difficulties and differences which can be found in the Scripture narratives, displayed them in their most glaring form, and merely observed, that as those with whom he was arguing could not solve these difficulties, but yet believed the Scriptures no less in spite of them, so the apparent unreasonableness of his doctrine about the priesthood was no ground why it should be rejected--a method of argument most blameable in any Christian to adopt towards his brethren; for what if their faith, being thus vehemently strained, were to give way under the experiment? and if, being convinced that the Scriptures were not more reasonable than Mr. Newman's system, they were to end with believing, not both, but neither?

Therefore the question is one of no small anxiety and interest; and it is not idly nor wantonly that we must speak the truth upon it, even if that truth may to some seem startling; for by God's blessing, if we do go boldly forward wherever truth shall lead us, our course needs not be interrupted, neither shall a single hair of our faith perish.

The same laws of criticism which teach us to distinguish between various degrees of testimony, authorize us to assign the very highest rank to the evidences of the writings of St. John and St. Paul. If belief is to be given to any human compositions, it is due to these; yet if we believe these merely as human compositions, and without assuming anything as to their divine inspiration, our Christian faith, as it seems to me, is reasonable;--not merely the facts of our Lord's miracles and resurrection; but Christian faith, in all its fulness--the whole dispensation of the Spirit, the revelation of the redemption of man and of the Divine Persons who are its authors--of all that Christian faith, and hope, and love can need. And this is so true, that even without reckoning the Epistle to the Hebrews amongst St. Paul's writings,--nay, even if we choose to reject the three pastoral epistles[18]--yet taking only what neither has been nor can be doubted--the epistles to the Romans, Corinthians, Galatians, Ephesians, Philippians, Colossians, and Thessalonians, we have in these, together with St. John's Gospel and First Epistle,--giving up, if we choose, the other two,--a ground on which our faith may stand for ever, according to the strictest rules of the understanding, according to the clearest intuitions of reason.

[18] I say this, not as having the slightest doubt myself of the genuineness of any one of the three, but merely to show how much is left that has not been questioned at all, even unreasonably.

I take the works of St. John and St. Paul as our foundation, because, in the first place, we find in them the historical basis of Christianity; that is to say, we find the facts of our Lord's miracles, and especially of his resurrection, and the miraculous powers afterwards continued to the church, established by the highest possible evidence. However pure and truly divine the principles taught in the gospel may be, yet we crave to know not only that we were in need of redemption, but that a Redeemer has actually appeared; not only that a resurrection to eternal life is probable, but that such a resurrection has actually taken place. This basis of historical fact, which is one of the great peculiarities of Christianity, is strictly within the cognizance of the understanding; and in the writings of St. John and St. Paul we have that full and perfect evidence of it which the strictest laws of the understanding require.

But the historical truth being once warranted by the understanding, other faculties of our nature now come in to enjoy it, and develop it; the highest reason and the moral and spiritual affections find respectively their proper field and objects, which, whenever presented to them in vision or in theory, they must instinctively cling to, but to which they now abandon themselves without fear of disappointment, because the understanding has assured them of their reality. We must suppose, on any system, the existence of reason and spiritual affections as indispensable to the understanding of the Scriptures; external authority can do nothing for us without these, any more than the mere faculties of the common understanding. But with these we apprehend the view which St. John and St. Paul afford to us: it opens before us one truth after another, one glory after another. St. John evidently supposes that his readers were familiar with another account of our Lord's life and teaching; and we find accordingly, another account existing in the writings of the three other evangelists. One and the same account is manifestly the substance of their three narratives, to which they thus bear a triple testimony, because none of the three has merely transcribed the others, and none of them apparently was the original author of it. Thus having now the full record of our Lord's teaching, we find that he everywhere refers to the Old Testament as to the word of God, and the record of God's earlier manifestations of himself to man. He has cleared up those especial points in it which might have most perplexed us, as I shall notice more fully hereafter, and he represents himself as the perpetual subject of its prophecies. We thus receive the Old Testament, as it were, from his hand, and learn while sitting at his feet to understand the lessons of the law and the prophets.

Thus we make Christ the centre of both Testaments, and by so doing, we cannot be blind to the divinity pervading both. For the amazing fact that God should come into the world and be in the world cannot by possibility stand alone; it hallows, as it were, the whole period of the world's existence, from the beginning to the end, placing all time and every place in relation to God; it disposes us at once to receive the fact of the special call of the people of Israel;--it gives, I had almost said, an *à priori* reason why there must have been in earlier times some shadows, at least, or images, to represent dimly to former generations that great thing which they were not actually to witness; it leads us to believe that there must have been some prophetic voices to announce the future coming of the Lord, or else "The very stones must have cried out."

But those writings of St. John and St. Paul which were our first lessons in Christianity, and those other accounts of our Lord's life and teaching to which they introduced us,--can we conceive it possible, that the real meaning of all these shall be hopelessly obscure and uncertain; that if we seek it ever so diligently, we shall not find it? With an humble mind ready to learn, with a heart fully impressed with the sense of God's presence, so as to be morally and spiritually in a condition to receive God's truth, can we believe, then, that the use of those intellectual means, which open to us certainly the sense of human writers, shall be applied in vain to those writers who were commissioned to be the very heralds of a divine message, whose especial business it was to make known what they had themselves heard? Surely if a sufficient certainty of interpretation be attainable in common literature, the revelation of God cannot be the solitary exception.

But we may be mistaken: we may *believe* that we interpret truly, but we cannot be *infallibly sure* of it; we want an authority which shall give us this assurance. This is no doubt the natural craving of our weakness; but it is no wiser a craving than if we were to long for the heaven to be opened, and for a daily sight of our Lord standing at the right hand of God. To live by faith is our appointed condition, and faith excludes an infallible assurance. We must earnestly believe that we have the truth, and die for our belief, if necessary, but we cannot*know* it. No device which the human mind can practise, can exclude the possibility of doubt. If we would find an armour which should cover us at every point from this subtle enemy, it would be an armour that would close up the pores of the skin, and stop our breath; our fancied security would kill us. Is it really possible that, with our knowledge of man's nature, our belief in any human authority can really be more free from doubt than our belief in the conclusions of our own reason? There must ever be the liability to uncertainty; we can put no moral truth so surely as that our minds shall always feel it to be absolutely certain. Where is the infallible authority that can assure us even of the existence of God? And will the scepticism that can believe its own conclusions in nothing else rest satisfied with one conclusion only--that the writers of the first four centuries cannot err? Surely to regard this as the most certain proposition that can be submitted to the human mind, is no better than insanity.

But we will consent to trust, it may be said, with God's help, to our own deliberate convictions that we have interpreted Scripture truly; but you tell us that the Scripture itself is not inspired in every part; you tell us that there are in it chronological and historical difficulties, if not errors; that there are possibly some interpolations; that even the apostles may have been in some things mistaken, as in their belief that the end of the world was at hand. Where shall we find a rest for our feet, if you first take away from us our infallible interpreter, and now tell us, that even if we can ourselves interpret it aright, yet that we cannot be sure that the very Scripture itself is infallibly true?

It is very true that our position with respect to the Scriptures is not in all points the same as our fathers'. For sixteen hundred years nearly, while physical science, and history, and chronology, and criticism, were all in a state of torpor, the questions which now present themselves to our minds could not from the nature of the case arise. When they did arise, they came forward into notice gradually: first the discoveries in astronomy excited uneasiness: then as men began to read more critically, differences in the several Scripture narratives of the same thing awakened attention; more lately, the greater knowledge which has been gained of history, and of language, and in all respects the more careful inquiry to which all ancient records have been submitted, have brought other difficulties to light, and some sort of answer must be given to them. Mr. Newman, as we have seen, has made use of those difficulties much as the Romanists have used the doctrine of the Trinity when arguing with Trinitarians[19] in defence of transubstantiation. The Romanists said,--"Here are all these inexplicable difficulties in the doctrine of the Trinity, and yet you believe it." So Mr. Newman argues with those who hold the plenary inspiration of Scripture, that if they believe that, in spite of all the difficulties which beset it, they may as well believe his doctrine of the priesthood; and many, if I mistake not, alarmed by this representation, have actually embraced his opinions.

[19] On this proceeding of the Romanists, Stillingfleet observes, "Methinks for the sake of our common Christianity you should no more venture upon such bold and unreasonable comparisons. Do you in earnest think it is all one whether men do believe a God, or providence, or heaven, or hell, or the Trinity, and incarnation of Christ, if they do not believe transubstantiation? We have heard much of late about old and new popery: but if this be the way of representing new popery, by exposing the common articles of faith, it will set the minds of all good Christians farther from it than ever. For upon the very same grounds we may expect another parallel between the belief of a God and transubstantiation, the effect of which will be the exposing of all religion. This is a very destructive and mischievous method of proceeding; but our comfort is that it is very unreasonable, as I hope hath fully appeared by this discourse."--*Doctrine of the Trinity and Transubstantiation compared*, at the end.

It has unfortunately happened that the difficulties of the Scripture have been generally treated as objections to the truth of Christianity; as such they have been pressed by adversaries, and as such Christian writers have replied to them. But then they become of such tremendous interest, that it is scarcely possible to examine them fairly. If my faith in God and my hope of eternal life is to depend on the accuracy of a date or of some minute historical particular, who can wonder that I should listen to any sophistry that may be used in defence of them, or that I should force my mind to do any sort of violence to itself, when life and death seem to hang on the issue of its decision?

Yet what conceivable connexion is there between the date of Cyrenius's government, or the question whether our Lord healed a blind man as he was going into Jericho or as he was leaving it; or whether Judas bought himself the field of blood, or it was bought by the high priests: what connexion can there be between such questions, and the truth of God's love to man in the redemption, and of the resurrection of our Lord? Do we give to any narrative in the world, to any statement, verbal or written, no other alternative than that it must be either infallible or unworthy of belief? Is not such an alternative so extravagant as to be a complete reductio ad absurdum? And yet such is the alternative which men seem generally to have admitted in considering the Scripture narratives: if a single error can be discovered, it is supposed to be fatal to the credibility of the whole.

This has arisen from an unwarranted interpretation of the word "inspiration," and by a still more unwarranted inference. An inspired work is supposed to mean a work to which God has communicated his own perfections; so that the slightest error or defect of any kind in it is inconceivable, and that which is other than perfect in all points cannot be inspired. This is the unwarranted interpretation of the word "inspiration." But then follows the still more unwarranted inference,--"If all the Scripture is not inspired, Christianity cannot be true," an inference which is absolutely entitled to no other consideration than what it may seem to derive from the number of those who have either openly or tacitly maintained it.

Most truly do I believe the Scriptures to be inspired; the proofs of their inspiration rise continually with the study of them. The scriptural narratives are not only about divine things, but are themselves divinely framed and superintended. I cannot conceive my conviction of this truth being otherwise than sure. Yet I must acknowledge that the scriptural narratives do not claim this inspiration for themselves; so that if I should be obliged to resign my belief in it, which seems to me impossible, I yet should have no right to tax the Scriptures with having advanced a pretension proved to be unfounded; their whole credibility as a most authentic history of the most important facts would remain untouched; the gospel of St. John would still be a narrative as unimpeachable as that of Thucydides, which no sane man has ever disbelieved.

So much for the unwarranted inference, that if the Scripture histories are not inspired, the great facts of the Christian revelation cannot be maintained. But it is no less an unwarranted interpretation of the term "inspiration," to suppose that it is equivalent to a communication of the Divine perfections. Surely, many of our words and many of our actions are spoken and done by the inspiration of God's Spirit, without whom we can do nothing acceptable to God. Yet does the Holy Spirit so inspire us as to communicate to us His own perfections? Are our best words or works utterly free from error or from sin? All inspiration does not then destroy the human and fallible part in the nature which it inspires; it does not change man into God.

In one man, indeed, it was otherwise; but He was both God and man. To Him the Spirit was given without measure; and as his life was without sin, so his words were without error. But to all others the Spirit has been given by measure; in almost infinitely different measure it is true: the difference between the inspiration of the common and perhaps unworthy Christian who merely said that "Jesus was the Lord," and that of Moses, or St. Paul, and St. John, is almost to our eyes beyond measuring. Still the position remains, that the highest degree of inspiration given to man has still suffered to exist along with it a portion of human fallibility and corruption.

Now, then, consider the epistles of the blessed Apostle St. Paul, who had the Spirit of God so abundantly, that never we may suppose did any merely human being enjoy a larger share of it. Endowed with the Spirit as a Christian, and daily receiving grace more largely, as he became more and more ripe for glory; endowed with the Spirit's extraordinary gifts most eminently; favoured also with an abundance of revelations, disclosing to him things ineffable and inconceivable,--are not his writings to be most truly called inspired? Can we doubt that, in what he has told us of things not seen, or not seen as yet,--of Him who pre-existed in the form of God before he was manifested in the form of man,--of that great day, when we shall arise incorruptible, and meet our Lord in the air, and be joined to him for ever,--can any reasonable mind doubt, that in speaking of these things he spoke what he had heard from God; that to refuse to believe his testimony is really to disbelieve God?

Yet this great Apostle expected that the world would come to an end in the generation then existing. When he wrote to the Thessalonians some years before his first

153

imprisonment at Rome, he warned them, no doubt, against expecting the end immediately: but he appears still to have supposed that it would come in the lifetime of men then living. At a later period, when writing to the Corinthians, his dissuasion of marriage seems to rest mainly upon this impression; it is good not to marry, "on account of the distress which is close at hand;" ([Greek: dia taen enestosan anankaen]; compare 2 Thess. ii. 2, [Greek: hos hoti enestaeken hae haemera tou Kyriou].) "The time is short," he adds; "the fashion of this world is passing away." And again, when speaking of the resurrection, he says emphatically, "the dead shall rise incorruptible, and *we* shall be changed;" where the pronoun being expressed in the original, [Greek: chai haemeis allagaesometha], shows that by the term "*we*," he does not mean the dead, but those who were to be alive at Christ's coming. So again, still later, when writing from Rome to the Philippians, he tells them "the Lord is at hand;" and later still, even in his first epistle to Timothy, he charges Timothy "to keep his commandment without spot, unrebukable, until the appearing of our Lord Jesus Christ." These and other passages cannot without violence be interpreted even singly in any other sense; but taking them together, their meaning seems absolutely certain. Shall we say, then, that St. Paul entertained and expressed a belief which the event did not verify? We may say so, safely and reverently, in this instance; for here he was most certainly speaking as a man, and not by revelation; as it has been providentially ordered that our Lord's express words on this point have been recorded--"Of that day and hour knoweth no man; no, not the angels in heaven." Or again, shall we say, that St. Paul advised the Corinthians not to marry, chiefly on this ground; and that this throws a suspicion over his directions in other points? But again it has been ordered, that in this very place, and no where else in all his writing, St. Paul has expressly said that he was only giving his judgment as a Christian, and not speaking with divine authority;--the concluding words of the chapter, [Greek: doko de kago pneuma theou echein] do not signify, as our Version renders them, "And I think also that I have the Spirit of God," as if he were confirming his own judgment by an assertion of his inspiration in a sense beyond that of common Christians; but the words say, "And I think that I too have the Spirit of God," "I too as well as others whom you might consult, so that my judgment is no less worthy of attention than theirs." But it is his Christian judgment only that he is giving, as he expressly declares, and not his apostolical command or revelation; a distinction which he never makes elsewhere, and which is in itself so striking, that we seem to recognise in it God's especial mercy to us, that our faith in St. Paul's general declarations of divine truth might not be shaken, because in one particular point he was permitted to speak as a man, giving express notice at the same time that he was doing so.

Now it is at least remarkable, that in the only two instances in which the existence of any absence of divine authority is to be discerned in St. Paul's epistles, provision is actually made by God's fondness to prevent them from prejudicing our faith in St. Paul's divine authority generally. And so in whatever points any error may be discoverable in Scripture, we shall find either that the errors are of a kind wholly unconnected with the revelation of what God has done to us, and of what we are to do towards Him; and therefore are perfectly consistent with the inspiration of the writer, unless we take that unwarranted notion of inspiration which considers it as equivalent to a communication of God's attributes perfectly; (and of this kind are any errors that may exist either in points of physical science, or of chronology, or of history;) or if there be any thing else which appears inconsistent with inspiration, in the sense in which we really may and do apply it to the Scriptures, namely, that they are a perfect guide and rule in all matters concerning our relations with God, then we shall find that God has made some special provision for the case, to remove what it otherwise might have had of real difficulty.

This merciful care is above all to be recognised with regard to one point, which otherwise would, I think, have been a difficulty actually insuperable: I mean the manifestly imperfect moral standard, which in some cases is displayed in the characters of good men in the Old Testament. Put the gospel by the side of the law and history of the Israelites; observe what the law permitted, and public opinion under the law did not condemn; observe the actions recorded of persons who are declared to have been eminently good, and to have received God's especial blessing; and it is manifest that had not our Lord himself vouchsafed his help, one of two things must have happened--either that we must have followed the old

154

heresy of rejecting the Old Testament altogether, or else that our respect for the Old Testament must have impeded the growth of the more perfect law of Christ. The true solution I do not think that we could have discovered, or ventured to admit on less authority than our Lord's. But his express declaration, that some things in the law itself were permitted, because nothing higher could then have been borne, and his stating in detail that in several points what was accounted good or allowable in the former dispensation was not so really, while at the same time he constantly refers to the Old Testament as divine, and confirms its language of blessing with respect to its most eminent characters, has completely cleared to us the whole question, and enables us to recognize the divinity of the Old Testament and the holiness of its characters, without lying against our consciences and our more perfect revelation, by justifying the actions of those characters as right, essentially and abstractedly, although they were excusable, or in some cases actually virtuous, according to the standard of right and wrong which prevailed under the law.

After observing God's gracious care for us in this instance, as well as in those which I have noticed before, I cannot but feel that we may safely trust Him for every other similar case, if any such there be, and that he will not permit our faith either in him or in his holy word to be shaken, because we do not attempt to close our eyes against truth, nor seek to support our faith by sophistry and falsehood. Feeling what the Scriptures are, I would not give unnecessary pain to any one by an enumeration of those points in which the literal historical statement of an inspired writer has been vainly defended. Some instances will probably occur to most readers; others are perhaps not known, and never will be known to many, nor is it at all needful or desirable that they should know them. But if ever they are brought before them, let them not try to put them aside unfairly, from a fear that they will injure our faith. Let us not do evil that evil may be escaped from; and it is an evil, and the fruitful parent of evils innumerable, to do violence to our understanding or to our reason in their own appointed fields; to maintain falsehood in their despite, and reject the truth which they sanction. If writers of Mr. Newman's school will persist in displaying the difficulties of the Scripture before the eyes of those who had not been before aware of them, let those who are so cruelly tempted be conjured not to be dismayed; to refuse utterly to surrender up their sense of truth,--to persist in rejecting the unchristian falsehoods which they are called upon to worship; sure that after all that can be said, that system will remain false to the end; and their Christian faith, if they do not faithlessly attempt to strengthen it by unlawful means, will stand no less unshaken.

In conclusion, Christian faith rests upon Scripture; and as it is in itself agreeable to the highest reason, so the authenticity of the Scriptures on which it rests is assured to us by the deliberate conclusions of the understanding; nor is any "mortal leap" necessary at any part of the process: nor any rejection of one truth, in order to retain our hold on another. And if it should happen, as in all probability it will, that we shall be called upon to correct in some respects our notions as to the Scriptures, and so far to hold views different from those of our fathers, we should consider that our fathers did not, and could not stand in our circumstances; that the knowledge which may call upon us to relinquish some of their opinions, was a knowledge which they had not. Till this knowledge comes to us, let us hold our fathers' opinions as they held them; but when it does come, it will come by God's will, and to do his work: and that work will, assuredly, not be our separation from our father's faith; but if we follow God's guidance humbly and cheerfully, clinging to God the while in personal devotion and obedience, we may be made aware of what to them would have been an inexplicable difficulty, and which was, therefore, hidden from their knowledge; and yet, "through the grace of our Lord Jesus Christ, we believe that we shall be saved even as they."

THE END.